MW00806887
LUCIFER BOOK THREE

Mike Carey
Writer

Peter Gross
Ryan Kelly
Dean Ormston
Craig Hamilton
David Hahn
Ted Naifeh
Artists

Daniel Vozzo
Colorist

Comicraft
Ken Lopez
Letterers

Christopher Moeller
Cover Art

Christopher Moeller
Tara McPherson
Original Series Covers

Based on characters created by Neil Gaiman, Sam Kieth and Mike Dringenberg.

Shelly Bond Editor – Original Series
Mariah Huehner Assistant Editor – Original Series
Jeb Woodard Group Editor – Collected Editions
Scott Nybakken Editor – Collected Edition
Steve Cook Design Director – Books
Louis Prandi Publication Design

Shelly Bond VP & Executive Editor – Vertigo

Diane Nelson President
Dan DiDio and Jim Lee Co-Publishers
Geoff Johns Chief Creative Officer
Amit Desai Senior VP – Marketing & Global Franchise Management
Nairi Gardiner Senior VP – Finance
Sam Ades VP – Digital Marketing
Bobbie Chase VP – Talent Development
Mark Chiarello Senior VP – Art, Design & Collected Editions
John Cunningham VP – Content Strategy
Anne DePies VP – Strategy Planning & Reporting
Don Falletti VP – Manufacturing Operations
Lawrence Ganem VP – Editorial Administration & Talent Relations
Alison Gill Senior VP – Manufacturing & Operations
Hank Kanalz Senior VP – Editorial Strategy & Administration
Jay Kogan VP – Legal Affairs
Derek Maddalena Senior VP – Sales & Business Development
Jack Mahan VP – Business Affairs
Dan Miron VP – Sales Planning & Trade Development
Nick Napolitano VP – Manufacturing Administration
Carol Roeder VP – Marketing
Eddie Scannell VP – Mass Account & Digital Sales
Courtney Simmons Senior VP – Publicity & Communications
Jim (Ski) Sokolowski VP – Comic Book Specialty & Newsstand Sales
Sandy Yi Senior VP – Global Franchise Management

LUCIFER BOOK THREE

Published by DC Comics. Copyright © 2014 DC Comics.
All Rights Reserved.

Originally published in single magazine form as LUCIFER 29-45. Copyright © 2002, 2003, 2004 DC Comics. All Rights Reserved. All characters, their distinctive likenesses and related elements featured in this publication are trademarks of DC Comics. The stories, characters and incidents featured in this publication are entirely fictional. DC Comics does not read or accept unsolicited submissions of ideas, stories or artwork.

DC Comics, 2900 W. Alameda Avenue, Burbank, CA 91505
Printed by RR Donnelley, Salem, VA, USA. Second Printing.
ISBN: 978-1-4012-4604-4

Library of Congress Cataloging-in-Publication Data

Carey, Mike, 1959- author.
Lucifer Book Three / Mike Carey ; [illustrated by] Peter Gross.
pages cm
Summary: "Cast out of Heaven, thrown down to rule in Hell, Lucifer Morningstar has resigned his post and abandoned his kingdom for the mortal city of Los Angles. Emerging from the pages of writer Neil Gaiman's award-winning series The Sandman, the former Lord of Hell is now enjoying a quiet retirement as the propretor of Lux, L.A.'s most elite piano bar. Still weak, with most of his power locked in the feathers stolen by Susano-O-No-Mikoto, Lucifer faces the challenge of single combat to the death with his brother, the angel of the Host Amenadiel. But when victory comes at the sacrifice of another, Lucifer embarks on a voyage that will take him to the depths of his former kingdom and beyond to retrieve their lost soul"-- Provided by publisher.
ISBN 978-1-4012-4604-4 (pbk.)
1. Graphic novels. I. Gross, Peter, 1958- illustrator. II. Title.
PN6728.L79C43 2014
741.5'973-dc23

2013046129

MIX
Paper from responsible sources
FSC® C101537

Table of Contents

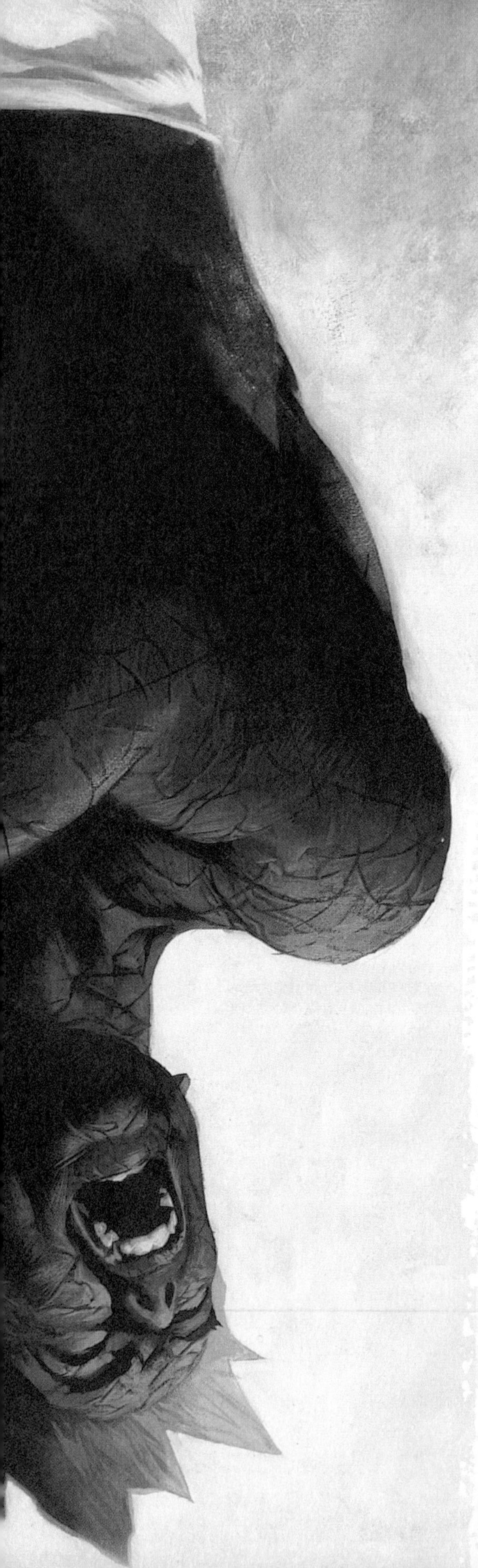

THE FATHER OF LIES

This third volume of the collected LUCIFER opens with issue 29 — midway through our third year, with a lot of story already told, a lot of characters moving on different (intersecting) trajectories and the groundwork laid for a lot of important revelations. We had a sense of gathering momentum and the confidence (maybe a little reckless, but, as it turned out, well placed) that we'd be able to finish the story exactly as we wanted to, at our own pace and to our own agenda.

The first order of business was to finish out the trilogy of interlinked tales that had begun with "Paradiso" and "Purgatorio." In "Inferno," Lucifer returns to Hell to keep the promise he made a year before — to fight a duel to the death with the angel Amenadiel. Unfortunately, he didn't anticipate when he made that promise that in the meantime he'd have his power and his immortality stolen from him through the machinations of the goddess Izanami. He's going naked into the conference chambers of the eternal realms — ultimately because he'd rather do that than break his word.

Promises are very central to this book. The swearing of oaths and the need to make good on them was a theme we kept coming back to. Sometimes it seemed as though our whole cast could be divided into the characters who were prepared to do anything — up to and including murder and self-immolation — to keep their word and those who, for whatever good or bad or equivocal reason, broke it.

Lucifer always fell into the first of those categories for us, and it was central to how we saw him. It's fair to say, however, that his honesty is a complicated artefact. On the face of it, it's a part of his massive arrogance and touchy pride. Lying, as David Easterman says when he first meets Lucifer, is a little bit demeaning — shaming, even. It makes you contingent to and lesser than the person you're lying to, which isn't something Lucifer would like at all.

But look a little harder at Lucifer's honesty and you start to see deeper and darker levels to it. The truth, in Lucifer's hands, is weaponized. He tells the truths that will get the job done, selecting them with absolute ruthlessness and fine discrimination. If he's talking to you, you're in trouble — all the more so since everything he says will stand up to the most rigorous examination. You won't find a hole in Lucifer's pitch. It will find a hole in you — as Easterman found to his cost in the "Children and Monsters" arc, contained in BOOK TWO.

In this third volume, Lucifer's path crosses that of two other characters who illuminate his honesty from two very different directions — Solomon and Bergelmir. Imagine them as angels sitting on his shoulders, whispering contradictory advice. Not that Lucifer would ever encourage that degree of intimacy. Or sit still long enough to be advised.

Solomon is the self-appointed judge of Heaven, carrying out in death the role for which he was famous when he was alive. He journeys through the world, seeking out sinners and finding punishments that fit their crimes. He believes that this is a divinely appointed mission — that God himself imposes the duty on him, sending him his instructions in dreams. He's probably insane, although we were never entirely explicit about that. What he definitely is, though, is unrelenting and fanatical, adhering to a code that's all about moral absolutes and the need to submit to them.

Solomon's integrity gives us a useful vantage point from which to observe Lucifer's, because it's the very opposite of self-interested. He does what he does because he has to, and he mostly experiences his mission as a sense of urgency and anger, a desperate need to act. He makes a point of pride out of the fact that he has even executed judgment on his own father — and you get the sense that if he ever fell short of his own standards he'd be equally merciless with himself.

Bergelmir is his polar opposite. The brother of Loki, he embodies the same love of mischief and the same gleeful moral relativism. His lies are part of a wider philosophy, a statement of allegiance. In the great debate between order and chaos, he knows which side he's on.

Again, this isn't primarily about self-interest. Bergelmir doesn't lie exclusively for advantage, he lies because it's his nature to do so and because he finds lies more congenial than truth. When Lucifer comes to him to demand the ship *Naglfar* for a voyage to the Mansions of the Silence, rather than say yes or no Bergelmir responds by concocting a plot that depends absolutely on Lucifer's unwillingness to break a promise — a plot which will effectively cause Lucifer to promise to kill himself.

I don't remember ever discussing any of this explicitly with Peter, but it's obvious in re-reading these stories that it's one of the things I was obsessing on. Seven years later, we'd be co-plotting THE UNWRITTEN, a story about stories and about why stories matter to us. But it turns out that LUCIFER also concerns itself with fictions — the intentional, extemporized fictions that are lies; and their opposite, oaths and promises and statements of unvarnished truth.

It's hard to say, though, why that should be such a central issue in a story about the devil. If we were presenting Lucifer in the traditional mold as "the father of lies" then yeah, okay, there'd be a clear through-line. But we weren't. This is Neil Gaiman's Lucifer, not John Milton's, and as far back as "Season of Mists" he made it very clear that he never tempted any man or woman to commit a single sin. That's not his thing at all.

His thing is freedom — the ultimate freedom of self-determination. He wants to be the author of his own fate, and so finds himself forever at odds with the logic of a deterministic universe defined by its creator's will.

But maybe that's the point. Lucifer is the goal of his own quest, the harbor towards which he's always sailing. The treasure he seeks is his own selfhood, and it would damage and denature that treasure if he were ever to utter the false coin of a lie. It's not that he would care about taking unfair advantage — he does that all the time. What he would never put at risk is his sense of himself, the absolute and inviolable boundaries of his own nature.

There's a moment in Robert Bolt's masterpiece, *A Man for All Seasons*, when his protagonist, Thomas More, is called on to explain why he won't sign the act of succession — the parliamentary instrument which declared King Henry VIII's marriage to Catherine of Aragon invalid and his daughter Mary a bastard. It's just a piece of paper, More is told by his friend Norfolk. You can sign it and still in your heart believe something different. But More replies that this is impossible for him to do. When you swear an oath, you hold your soul in your hands like water. If you open your hands at that point, there's no going back. You're lost, and you'll never find yourself again.

Lucifer would understand that intimate and irrevocable link between your word and your self. God's word, the *logos*, created the universe. Our words create us, from one moment to the next. When you lie, it's that act of self-creation that's sabotaged and corrupted.

If this sounds dry or abstract, please believe me when I say that in the stories you're about to read, it's anything but. Truth and falsehood are battlefields here, but there are plenty of real battlefields too — on Earth, in Hell, and in places still further and stranger. And the stakes, for Lucifer and the rest of our cast of thousands, just keep on getting higher.

— Mike Carey
London, November 2013

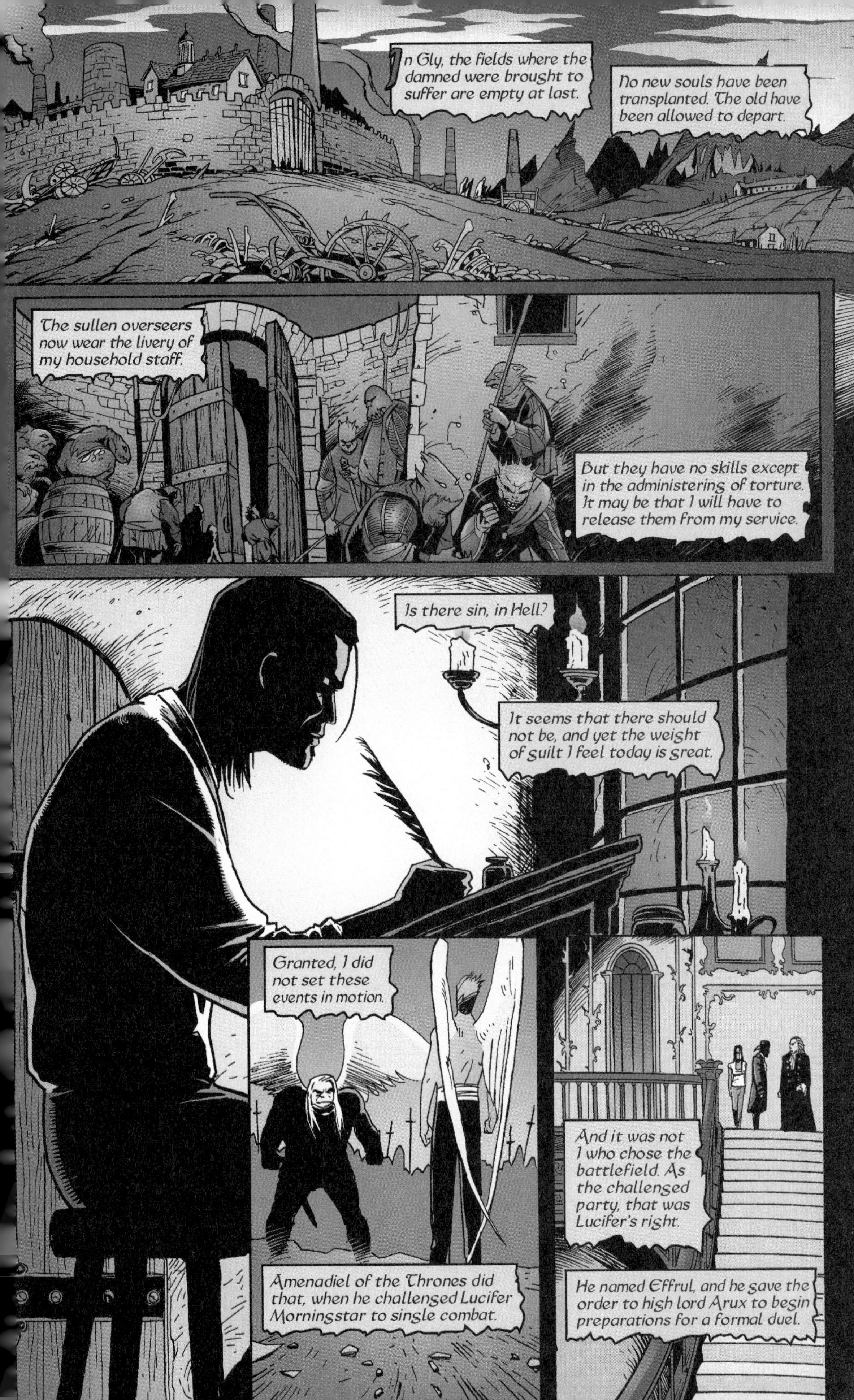
In Gly, the fields where the damned were brought to suffer are empty at last.
No new souls have been transplanted. The old have been allowed to depart.
The sullen overseers now wear the livery of my household staff.
But they have no skills except in the administering of torture. It may be that I will have to release them from my service.
Is there sin, in Hell?
It seems that there should not be, and yet the weight of guilt I feel today is great.
Granted, I did not set these events in motion.
Amenadiel of the Thrones did that, when he challenged Lucifer Morningstar to single combat.
And it was not I who chose the battlefield. As the challenged party, that was Lucifer's right.
He named Effrul, and he gave the order to high lord Arux to begin preparations for a formal duel.

But as to what happened when he came here -- here to Hell -- for that I bear sole responsibility.
I have abused the holy laws of hospitality.
I have betrayed the trust of one who offered me no harm.
Who had in fact professed himself my patron and my friend.
And I have brought an angel to his death.
If I ever harbored any hope of redemption, it ends here. Now.
INFERNO
PART 1 of 3
MIKE CAREY WRITER
PETER GROSS & RYAN KELLY ARTISTS
COMICRAFT LETTERS
DANIEL VOZZO COLORS & SEPARATIONS
CHRISTOPHER MOELLER COVER PAINTING
MARIAH HUEHNER ASSISTANT EDITOR
SHELLY BOND EDITOR
LUCIFER IS BASED ON CHARACTERS CREATED BY
GAIMAN, KIETH, AND DRINGENBERG

HELL.
THE TOWER OF RULE.
How many times do I have to *say* this?
He must not win.
REMIEL, I WOULD DEARLY *LOVE* TO PROMISE YOU A VICTORY.
BUT IT WOULD HURT MY PRIDE TO BE *FORSWORN* AS WELL AS DEAD.
Then perhaps the challenge was a poor idea in the *first* place.
Can you envision what they might *mean* for our rule over Hell's legions.
If Lucifer fights an angel of the *host,* and brings him down? How will I *command* them afterwards?
INDULGE MY CURIOSITY.
HOW DO YOU COMMAND THEM *NOW?*
Your jest is a poor one. *I* am the agent of God here, Amenadiel-- you are merely pursuing a private *vendetta.*
I repeat. Lucifer must *lose* this duel.

MY LORD REMIEL, I WAS NOT IN A POSITION TO *REFUSE* YOUR INVITATION. BUT I THINK I HAVE LITTLE TO CONTRIBUTE HERE.
AS TO THE PRACTICALITIES, HE IS *LUCIFER*. HE DOES NOT LOSE.
In case you have forgotten, Arux I am your master. Your power *devolves* from me.
I HAVE *NOT* FORGOTTEN.
Now, it may be that the Lightbringer is *weak* after his struggle against the Basanos.
We will *test* him with a feint. That should be easy enough to arrange.
If he seems vulnerable, then we will consider what *more* might be done.
MY LORD, I BEG YOUR *INDULGENCE*.
YOU ARE NEW TO HELL, AND IN SOME MATTERS YOUR *UNDERSTANDING* IS STILL IMPERFECT.
THERE ARE *ALLIANCES* AND OBLIGATIONS BETWEEN MY VASSAL LORDS THAT GO BACK TO THE DARKNESS BEFORE LIGHT.
IF THEY SUSPECT THAT I HAVE *CONSPIRED* AGAINST ONE OF THEIR NUMBER, THERE WILL BE CIVIL WAR. THEY WILL *UNSEAT* ME.
My dear lord Arux, you concern yourself over *nothing.*
I have already *chosen* who shall play host to Lucifer.
And trust me, he has no *allies* at all.

I am able to fill in the gaps in the story with later knowledge.
In the realms unnamed, at exactly this time, a hunt was in progress. It was led by Mazikeen, daughter of Ophur.
And coordinated by her aide de camp--
WHAT NEWS?
BOTH SWEET AND BITTER, WAR LEADER!
--a tiny demon of the Elokim.
You will have heard of him since of course. Of the bone he sings to, of his cruel loss and his crueler revenge.
WE HAVE DRIVEN HIM EAST, AWAY FROM HIS MOTHER'S BORDERS.
BUT HE IS A THUNDER GOD, AND THE STORM IS BUILDING. HE INTENDS TO FIGHT.
Elokim Shaer. Mazikeen's arrow.
TELL MISRAN TO SPREAD AS THINLY AS HE CAN, BUT TO KEEP LINE OF SIGHT.
SUSANO MUST NOT DOUBLE BACK THROUGH OUR LINES.
AS FOR THE STORM--
--IT BRINGS US TO HIM, MORE SURELY THAN ANY MAP.

Elsewhere under the snarling clouds, the god Susano-O-No-Mikoto had finished his traveler's meal of rice and dried fish.
With no servants to cook for him, he had eaten it cold.

It was now time to pray to his brother's souls, as he did four times each day.
Promising them peace. Peace and quittance.

While he was thus engaged, a white bird came and sat upon his forearm.
It asked him a question, in slightly accented Ainu.

When his devotions were done, he penned a letter in perfect calligraphy on a fallen leaf. It contained the single word "yes," under his seal.
He tied it to the bird's leg with a thread taken from his robe.

His thirst was great, but there was no question of drinking the water in his last canteen.
He needed it to slow his pursuers.

for the road was still long before him. His enemies compassed him about.
And his brothers' shades would be angry if he broke his promise.

I had thought that he would fly down out of the sulfurous sky.
But this proved not to be the case.
And where the damned are farmed like cattle for their pain--
--the devil rides out like lord of the manor.
LUCIFER MORNINGSTAR. YOU ARE MOST WELCOME AT MY HOUSE.
DUKE OF GLY, I APOLOGIZE IN ADVANCE FOR YOUR TROUBLE.
IT'S GOING TO BE CONSIDERABLE.
AH. HIGH LORD ARUX INFORMED ME ONLY AN HOUR SINCE THAT I WAS TO BE YOUR HOST.
I REGRET THAT I'VE HAD SCANT TIME TO--
THAT'S NOT WHAT I MEANT.

I'VE COME ALONE, AS THE CUSTOM IS ON SUCH OCCASIONS.
ALL I NEED IS A ROOM. WE CAN SORT OUT THE DETAILS LATER.
YOU WERE IN EFFRUL WHEN I SAW YOU LAST. IN THE COMPANY OF THE LADY LYS.
AYE, I WAS.
THAT LIAISON IS NOW CONCLUDED.
IT'S UNUSUAL FOR A HUMAN SOUL TO WIN A TITLE IN HELL.
I'D BE INTERESTED TO HEAR--
LORD LUCIFER, KEEP YOU AND SAVE YOU!
YOUR BLESSING ON US, MORNINGSTAR.
MY BLESSING? AN ODD CHOICE OF WORDS.
GOD'S WOUNDS!

GUUUH!

WHO ARE THESE MEN? HOW COULD THIS HAPPEN?
MY LORD, THEY--THEY'RE OF YOUR OWN HOUSEHOLD. I COULDN'T KNOW--

LUCIFER! YOU BLEED.
IT'S NOTHING. SHOW ME THAT ROOM, AND I'LL WASH FROM THE ROAD.

AND THEN PERHAPS WE CAN REVIEW YOUR SECURITY ARRANGEMENTS.

The storm broke.
It caught the Lilim on the bald flank of a ridge.
The first bolt ripped the ground away from their horses' hooves.
There was nowhere for them to go.
The lightning was like the tail of some demonic scorpion, striking where it pleased.

They might have panicked then, and been lost, had it not been for their general.
They saw her riding forward, into the swag-bellied clouds, the half of her face that was visible twisted in a grin.
And so they followed her into the heart of the maelstrom.
Like surgeons feeling blindly for a cancer.

A dangerous opponent-- Susano-O-No-Mikoto.
They thought the storm his greatest weapon.
Therefore they were unlikely to see it as a feint.

Lucifer's thoughts rested on her, doubtless, as he wipes away the stains of his mortality.
YOU MUST NOT GO ON WITH THIS.
WHY? BECAUSE I MIGHT LOSE?
A STRANGE REASON FOR CALLING OFF A DUEL.
WHAT IF I WERE TO INTERCEPT SUSANO? BRING THE FEATHERS BACK TO YOU?
THEN WOULD YOUR STRENGTH BE RESTORED?
NO NEED EVEN FOR THAT.
IF THEY WERE TO BE DESTROYED, EVERYTHING STORED UP IN THEM WOULD FLOW BACK TO ME.
It was an irony very much to his taste, that he could no longer live without her.
THEN COMMAND ME, LORD.
AS YOU DID BEFORE.

THIS WAS A *FORTRESS* BEFORE IT WAS A CHATEAU.
THE INNER AND OUTER WALLS ARE TWENTY SPANS APART, AND THE SPACE IN BETWEEN WAS LEFT *CLEAR*, AS A KILLING GROUND.
YES. SO I SEE.
BUT I DOUBT THAT INVADING *ARMIES* WILL BE AN ISSUE HERE.
ANYONE TRYING TO *FORESTALL* THIS DUEL--
--WILL PROBABLY SEND SINGLE ASSASSINS.
I HAVE CONSIDERED THAT, TOO.
THE TOWER IN WHICH I HAVE LODGED YOU IS MY *OWN* ADDITION TO THE CASTLE OF GLY.
IT HAS A UNIQUE *FEATURE*, WHICH I WILL DEMONSTRATE FOR YOU LATER.
YOU'VE MADE *OTHER* CHANGES TOO, I SEE.
I USED TO COME THIS WAY QUITE *OFTEN* ONCE. AS I REMEMBER, THOSE WERE *PAINFIELDS*.
THEY ARE *STILL* PAINFIELDS.
IT IS JUST THAT I HAVE ORDERED A *FALLOW* SEASON, LORD LUCIFER.
TO ADD *SAVOUR* TO THE NEXT YEAR'S CROP.
AH. OF COURSE.
THEN IT DOESN'T *BOTHER* YOU, THE HARVESTING OF PAIN?
NO PRICKINGS OF *CONSCIENCE*--

--NOW THAT YOU FIND YOURSELF AT THE OTHER END OF THE LASH?
YOU ARE QUICK AND YOU ARE STRONG, SIR DEVIL. BUT THIS MORNING A DAGGER THRUST MADE YOU BLEED.
AND YOUR POINT IS--?
I BELIEVE YOU SEE MY POINT.
I KILLED AN INNOCENT, ONCE. AND THREE HUNDRED YEARS OF TORMENT HAVE NOT WASHED THAT STAIN FROM MY SOUL.
I WOULD NOT MAKE THE SAME MISTAKE AGAIN.
SO TELL ME, LUCIFER, FOR I CRAVE TO KNOW. ARE YOU, AS THE BIBLE SAYS, THE ARCHITECT OF HELL?
WHETHER AS JOKE OR VENGEANCE OR I KNOW NOT WHAT, IS THIS MONSTROSITY YOUR HANDIWORK?
I SUPPOSED IT DEPENDS ON YOUR PRIORITIES. KILLING ME WOULD LOOK GOOD ON YOUR RÉSUMÉ--IF YOU COULD MANAGE IT.
BUT THIS PLACE? IT'S GOT ITS OWN MOMENTUM.
IT ACCRETED AROUND ME.
CERTAINLY I DID NOTHING TO STOP IT.

HAH! WELL, I AM ANSWERED. THE TEMPTATION WAS TOO GREAT. TO STRIKE THE HEAD OFF WITH ONE THRUST.
YOU WERE SENT HERE TO TEST ME, THEN.
NOBODY SENDS ME ANYWHERE. AND YOUR PLANS TO TOPPLE HELL ARE YOUR OWN BUSINESS.
MY--MY OWN--?
I DON'T EVEN LIVE HERE ANYMORE.
IT'S A SYSTEM, THAT'S ALL. IT MATCHES SUPPLY AND DEMAND IN THE MATTER OF AGONY.
REMOVE IT AND HE'LL PUT SOMETHING ELSE IN ITS PLACE.
AYE, SIR. BUT THE HEAT OF THE FORGE IS NOT THE SAME FOR THE HORSESHOE AS FOR THE SMITH.
YOU UNDERSTAND.
YES, I SUPPOSE I DO.
WE MIGHT EVEN TALK STRATEGIES AT SOME POINT.
IF NOTHING ELSE, WE CAN GIVE EACH OTHER THE LUXURY OF A NEW PERSPECTIVE.

Her friends call her warrior. Her enemies berserker.
All agree that Mazikeen of the Lilim will fight on until her body is rendered tallow. And will then spit as she burns.
But when she hacked off a score of the bodiless limbs, and a hundred more had grown to replace them--
--she was obliged to take the battle to a different front.
WAR LEADER, WAIT! WE WILL JOIN YOU!
STAY WHERE YOU ARE.
THERE MUST BE ANOTHER PATH FURTHER DOWN THE SLOPE. GO SLOWLY AND TEST THE GROUND.
LOOK FOR MY TRAIL. I'LL MAKE IT OBVIOUS.
HE'S LEFT THE ROAD-- STRIKING OFF SOUTH.
GOOD. MISRAN WILL BE AHEAD OF HIM BY NOW. HE HAS NOWHERE TO GO.

AYE, BUT HE DOES.
HE IS HEADING FOR A HOUSE, ON THE FAR SIDE OF THIS PEAK. SCARCELY A LEAGUE AWAY.
A HOUSE? NOBODY BUILDS OUT HERE.
NOBODY COULD LIVE--
SEE, WAR LEADER. THERE!

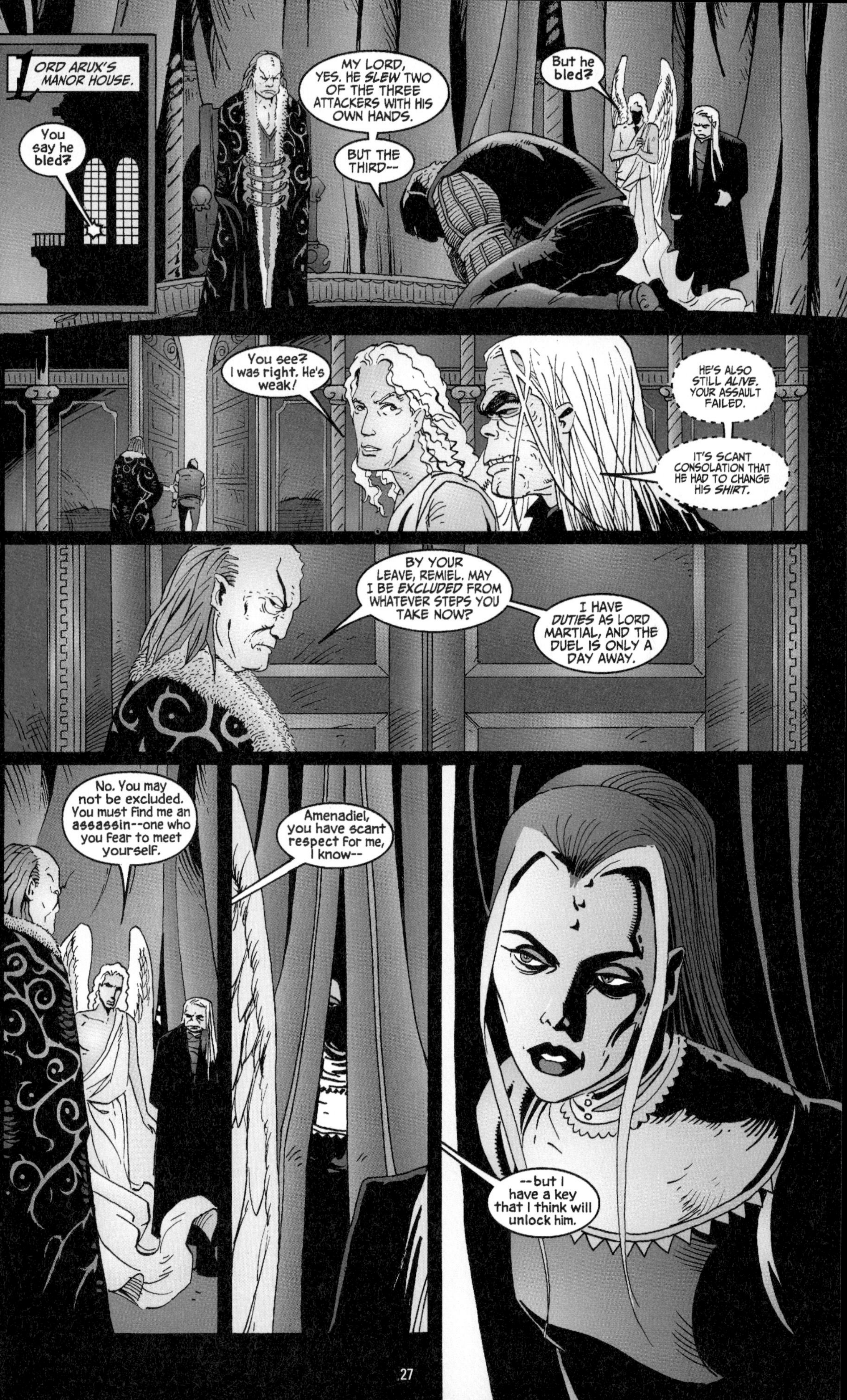
LORD ARUX'S MANOR HOUSE.
You say he bled?
MY LORD, YES. HE SLEW TWO OF THE THREE ATTACKERS WITH HIS OWN HANDS.
BUT THE THIRD--
But he bled?
You see? I was right. He's weak!
HE'S ALSO STILL ALIVE. YOUR ASSAULT FAILED.
IT'S SCANT CONSOLATION THAT HE HAD TO CHANGE HIS SHIRT.
BY YOUR LEAVE, REMIEL. MAY I BE EXCLUDED FROM WHATEVER STEPS YOU TAKE NOW?
I HAVE DUTIES AS LORD MARTIAL, AND THE DUEL IS ONLY A DAY AWAY.
No. You may not be excluded. You must find me an assassin--one who you fear to meet yourself.
Amenadiel, you have scant respect for me, I know--
--but I have a key that I think will unlock him.

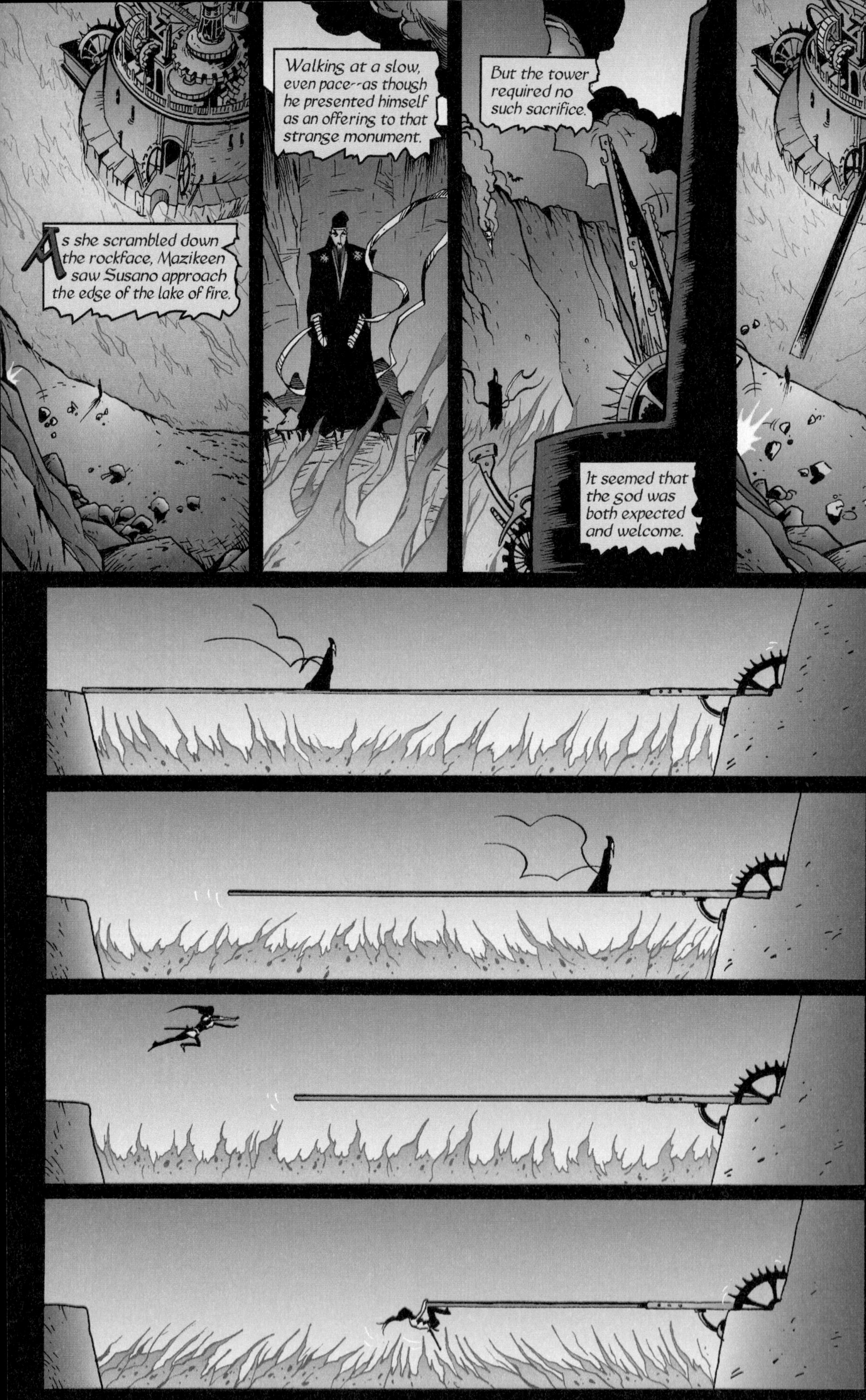
As she scrambled down the rockface, Mazikeen saw Susano approach the edge of the lake of fire.
Walking at a slow, even pace--as though he presented himself as an offering to that strange monument.
But the tower required no such sacrifice.
It seemed that the god was both expected and welcome.

YOU MUST UNDERSTAND THAT I DETEST COMPANY. *ALL* COMPANY.
YOUR VERY *PRESENCE* MAKES MY SKIN CRAWL.
I HAD HEARD THIS, GREAT ARTIFICER. NOR DO I COME HERE *LIGHTLY*, OR WILLFULLY.
BUT YOU YOURSELF GAVE ME LEAVE, AND MY *ADMIRATION* FOR YOUR WORK--
YES, YES. ENOUGH.
I SAID YOU COULD HAVE SANCTUARY HERE IF YOU COULD *DELIVER* WHAT YOU PROMISED.
HAVE YOU?
SEE FOR YOURSELF.
OH, THE GEMSTONES AND THE PRECIOUS METALS WILL COME LATER. BUT THE *SUBSTANCE* OF OUR AGREEMENT--
YES. THE SUBSTANCE.
BRING HER FORWARD, INTO THE *LIGHT*.

I HAVE WAITED SO LONG TO SEE YOU AGAIN, MAZIKEEN, THAT I COULD ALMOST *FORGIVE* YOU.
BUT I SUPPOSE YOU'LL HAVE TO BE *PUNISHED*.
AS AN EXAMPLE TO *OTHER* UNDUTIFUL WIVES.

She whom I love and hate most in the world went out riding-with such mischief in her heart.
Lys. The Lady Lys. Who had surfeited on cruelty and then almost died of compassion.
In Effrul, as in most of Hell, an unguarded coach is at worst a diversion, at best a banquet.
The gossamer-winged dwellers of the middle heights paused in their internecine wars to fall on her coach and feast.
But the coachman just laughed as they stooped over him.
And the black armorial crest on the carriage's side bore a legend which to the eyes of the demons reads "Do it then, and be dust."
Whereupon it occurred to the sky-demons that to risk the final death for the sake of a hearty breakfast is a fool's transaction.
Even in Hell, there are far easier meals to be had.
Lys's heart called out to them, for she had been like them once. A creature of air and appetite.
Until she met with me.

Until I poisoned her.
Her father had swallowed poison too, but it was none of mine.
I did not love him enough for that.
LORD ARUX, THE ASSASSIN AWAITS YOUR PLEASURE.
THANK YOU, PRACKSPOOR. LET HIM COME.
I ADVISE YOU AGAIN TO RECONSIDER. YOU ALIGN YOURSELF AGAINST THE MORNINGSTAR.
IF YOUR HAND IS SEEN IN THIS, THE ANGELS WILL NOT BE ENOUGH TO PROTECT YOU.
AND WHAT PROTECTION WILL I ENJOY IF I DEFY THEM? LIKE ALL THE LORDS OF HELL, I ONLY RULE BY THEIR PATRONAGE.
SEND HIM IN. AND THEN LEAVE US.
GOOD DAY TO YOU, BRAID.
I HEAR IMPRESSIVE REPORTS OF YOUR SKILLS.
YOU HEAR NOTHING FROM THOSE I HAVE VISITED. GOD AND ANGEL AND DEMON, THEIR SILENCE SPEAKS LOUDEST FOR ME.
WHO WOULD YOU HAVE DEAD?
YOUR PROFESSIONAL ATTENTIONS ARE REQUIRED FOR LUCIFER MORNINGSTAR.
THIS IS VIRTUS, BY THE WAY. HE IS TO BE YOUR PARTNER IN THE ENTERPRISE.

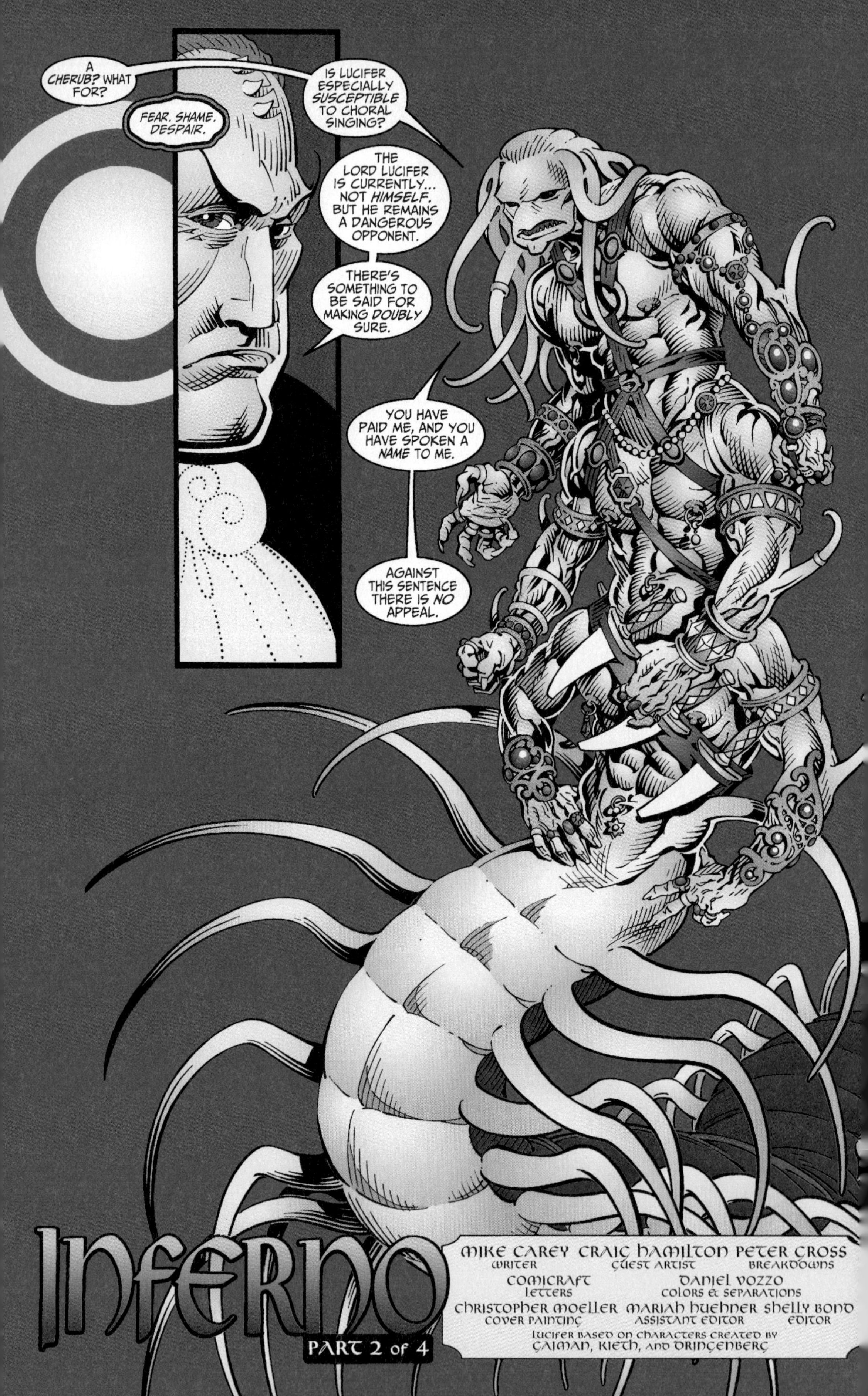

A CHERUB? WHAT FOR?
IS LUCIFER ESPECIALLY SUSCEPTIBLE TO CHORAL SINGING?
FEAR. SHAME. DESPAIR.
THE LORD LUCIFER IS CURRENTLY... NOT HIMSELF. BUT HE REMAINS A DANGEROUS OPPONENT.
THERE'S SOMETHING TO BE SAID FOR MAKING DOUBLY SURE.
YOU HAVE PAID ME, AND YOU HAVE SPOKEN A NAME TO ME.
AGAINST THIS SENTENCE THERE IS NO APPEAL.
INFERNO
PART 2 of 4
MIKE CAREY WRITER
CRAIG HAMILTON GUEST ARTIST
PETER CROSS BREAKDOWNS
COMICRAFT LETTERS
DANIEL VOZZO COLORS & SEPARATIONS
CHRISTOPHER MOELLER COVER PAINTING
MARIAH HUEHNER ASSISTANT EDITOR
SHELLY BOND EDITOR
LUCIFER BASED ON CHARACTERS CREATED BY GAIMAN, KIETH, AND DRINGENBERG

As for Susano? His manners, normally equal to any situation, were put under the severest strain.
WATCH.
BAROOM

WELL...?
EXTRAORDINARY. YOU FOUND A WAY TO MOVE YOUR CLOCK BACKWARDS WITHIN TIME'S TORRENT.
DON'T BE ABSURD, SUSANO-O-NO-MIKOTO. THAT WOULD BE BANAL.
IT IS THE SLIPSHOD MATERIALS OF REALITY THAT THE CLOCK MANIPULATES. DIRECTLY.
AND IT IS NOT LIMITED TO TIME.
AH. OF COURSE.
IF I WERE STAYING HERE LONGER, I WOULD BEG YOU TO EXPLAIN ITS FUNCTIONING.
BUT ALAS, MY BUSINESS COERCES MY MANNERS TO A DISTRESSING EXTENT, AND I MUST NOW DEPART.
YOUR PARDON, GREAT SCORIA?
I WAS SPEAKING TO THE AUTOMATON. THEY RESPOND ONLY TO RUHOK, THE LANGUAGE OF MY DEMON FOREFATHERS.
THE DEMONSTRATION I JUST GAVE YOU WILL HAVE A DESTABILIZING EFFECT ON THE LAND AROUND US.
YOU CANNOT LEAVE. NOT YET.
WHEN THE THIRD BRASS ARMATURE IS AT THE VERTICAL, THEY WILL READY SUPPER. I'LL SEE YOU THEN.
LIKE YOU, I HAVE OTHER BUSINESS THAT CALLS ME FIRST.

WHY NOT JUST --
-- TO THE DEATH?
IN THE CASE OF SOME OF THE DUELISTS, DEATH PROVED TO BE A LITTLE DIFFICULT TO DEFINE.
THE LORDS OF EFFRUL AGREED ON THIS WORDING BECAUSE IT WORKS. MOST OF THE TIME.
WE'LL FIGHT UNTIL ONE OF US TEARS OUT THE OTHER'S HEART. AND EATS IT.
ANY BREACH OF THE RULES, AND THE LORDS MARTIAL WILL COMBINE THEIR POWERS TO KILL THE TRANSGRESSOR.
AND IS THE ANGEL... HUF... STRONGER THAN YOU, LUCIFER? IN YOUR CURRENT STATE?
YOU MIGHT LEND YOUR WEIGHT TO THIS WHILE YOU ANSWER.
MY STRENGTH AT THE MOMENT IS SCARCELY GREATER THAN YOURS.
AND AMENADIEL COULD TEAR YOU LIKE PAPER.

WELL, MIGHT NOT A DEVIL LAY BY HIS HEART, AND FIGHT *WITHOUT* IT?
CRASH!!
POSSIBLE. BUT AGAINST THE RULES.
AND **OBVIOUS** EVEN TO THE MOST CURSORY INSPECTION.
YOU'VE OPENED YOUR *WOUND* AGAIN. HERE.
THANK YOU.
MY LORD! MY LORD!

I TOLD HER YOU WEREN'T *RECEIVING*, MY LORD, BUT SHE INSISTED. AND I COULD NOT REFUSE HER.
SPEAK SENSE, MAN.
WHO INSISTED? WHO'S COME?
THE LADY LYS.

MAZIKEEN.
MY LOVE.
YOU'VE CHANGED YOUR FACE. THE NEW ONE MAKES A *CURIOUS* EFFECT.
LOOSEN MY CHAINS, THEN, AND LET ME SEE WHAT I CAN MAKE OF YOURS.
COULD YOU FIND IT IN YOUR HEART TO BEG MY *FORGIVENESS?*
FOR THE *BETRAYAL.* FOR THE BREAKING OF YOUR VOWS.
THERE WERE NO VOWS. WE SHARED BLOOD AND WE RUTTED TOGETHER.
WE *CHOSE* EACH OTHER FOR A TIME. THAT'S ALL.

NO. THAT IS NOT ALL. FOR US IT WAS DIFFERENT.
RRRIP!
RRRIP!
IF YOU WERE TO ASK FOR FORGIVENESS, IT WOULD NOT REMOVE THE NEED TO LASH YOU.
BUT IT WOULD MAKE THE LASHING AN ACT OF RECONCILIATION BETWEEN US, NOT A PUNISHMENT.
DON'T WASTE YOUR BREATH.
EVERY WORD COULD BE A STROKE.

I APOLOGIZE *PROFUSELY*, LADY. I WOULD NOT HAVE MADE YOU WAIT.

IT'S NO MATTER, DUKE OF GLY. I *AMUSED* MYSELF BY LOOKING AT THE PORTRAITS.

I NOTICE YOU HAVEN'T YET SAT *YOURSELF*.

GOD FORBID. I STAND IN NO LINE OF *DESCENT*, AND I WILL NEVER PUT MY LIKENESS HERE.

NO? WELL, PERHAPS IT'S FOR THE *BEST*.

A PAINTER MUST CAPTURE THE *ESSENCE*, NOT MERELY THE LIKENESS.

SOMETHING OF A *CHALLENGE*, WHEN THE SUBJECT IS SO MERCURIAL AND UNPREDICTABLE.

AND THE LORD *LUCIFER* IS HERE TOO. HOW PERFECT. IT'S BEEN AN AGE, MORNINGSTAR.

A SCORE OF AGES.

I'VE LOST COUNT. BUT YOU HAVEN'T *CHANGED*, LYS.

NOT TRUE.

I HAVE CHANGED BEYOND ALL REACH OR *FATHOM*.

YES. PERHAPS YOU HAVE AT THAT.
HAVE YOU PASSED THROUGH ANY FIRES LATELY?
NONE SO HOT AS YOURS. BUT HELL IS A COLD PLACE, THESE DAYS.
MADAM, WHAT IS IT THAT BRINGS YOU HERE?
PAINFUL AS IT MUST SURELY BE TO YOU...
WHY, I THANK YOU FOR YOUR SOLICITUDE, MASTER RUDD.
KLAK
I AM COME TO TELL YOU THAT MY FATHER IS SUBORNED. HE INTENDS TO ENSURE THAT THE VICTORY IN THE COMING DUEL GOES TO AMENADIEL.
ASSUMIN IT IS FOU AT ALL
AND NOW PERHAPS YOU WILL SEE ME BACK TO MY COACH. IF MY ABSENCE IS NOTICED, IT WILL GO HARD ON ME.
AND AS GENTLEMEN I'M SURE YOU COULDN'T BEAR TO SEE ME SUFFER.

MY LIFE--
--IS A MONUMENT.
A MONUMENT TO OUTLAST BRONZE, GREAT SCORIA.
ALL THESE THINGS I HAVE MADE, THAT NOBODY ELSE HAS DARED TO DREAM OF!
EVEN THESE IRON HOMUNCULI THAT SERVE MY NEEDS.
TRIVIAL. TRIVIAL! BUT THE MIND LABORS, AND THE HAND GIVES BIRTH.
UUUUUUURGGH!
SKLANG! SKLANG! SKLANG! SKLANG!
SHE MOCKED ME. EVEN AS I WAS BEATING HER.
AND SHE WOULDN'T STOP.

INESTIMABLE MAKER, THE PERFIDY OF WOMEN--
YOU WANT TO KNOW HOW IT WORKS? THE CLOCK?
YOU WANT TO SEE HOW WONDROUSLY I HAVE WROUGHT?
I CURSE THE URGENCY OF MY ERRAND, THAT MAKES EXPLORATIONS IMPOSSIBLE.
I CAME HERE ONLY TO DELIVER YOUR WIFE, AND TO FREE MYSELF FROM HER PURSUIT. NOW I FEAR I MUST--
COME.
I'LL SHOW YOU HOW PITIFULLY WIDE OF THE MARK THE BITCH'S TAUNTS WENT.
I AM...AT YOUR DISPOSAL, GREAT SCORIA.
BRING HER, TOO.
YOU WILL WORSHIP ME, MAZIKEEN.
YOU WILL YET WORSHIP ME.
I HAVE STARED INTO THE LIGHT--
--AND YOU ARE ALL MY SHADOWS.

NOTHING TO SAY, MASTER RUDD?
NOTHING TO ANY PURPOSE. I DID NOT KNOW THAT YOU AND LUCIFER HAD--
--HAD KNOWN EACH OTHER.
AH! YOU MUST GIVE UP THESE EUPHEMISMS NOW. THE ARISTOCRACY DISDAIN SUCH NICETIES.
THERE WAS A TIME WHEN I WAS KNOWN FOR KNOWING EVERYBODY.
LYS, I HURT YOU ALMOST BEYOND BEARING, I KNOW.
I CANNOT BELIEVE THAT YOU'VE COME HERE AS A FRIEND.
BUT PAIN IS A CONUNDRUM, CHRISTOPHER. TO YOU MORE THAN ANYONE.
I USED TO FIND IT EROTIC.
BUT THEN, I HAD NEVER ENCOUNTERED A PAIN OF THE SPIRIT THAT THE BODY COULD NOT QUENCH.

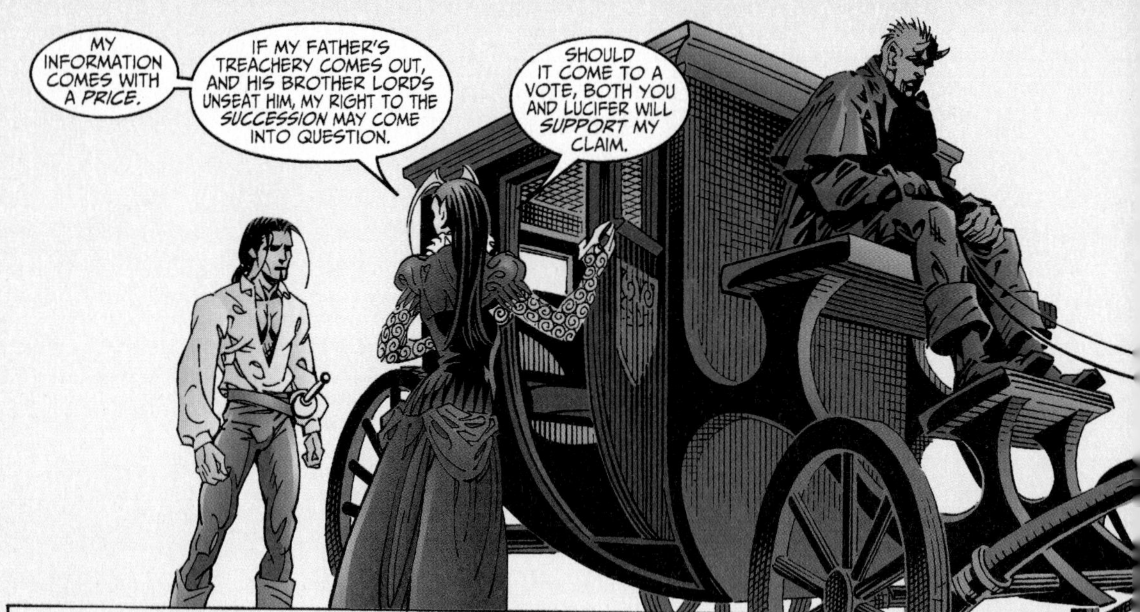
MY INFORMATION COMES WITH A PRICE.
IF MY FATHER'S TREACHERY COMES OUT, AND HIS BROTHER LORDS UNSEAT HIM, MY RIGHT TO THE SUCCESSION MAY COME INTO QUESTION.
SHOULD IT COME TO A VOTE, BOTH YOU AND LUCIFER WILL SUPPORT MY CLAIM.

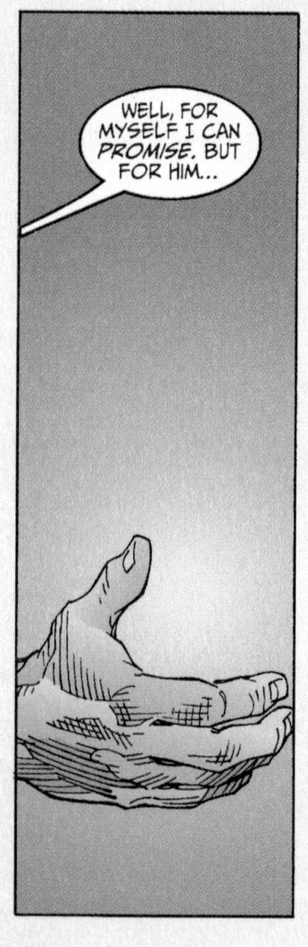
WELL, FOR MYSELF I CAN PROMISE. BUT FOR HIM...

DO NOT THINK TO TOUCH ME, MASTER RUDD!
I WILL HOOK OUT YOUR EYES WITH MY THUMBNAILS BEFORE YOU TOUCH ME AGAIN!

I MEANT ONLY TO ASSIST YOU INTO THE CARRIAGE. I KNOW WELL ENOUGH THAT'S ALL SPENT BETWEEN US.

ALL SPENT? NO, I HAVE BUSINESS WITH YOU YET, CHRISTOPHER.
BUT NOT TONIGHT.
TONIGHT YOU MAY SLEEP.
SO LONG AS CONSCIENCE AND CIRCUMSTANCE ALLOW.

PITY. ANGUISH. FEAR.
BE SILENT, CREATURE, AND LET ME WORK. THE CIRCLETS ARE SENSITIVE TO MAGIC, BUT THERE'S NOTHING HERE.
NOTHING THAT THREATENS US--
--BUT PERHAPS ENOUGH TO LIGHT OUR WAY.
I SENSE A WARD AND A MAKING. IF THEY'RE GUARDING LORD LUCIFER, THEN HE'S UP THERE.

DOOR'S OPEN.
FOR WHAT IT'S WORTH.
I'D RATHER HAVE YOU ALIVE, GIVEN THE CHOICE.
THAT WAY YOU CAN BETRAY YOUR EMPLOYERS.
BRAVE WORDS. BUT YOU'VE ONLY TWO SMALL WEAVINGS TO PROTECT YOU, LUCIFER.
ARMIES AND CITADELS WOULD NOT BE ENOUGH.
TAKE IT UP WITH THE OWNER.
THEY'RE HIS SPELLS, NOT MINE.
AH. SO THIS IS THE WARD.
THE MIGHTY MORNINGSTAR HIDING BEHIND HEDGE MAGICS.
BUT LOOK NOW, LUCIFER--
--AT WHAT WAS HIDING BEHIND ME!

THIS CREATURE IS A CHERUB. BUT APPARENTLY IT IS *MAD*. SICK WITH PARANOIA AND SELF-HATRED.
ITS WEAKNESS INFECTS ALL IT *TOUCHES*.
AND NOW IT IS *INSIDE* YOU.

DOWN, DOWN, DOWN. MORE THAN A MILE. I BUILT INTO BEDROCK, BUT THAT'S NOT THE WONDER.
ANY MOLE CAN DIG. ANY FOOL WITH A *SHOVEL* CAN DIG.
THERE! WHAT WAS LUCIFER'S REBELLION COMPARED TO *THIS?*
WHAT HAS *ANYONE* DONE EQUAL TO THIS?
CELESTIAL ARTISAN, I *SEE* BUT DO NOT COMPREHEND.
YOU MUST *EXPOUND* THIS MARVEL TO ME.

EXPOUND IT? IT'S *OBVIOUS.* I DUG INTO HIS MIND.

THESE ARE THE THOUGHTS OF GOD.

I BELIEVE I COULD HAVE BESTED YOU ANYWAY, MORNINGSTAR.
BUT IT WAS LORD ARUX'S WISH THAT I TAKE NO UNNECESSARY RISKS.
A RISK... IMPLIES...THAT THIS COULD HAVE ENDED... DIFFERENTLY.
VERY TRUE. AND THAT IS WHAT I TOLD HIM.
THEY SAY YOU WERE AN ANGEL ONCE. WELL, SO AM I.
I AM THE ANGEL OF MERCY, WHOSE HANDS BRING THE END OF ALL PAIN.
THE...LAST TIME I MET ONE OF YOUR RACE... I WAS ABLE TO STRIKE A DEAL WITH HER.
ARE YOU... AMENABLE...TO REASON?
BY NO MEANS.

WELL, IT WAS WORTH TRYING. MARGINALLY.
"SISYPHUS."
THE--THE TOWER--
--WAS MADE OF SPELLS, NOT STONE. THAT WAS THE MAKING YOU SENSED. GOODBYE, ASSASSIN.

I came on the scene too late. But made up for it by issuing a great many unnecessary commands.
HAVE THIS OFFAL CLEARED AWAY.
AND DOUBLE THE GUARD.
AYE, MY LORD. AT ONCE.

HAVE YOU SUSTAINED SOME FURTHER INJURY, LORD LUCIFER? I HAVE SURGEONS--
NO. NO INJURY.
THIS IS SOMETHING I'M GOING TO HAVE TO WORK OUT FOR MYSELF.

THEN I'LL BID YOU GOODNIGHT. PERHAPS IN THE MORNING WE CAN--
...
WELL, TOMORROW IS TIME ENOUGH, TO BE SURE.

As I walked away from him, I drew it forth from my sleeve. The kerchief with which he stanched his wound in the torture shed.
In truth, I had forgotten I had it.

To the north west of Hell, where now I write--close to the disputed border between Effrul and Amsath--there is a valley, through which a poisoned river runs.
Stands of poisoned trees, feeding on its waters, thrust up their pleading hands as they die.
The laws of Effrul call for "a dueling ground in open air, twice ten leagues across"--their infernal lordships desiring to see a hunt as well as a kill.
The space was duly marked with blood and salt.
The carpenters of Lord Arux had been told to build accommodations for a million spectators.
More than twice that number had arrived before the building even commenced.
But the carpenters could have begun their hammering before Adam fell, and leveled all of Eden for wood.
It would not have been enough. Not for this fight.
What matter that Lucifer had abandoned these realms for Earth? Or that Amenadiel had given control of the angelic host back to its several generals?
In their minds, this was Hell against Heaven.

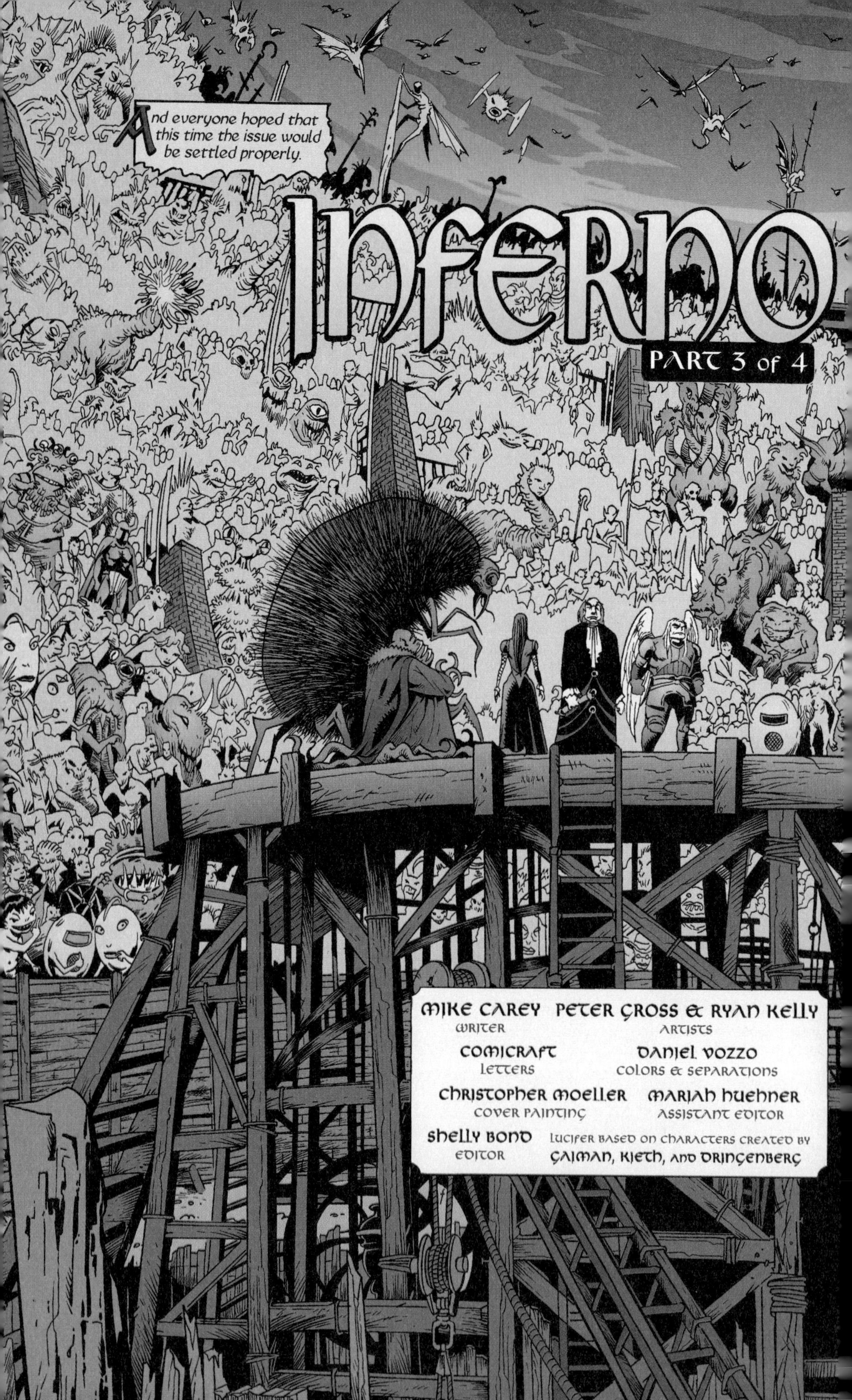
And everyone hoped that this time the issue would be settled properly.
INFERNO
PART 3 of 4
MIKE CAREY
WRITER
PETER GROSS & RYAN KELLY
ARTISTS
COMICRAFT
LETTERS
DANIEL VOZZO
COLORS & SEPARATIONS
CHRISTOPHER MOELLER
COVER PAINTING
MARIAH HUEHNER
ASSISTANT EDITOR
SHELLY BOND
EDITOR
LUCIFER BASED ON CHARACTERS CREATED BY
GAIMAN, KIETH, AND DRINGENBERG

LOOK AT THAT HEAVEN-SPEWED BASTARD. STANDING THERE LIKE HIS SHIT DON'T STINK.
IT DOESN'T. IT SINGS HOSANNAS.
HOW CAN HE HOPE TO STAND AGAINST LUCIFER?
TEN SOULS SAYS THE FIGHT IS OVER BEFORE HE STRIKES A BLOW.
I'LL TAKE THAT WAGER.
YOU ARE PENSIVE, MY DAUGHTER.
NO, FATHER. MERELY BORED.
THIS FUTILE POMP AND CEREMONY WEARIES ME TO DEATH.
BLOOD!
GIVE US BLOOD!
THE CROWD GROWS RESTLESS. EXCUSE ME, LYS.

I AM ARUX OF EFFRUL, AND I STAND AS LORD MARTIAL HERE.
THE DUKES DUROVALLIS AND CLOY STAND LIKEWISE, THEIR AUTHORITY NO LESS THAN MINE.
WHO SPEAKS FOR AMENADIEL, OF THE THRONES?
HIMSELF.
AND DO YOU HERE ABIDE BY THE CHALLENGE YOU HAVE ISSUED?
YES.
I DO.
AND WHO IS IT THAT SPEAKS FOR LUCIFER MORNINGSTAR?

I ASK AGAIN.
WHO SPEAKS FOR LUCIFER MORNINGSTAR?

I DO!
I SPEAK FOR HIM!

WHAT? DUKE OF GLY, THERE IS NO PRECEDENT FOR THIS.
THE RESPONDENT MUST ANSWER THE CHALLENGE OR HIS LIFE IS FORFEIT.

AYE, MY LORD. I KNOW THAT--
"BUT THE RESPONDENT IS INDISPOSED."

Indisposed! The cherub Virtus had infected his soul and his volition. He could not summon the will to move.
His mind kept trying to grasp its present predicament, only to slip away obliquely into other places.
THIS IS NOT OVER, MORNINGSTAR. AND IT MUST BE OVER. WHILE YOU LIVE, THERE IS NO JOY FOR ME.
I CHALLENGE YOU TO FACE ME-- ALONE. WHEREVER AND WHENEVER YOU LIKE.
VERY WELL. IN EFFRUL, A YEAR FROM NOW. WHEN I AM RAW AND CRIPPLED FROM THE FIRE.
WHEN THE TOWER HAS BEEN STRUCK BY LIGHTNING.
DO NOT... MOCK ME... CREATURE.
I KNOW YOU...FOR WHAT YOU ARE. AND YOU ARE NOTHING.
In a moment of lucidity, he saw what he would have to do.
But it would mean dragging the dead weight of his body out of the castle to the fields beyond.
He did not even reach the doorway of his room.

"THE MIND OF GOD?"
EXACTLY. MY PROBLEM WAS A METAPHYSICAL ONE, YOU SEE.
AND THE METAPHYSICS OF ENGINEERING, MY DEAR SUSANO, IS STILL IN ITS INFANCY.
I WISHED TO MEASURE TIME AND SPACE BY REFERENCE TO SOME ABSOLUTE POINT.
YET TIME AND SPACE LIE IN AN UGLY HEAP, ALL TANGLED UP WITH EACH OTHER AND EVERYTHING ELSE.
BUT GOD! MEASURED FROM HIM, THE DISTANCE IS ALWAYS ZERO.
THE TIME IS ALWAYS NOW.
I USED A DRILL SO SMALL. SO VERY SMALL.
ITS TIP A MOUNTAIN OF DIAMOND SHARPENED DOWN TO AN INVISIBLE SPLINTER.

BUT... GREAT SCORIA. THE MIND OF YAHWEH!
HOW WOULD SUCH A THING BE POSSIBLE? ONLY A MIRACLE--
A MIRACLE! YES!
AND THOSE WHO SNEER AT MIRACLES REVEAL THEIR OWN INADEQUACIES. THEIR OWN SMALLNESS.
STILL NO WORDS, MY WIFE? STILL NO WORSHIP?
IS YOUR SOUL TOO SHRIVELED TO SEE THE GREATNESS OF WHAT I'VE DONE HERE?
LOOK! LOOK DOWN!
CAN YOU GUESS WHAT GOD IS THINKING OF?
HERE.
LET ME SHOW YOU.

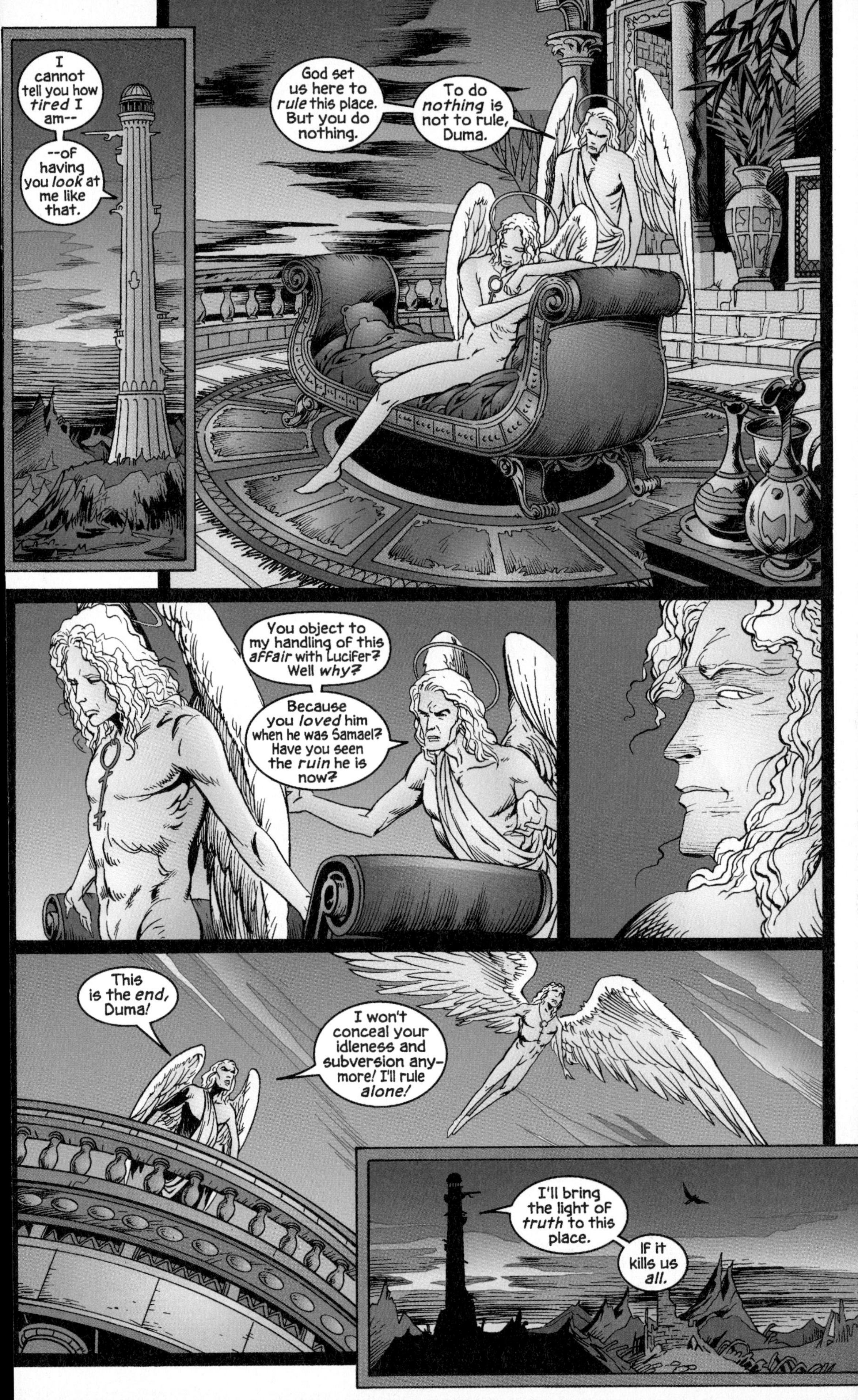
I cannot tell you how *tired* I am--
--of having you *look* at me like that.
God set us here to *rule* this place. But you do nothing.
To do *nothing* is not to rule, Duma.
You object to my handling of this *affair* with Lucifer? Well *why?*
Because you *loved* him when he was Samael? Have you seen the *ruin* he is now?
This is the *end,* Duma!
I won't conceal your idleness and subversion any-more! I'll rule *alone!*
I'll bring the light of *truth* to this place.
If it kills us *all.*

FATHER, THESE PEOPLE HAVE CROSSED HALF OF *HELL* TO SEE A DUEL. THEY'LL ACCEPT NOTHING LESS.
YOU MUST *WAIT* UNTIL LUCIFER APPEARS, HOWEVER LONG IT TAKES.
THE RULES ARE *CLEAR*, LYS. THERE IS NO LEEWAY.

I BEG TO *DIFFER*.
THE RULES ALLOW FOR *EITHER* NAME TO BE CALLED THRICE.
AYE, THREE TIMES, WITH A FULL TURN OF THE *GLASS* IN BETWEEN.
DON'T BE TOO QUICK TO GIVE THE GAME TO HEAVEN, ARUX.

WELL. I DEFER TO MY BROTHER LORDS.

BUT PERHAPS ONE OF *YOU* WILL TELL THE CROWD THAT THEY MUST WAIT ON LUCIFER'S PLEASURE.

LORD ARUX. VOUCHSAFE ME A WORD.
I BEG YOUR *INDULGENCE*, MASTER RUDD.
I'M SCARCE IN *HUMOR*.

WELL, IF IT'S THE UNCERTAINTY OF THIS *CONTEST* THAT TROUBLES YOUR HEART, MY LORD--
--I'VE SOMETHING HERE THAT WILL BE BETTER THAN ANY *MEDICINE*.
SPEAK *PLAINLY*, MASTER RUDD.
LUCIFER'S *POWER* IS ALL BUT GONE.
IF HE ENTERS THE ARENA AT ALL, HE WILL TRY TO *AVOID* THE ANGEL FOR AS LONG AS HE CAN.
HE TOLD ME THAT HIS SERVANT, *MAZIKEEN*, IS SEEKING TO RESTORE HIS STRENGTH. HIS AIM WILL BE TO *DELAY* THE FIGHT UNTIL SHE SUCCEEDS.
BUT FROM THIS HE *CANNOT* HIDE.
WHAT IS IT?
SOMETHING OF HIS THAT IS NOW *YOURS*. SOMETHING THAT WILL YEARN *TOWARDS* HIM, WHEREVER HE IS.
IT WORKS BY THE MAGIC OF *SYMPATHIES*, MY LORD.
YOU HAVE FOUND SOME OF HIS *HAIR* OR HIS BLOOD. OR THE PARING OF A NAIL. REMARKABLE.
IT MAY NOT *COME* TO A FIGHT, OF COURSE. BUT STILL--
TO OPEN IT WILL PROBABLY BREAK THE CHARM. BUT MY LORD, IN THE MATTER OF MY REWARD--
YES, YES.
--THAT DISCUSSION WE CAN CONVENIENTLY POSTPONE. AFTER ALL--
--THIS MAY NOT EVEN COME TO A FIGHT.

DUKE OF GLY.
AHH! LADY LYS! I DIDN'T HEAR YOU APPROACH.
GOOD MORROW TO YOU.
WHATEVER GIFT YOU GAVE MY FATHER...
...IT SEEMED TO LIGHTEN HIS MOOD CONSIDERABLY.
IT WAS A CURIO, ONLY. A SHARED INTEREST THAT WE--
SLAP
CURSE YOU! YOU'VE BETRAYED LUCIFER, HAVEN'T YOU? AND ME WITH HIM.
I SHOULD HAVE REMEMBERED HOW EAGERLY YOU CLIMBED OVER ME TO REACH MY FATHER'S FAVOR.
Lys was my lover and my patron. Until I poisoned her joys with human grief and guilt.
LYS, I SAID NOTHING ABOUT YOU. YOU'RE SAFE.
I CARE NOT. I WILL SEE YOU PAID OUT IN FULL FOR THIS, RUDD. BY MY MOTHER'S BLOOD, I SWEAR IT.
The unthinkable harm we have done one another is the foundation of our intimacy.
As I believe is the case in many relationships.

I have tried since these events transpired to put myself in Mazikeen's place.
I have struggled to imagine what she felt.
Immersed in the effluent of God's living mind.
Drowning in his vast, slow thoughts.
These are mysteries that I cannot fathom, and was not meant to.
But I warrant it was more like Hell than Heaven.
To stand in a light so harsh must make everything else seem like pitch dark.
And leave you blinded to your own life.
KHHHHHHHH!

LUCIFER, YES? THE SPOILED BASTARD SON OF HEAVEN WHO COVERS YOU LIKE A STALLION, AND HIS WITLESS BROTHER MICHAEL.
OVER AND OVER AGAIN. YAHWEH'S FAVORITES, WHO HE TAUGHT TO HATE HIM.
IT IS AS IF HE IS OBSESSED. AS IF HE CANNOT EVEN SEE THE REST OF WHAT HE HAS MADE.
NOTHING IS REAL EXCEPT FOR LUCIFER AND MICHAEL.
YOU HAVE A KNIFE. INSIDE THE SLEEVE OF YOUR ROBE.
NO, GREAT SCORIA. I WAS MERELY--
YOU ARE MY GUEST, AND YOU WOULD OFFER VIOLENCE TO ME?
HAVEN'T YOU LISTENED TO ME? HE'S BEEN PREPARING FOR THIS SINCE THE WORLDS BEGAN.
NOW HE'S GOT WHAT HE WANTS, HE'S DONE WITH US. SO NOW I CAN BE GOD.
BRING THEM BOTH TO THE WORKROOM.
I AM AN ARTIFICER, YOU MUST REALIZE. A MAKER. AND YOU--
--YOU ARE ONLY MATERIALS.

DUMA...THE PAINFIELDS...
I NEED TO...

THE GLASS IS EMPTY.
INDEED. IT HAS BEEN FOR SOME SEVERAL MOMENTS NOW.
BUT I WOULD NOT HAVE IT SAID THAT I FAVORED HEAVEN.
THIS IS THE SECOND CALL. WHO IS IT SPEAKS FOR LUCIFER MORNINGSTAR?
WILL HE MAKE ANSWER TO THIS CHALLENGE OR NO?
IT IS STRANGE THAT HE SHOULD NOT APPEAR.
AYE. HE COULD NEVER ABIDE TO BE FORSWORN.
THAT WAS IN TIMES PAST, DUROVALLIS.
HE IS NO LONGER THE POWER HE WAS.

SET ME DOWN THERE. WHERE THE BLADES ARE.
The cherubim are emotional lattices, nothing more.
So I was told much later, by a creature who claimed to have been one.
They respond to emotion as a boat responds to a following wind.
Or a crosswind, for that matter.

Or a hurricane.

HAMMER. BRADAWL. CHISEL. KNIFE.
CHAIN THEM. MY WIFE TO THE BENCH. THE STORM GOD TO THE PILLAR.
SCORIA, THIS IS A BREACH OF HOSPITALITY.
IT WILL HAVE CONSEQUENCES.
A HUSBAND HAS RIGHTS, MAZIKEEN. SOLACES. HAVE YOU THOUGHT ABOUT THEM ONCE?
WHAT IF MY SEED WERE TO DIE? WHAT IF ALL MY GREATNESS WERE TO DIE?
WELL, IT WILL NOT DIE!
NO.

NOT LIKE THIS. NOT IN A LABORER'S APRON. I WILL COME TO YOU AS A GOD SHOULD.
I WILL PUT OUT YOUR EYES WITH MY BRIGHTNESS.
BUT I WILL FILL YOUR WOMB BY WAY OF RECOMPENSE.
SUSANO. IF YOU DESTROY THE FEATHERS WE CAN MAKE TRUCE...
...FIGHT HIM TOGETHER.
BUT MY MOTHER HAS TASKED ME TO BRING THE FEATHERS BACK INTACT.
AND ONCE SCORIA'S PASSION IS SPENT, I HOPE TO FIND HIM MORE... TRACTABLE.
SO I THANK YOU FOR YOUR CONSIDERATION, BUT I DECLINE.
MORE TRACTABLE? YOU THINK SO?
VERY WELL, SUSANO-O-NO-MIKOTO.
REMEMBER THAT I OFFERED.

I CALL UPON LUCIFER MORNINGSTAR.
FOR THE *THIRD* TIME, WILL HE RESPOND TO THE CHALLENGE?
THEN IN ACCORDANCE WITH THE LAWS OF EFFRUL, I PROCLAIM HIM *RENEGADE* TO HIS OATH.
THE DUEL AND HIS LIFE ARE *FORFEIT*. HIS PRESENCE ANATHEMA THROUGHOUT THESE--
LUCIFER MORNINGSTAR SPEAKS FOR *HIMSELF*.

I am sorry to have delayed you, Lord Arux.
Shall we *begin?*

A hush fell upon the crowd, then.
For they had seen their champion for the first time, and they were dismayed.
THE COMBATANTS MUST BE SEARCHED BEFORE THEY ENTER THE ARENA.
LOOK TO THE LORD LUCIFER.

RUDD STOLE A LITTLE OF HIS FLESH, OR BLOOD. IT WILL POINT TO HIM LIKE A LODESTONE.
THE REST IS YOUR AFFAIR.

TAKE YOUR PLACES. LUCIFER TO THE NORTH AND AMENADIEL TO THE SOUTH.
YOU MAY ENTER THE DUELING GROUNDS WHEN THE HORNS HAVE SOUNDED THRICE.

A FOOL MIGHT UNDERESTIMATE YOU, LIGHTBRINGER, AND DRAW THIS OUT FOR THE SHEER PLEASURE OF IT.

BUT I AM NOT A FOOL.

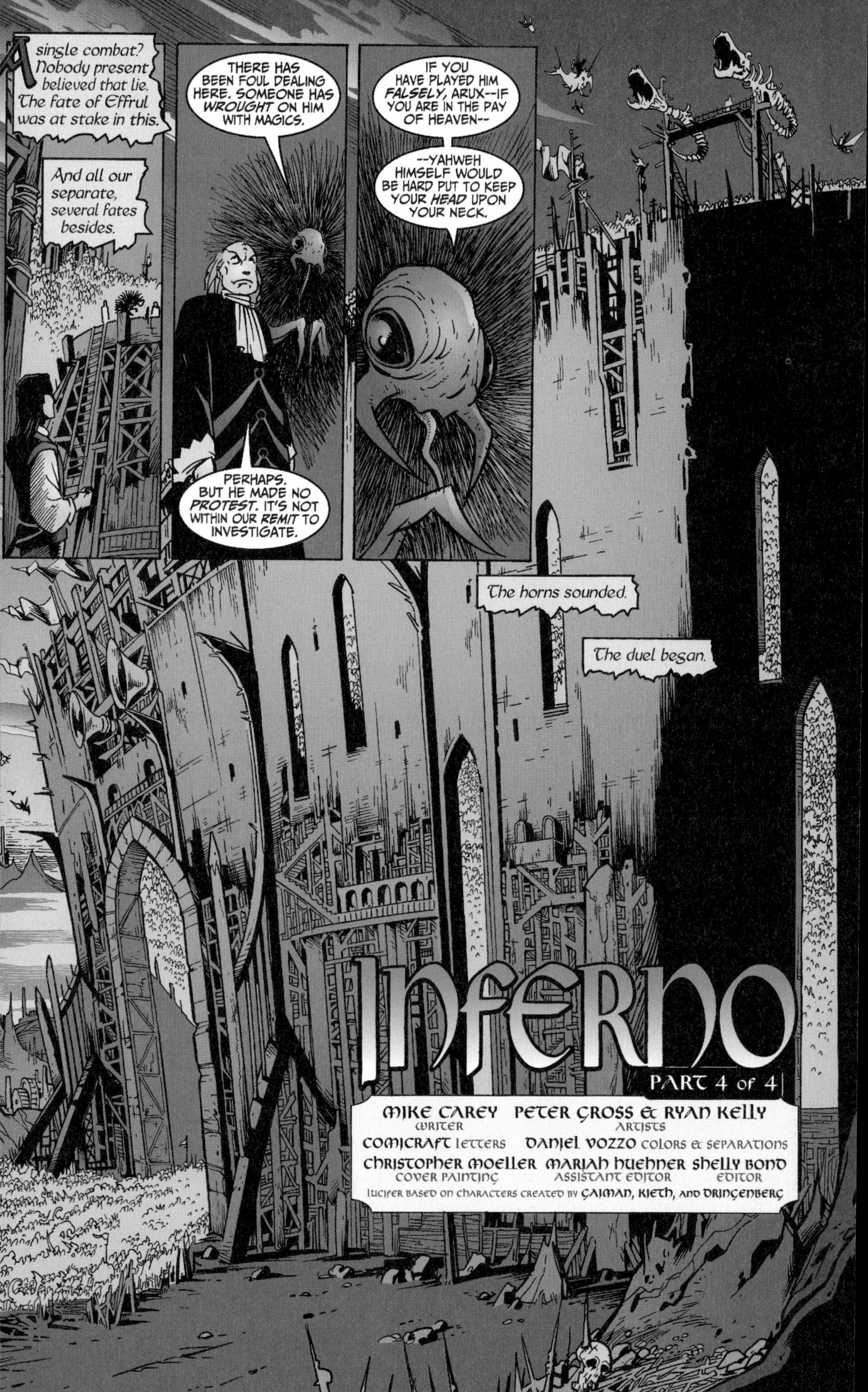
A single combat? Nobody present believed that lie. The fate of Effrul was at stake in this.
And all our separate, several fates besides.
THERE HAS BEEN FOUL DEALING HERE. SOMEONE HAS WROUGHT ON HIM WITH MAGICS.
PERHAPS. BUT HE MADE NO PROTEST. IT'S NOT WITHIN OUR REMIT TO INVESTIGATE.
IF YOU HAVE PLAYED HIM FALSELY, ARUX--IF YOU ARE IN THE PAY OF HEAVEN--
--YAHWEH HIMSELF WOULD BE HARD PUT TO KEEP YOUR HEAD UPON YOUR NECK.
The horns sounded.
The duel began.
INFERNO
PART 4 of 4
MIKE CAREY WRITER
PETER GROSS & RYAN KELLY ARTISTS
COMICRAFT LETTERS
DANIEL VOZZO COLORS & SEPARATIONS
CHRISTOPHER MOELLER COVER PAINTING
MARIAH HUEHNER ASSISTANT EDITOR
SHELLY BOND EDITOR
LUCIFER BASED ON CHARACTERS CREATED BY GAIMAN, KIETH, AND DRINGENBERG

The combatants entered the valley from two separate points, twenty leagues apart.
It was the rule and the custom for contests of this kind.
At another time, in other circumstances, this would have provided the thrill of a chase.
But the angel, Amenadiel, stooped over the dueling ground like an armored hawk.
And delay suited neither his purpose nor mine.
Not at all.
No foreplay, this time.
No honing of the pleasure through the exquisite agony of anticipation and delay.
Just the climax.
Which was always the point, after all.

LOOK UPON ME, MAZIKEEN.
I HAVE WASHED IN THE BLOOD OF WILLING SACRIFICES, AND CLOTHED MYSELF IN THE RAIMENT OF THE SUN.
LOOK UPON YOUR HUSBAND IN THE FULLNESS OF HIS PERFECTION.
SCORIA, I AM WAR LEADER OF THE LILIM. YOU ACT AGAINST YOUR WHOLE RACE NOW.
BUT GIVE ME SUSANO, AND YOU MAY YET LIVE.
I MAY YET LIVE? YOU SPEAK BLASPHEMY, MAZIKEEN.
LIFE IS MY GIFT.
AND I WILL PLANT LIFE IN YOUR BODY NOW.
MY FIRST MIRACLE WILL BE A HUMBLE, MUNDANE ONE.

The storm god Susano-O-No-Mikoto looked away fastidiously.
These events had no bearing on his errand, the burden he carried, or his vengeance against the Morningstar.
His hands were almost able to meet around the girth of the pillar. He continued to unwind his bandages.
I WILL NOT *SUBMIT* TO YOUR EMBRACE.
IT IS TOO GREAT AN *HONOR* FOR YOU, WHORE.
BUT THERE ARE NO *OTHER* VESSELS HERE THAT WILL SERVE.

Between the prayer and the headman's stroke falls the shadow.
Between the blind instinct and the uncertain act.
Between the hope of salvation--
--and the hungry dust.
LOOK. IT WAS THIS. A LITTLE OF YOU, IN A SILVER BOX, CHARMED SO THAT IT WOULD PULL TOWARDS ITS SOURCE.
THE MAN RUDD BETRAYED YOU.
YOU HAVE NOT INSPIRED LOYALTY, MORNINGSTAR.
YOU HAVE NOT INSPIRED LOVE.

I...NEVER *ASKED* FOR EITHER.
BUT WHAT ELSE HAVE WE *LIVED* BY, AFTER ALL?
WHERE ELSE IS OUR LEGACY TO BE FOUND?
YOU CHOOSE TO LIVE *ALONE*--
--TO *REJECT* ALL OPINIONS, ALL REALITIES, BUT YOUR OWN.
SO YOU HAVE NOT LIVED AT ALL. AND THIS IS NOT *DEATH*--
--BUT THE *CONFIRMATION* OF DEATH.

HOLD FAST TO HIS WINDPIPE. DON'T LET HIM SPEAK.
BECAUSE I'M A WOMAN, MY FATHER WOULD NOT TEACH ME RUHOK.
BUT HE SPOKE IT OFTEN ENOUGH, SCORIA. AND I LISTENED.

HERE IS YOUR APOTHEOSIS, HUSBAND.
YOU'VE EARNED IT.
KLUDKLUDKLUDKLUDKLUDKLUD
The pistoning motion of her arm was hypnotic.
Susano tore his eyes from it with difficulty.
Under the bandages his hands were seared bone, moved only by his divine will.
And she was too deeply involved in her catharsis to see him go.

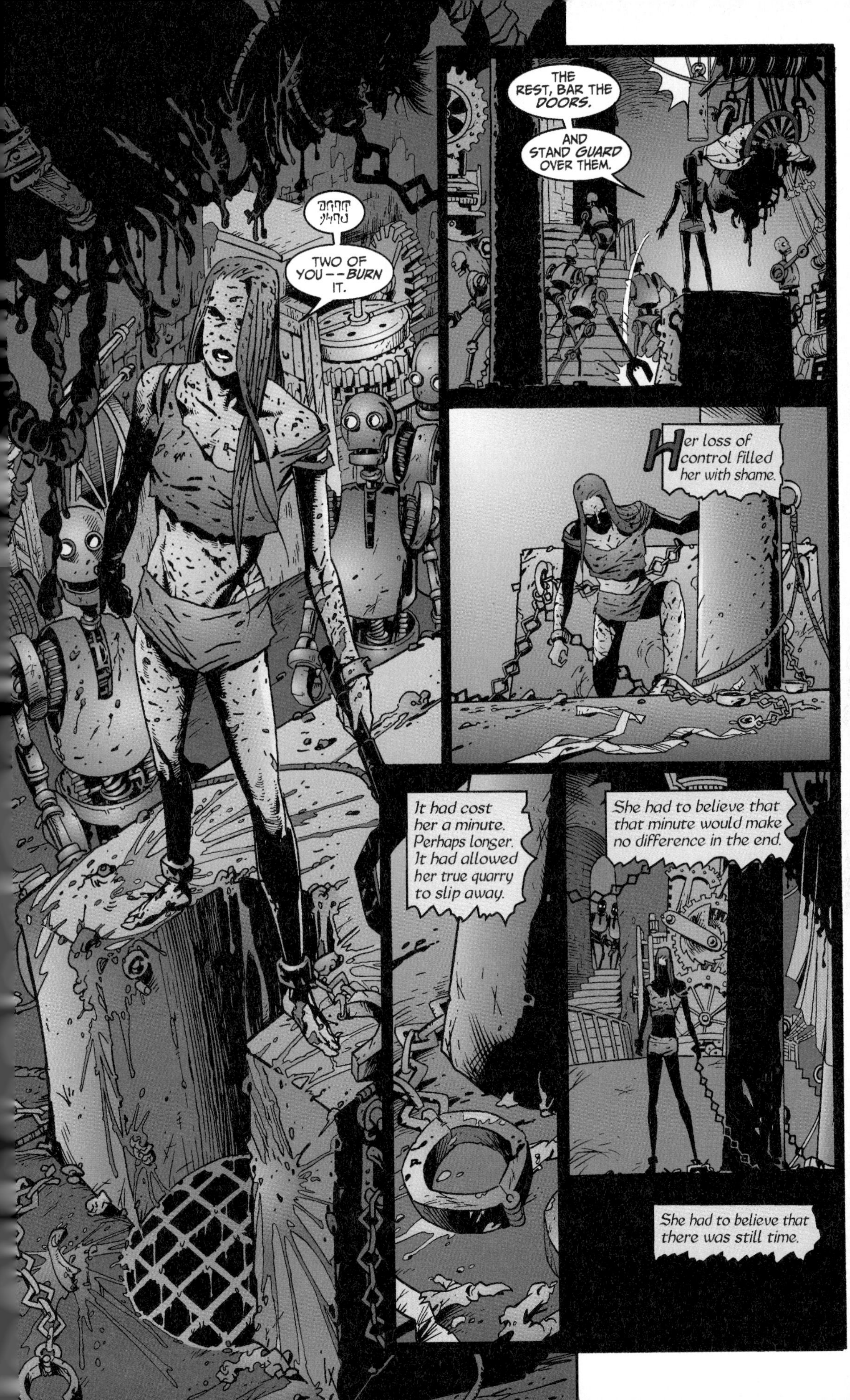

TWO OF YOU--*BURN* IT.
THE REST, BAR THE *DOORS.*
AND STAND *GUARD* OVER THEM.
Her loss of control filled her with shame.
It had cost her a minute. Perhaps longer. It had allowed her true quarry to slip away.
She had to believe that that minute would make no difference in the end.
She had to believe that there was still time.

ALL I KNOW OF JOY HAS ITS SOURCE AND ITS FRUITION IN THIS MOMENT.
YOU HAVE GIVEN ME BACK MY LIFE, LUCIFER. I MUST LOVE YOU FOR THAT.

NO.
NO.
THE--THE HEART--
I RETURN IT TO YOU FREELY. IT BELONGED TO YOUR ASSASSIN.
AND THE TOXIC CHERUB I BOUND INSIDE IT. THAT WAS ALSO YOURS, I THINK.
NO. IT WAS REMIEL'S. AAAAARH!
THIS IS -- WHAT IT FELT LIKE THEN? I CANNOT MOVE...
YOU WON'T BE NEEDING TO.

BUT YOU BROKE THE CODE DUELLO. YOU WILL DIE, TOO.
POSSIBLY. HOLD STILL, AMENADIEL.
THIS WILL PLAY BETTER IN THE BACK SEATS IF I DO IT IN ONE STROKE.
A MALEDICTION ON YOU, LUCIFER!
MAY YOU ROT BY INCHES AND OUNCES. MAY YOU --

RULES ARE RULES.
LUCIFER!
LORD LUCIFER!
EFFRUL FOR LUCIFER!

EXCELLENT! STAND FORWARD, ARUX, AND PROCLAIM HIM VICTOR.
IT'S YOUR PRIVILEGE.
No.
The privilege is mine.
No one here is to move from his place. Secure the dueling ground, Lord Arux.
And have Lucifer brought to me.

At this point we enter the intricacies of endgame.

Susano-O-No-Mikoto fled through the labyrinth of Scoria's tower. Always upwards.

With the doors barred, the roof offered the only hope of escape.

But the tower stood at the center of a lake of fire, and his ruined hands would not permit him to climb.

SUSANO.

GIVE ME THE *FEATHERS.*

It appears that there has been an *irregularity* in this contest, Lucifer Morningstar.
HAS THERE? NOT ON *MY* PART.
HE'S *WON,* ANGEL!
HE'S WON BY *OUR* RULES!

Ah, but I fear he has *not.*

His heart was not *present* in the arena.
This is a *breach* of the code duello, and his life is forfeit.

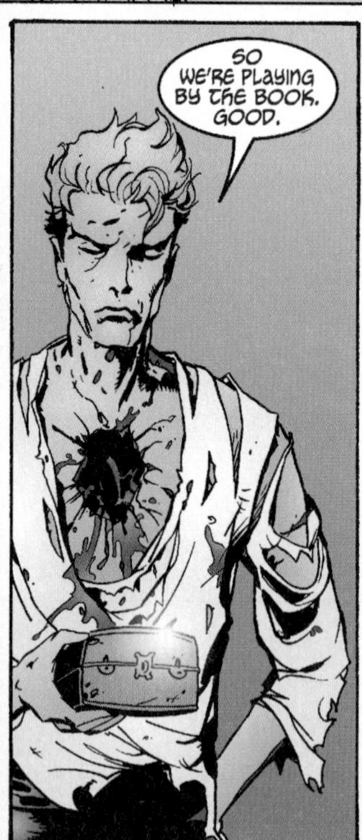
SO WE'RE PLAYING BY THE BOOK. GOOD.

I READ IT TOO. LOOK.

I OFFERED YOU YOUR *LIFE* A WHILE AGO.

YOU *REFUSED* IT.

YOU MANIPULATED ME. INTENTIONALLY!
AYE, MY LORD. TO PREVENT A GREATER INJUSTICE.
Nonetheless. Lucifer's heart was not in his own chest.
A case could still be made--
YOU'D HAVE ME EXECUTED ON A TECHNICALITY.
It is a matter of the code, Morningstar.
You understand the importance of obedience.

WELL.
IT SEEMS YOU'LL HAVE TO FIND SOME *OTHER* SOLUTION TO YOUR DILEMMA.
As I was about to say. Guards, take Lord *Arux* into custody--
--for treasonous *subversion* of the code duello.

There remains but little to say.
And all of it hard.
You have treated me with kindness, I know. And I have repaid it badly.
However hypocritical it sounds, I beg your forgiveness.
The truth is that I have a plan. A grand design.
The patronage of Lucifer Morningstar moves me forward in that design.
He nominated Lys as your successor, as he had agreed to do when she came to warn us against you.
Most, if not all, of your household have stayed on and pledged their service to her.
It was my mediation that saved you from a death sentence. I am aware that you will hardly thank me for that.
And neither will she, of course.
Neither will she.
But sometimes one tries to balance a great sin--
--with a thousand inadequate charities.

There are two of us now.
Two who have defied our father's will.
I was perfectly comfortable standing alone, of course. But still, that pleases me more than I'd have expected.
Three of us?
Well, I've been out of touch for a while, Duma, and things are changing fast now.
"I wonder if he's begun to be afraid yet."

MARKET

SO THERE IS A STORY ABOUT A MAN. A MAN IN A WESTERN CITY.

NOT HIS BIRTHPLACE, BUT STILL, HIS HOME.

HE WAS A MAN WHO BELIEVED IN A BOOK, AND TRIED TO LIVE BY ITS WORDS.

AND THE REWARD OF VIRTUE NOT SO VERY LONG POSTPONED.

Dear Mr. Al-Dabagh,
It is with great regret that we
have to i... you that the results
of ...s (attached)
...e. The tests
...hrough 13

BEARING GIFTS

MIKE CAREY writer **DEAN ORMSTON** art
COMICRAFT letters
DANIEL VOZZO colors & separations
CHRISTOPHER MOELLER cover painter
MARIAH HUEHNER assistant editor
SHELLY BOND editor
based on characters created by
GAIMAN, KIETH & DRINGENBERG

SIGN SAYS TWENTY-FOUR HOURS. DON'T EXPECT TO COME BY AND FIND YOU CLOSED.
I AM SORRY, MR. SKOLNICK. I GIVE SANDWICHES TO CORA, THE HOMELESS LADY ON THE CORNER.
THIS IS A DUTY TO GOD.
$1.75

TZEDAKAH, YOU MEAN. WELL, I'M ALL FOR THAT, I GUESS.
IF YOU DO YOUR MITZVOT AT A FIXED TIME, I CAN WORK AROUND YOU.

TCHING

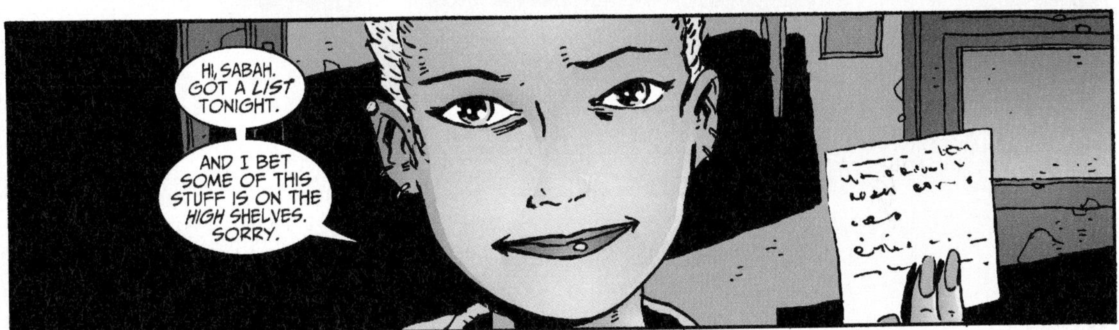
HI, SABAH. GOT A LIST TONIGHT.
AND I BET SOME OF THIS STUFF IS ON THE HIGH SHELVES. SORRY.

THE LONGER THE BETTER, MISS ZIM'ET. I WILL SERVE YOU SLOWLY, SO YOU STAY IN MY STORE EVEN LONGER.
YOU JUST LOVE TO SEE ME BLUSH, DON'T YOU?
SOME BEEF JERKY, PLEASE. AND TWO BOTTLES OF SCOTCH WHISKEY.

A COUPLE DOZEN CANDY BARS--ANYTHING YOU HAVE. CHARCOAL, COOKING OIL.
A PACK OF RAZOR BLADES.

WHISKEY? AND CANDY? YOU ARE HAVING PERHAPS A PARTY, MISS ZIM'ET?
I HAVE NOT KNOWN YOU TO BUY THESE THINGS BEFORE.

THEY'RE FOR MY SISTER. THE ONE WHO'S PREGNANT.
SHE'S STARTING TO HAVE CRAVINGS. YOU KNOW.

YES, WITH MY WIFE IT WAS PICKLES. AND MOUTHWASH.
THE MOUTHWASH WAS FORTUNATE FOR ME, I THINK.

HEY. CAN WE GET SOME SERVICE?
CERTAINLY YOU CAN.
ONCE I HAVE FINISHED THE LADY'S ORDER.

WE'RE IN A HURRY. EMPTY THE REGISTER--
--BEFORE I PEEL YOUR FUCKING FACE OFF.

I DON'T *LIKE* THAT FUCKIN' FOREIGN DOUBLETALK.

NOW OPEN YOUR FUCKIN'--

IF THE MAN HAD A FAULT, IT WAS COWARDICE.
IN THE THROAT-SPOKEN FRENCH OF HIS NATIVE GABON, SHE HAD TOLD HIM TO COVER HIS EYES. SO HE DID.
HE HEARD SOUNDS, BUT THEY WERE MUFFLED AND UNCLEAR.
A CHOKED CRY. A SIGH LIKE TEARING CLOTH.
A HEAVY, LIQUID IMPACT. A METALLIC PERCUSSION.
A SINGLE SYLLABLE, WHISPERED IN A WAVERING VOICE.
AND THEN, FINALLY--
--SILENCE.
MISS ZIM'ET! WHAT HAPPENED?
THEY HEARD A SIREN AND RAN AWAY. COULD YOU FILL MY ORDER, PLEASE, SABAH?
I DON'T LIKE TO LEAVE MY SISTER ALONE TOO LONG.

LATER, WHEN SHE HAD GONE, HE THOUGHT ABOUT CALLING THE POLICE. BUT NOTHING HAD BEEN STOLEN.
WHAT WOULD THE POLICE DO BESIDES SCARE AWAY MORE CUSTOMERS?

THERE WAS A SECURITY CAMERA IN THE SHOP WHOSE WORKINGS HE BARELY UNDERSTOOD.
HE SUCCEEDED IN MAKING IT PLAYBACK.

HE SAW MISS ZIM'ET THREATENED BY THE GUN. THE MUZZLE PRESSED AGAINST HER FACE.
HE EXPECTED HER TO LEAN BACK AWAY FROM IT, BUT SHE DIDN'T. HE SAW HER LIPS PART.

BUT THEN THE CAMERA MALFUNCTIONED.
STILL, THERE WERE SHAPES WITHIN THE SWIRLING DARKNESS. PERHAPS IF HE INCREASED THE BRIGHTNESS--

SABAH.
AAAAAA!

MISS ZIM'ET. YOU CAME BACK!
YES. MY SISTER IS COMING TO TERM, BUT SHE'S IN A LOT OF PAIN.
I NEED YOUR HELP.

MY HELP? I KNOW NOTHING ABOUT THESE THINGS.
SHE MUST GO TO A HOSPITAL AND THE DOCTORS WILL BRING OUT THE BABY.
AN EPIDURAL'S NOT GOING TO CUT IT, SABAH.
I NEED YOU TO SWEAR INTO THIS SKIN BAG. ALL THE CURSE WORDS YOU KNOW.
SWEAR?
SWEAR.
BUT... MISS ZIM'ET, IN FRONT OF A WOMAN...

JUST CURSE WORDS, THOUGH. IN ANY LANGUAGE. AND NOTHING YOU THINK YOU MIGHT NEED AGAIN.
OH. OKAY. I'LL GO IN THE BACK HERE.

NOT MANY OF THE CHERUBIM FELL. YOU'RE PROBABLY GAUDIUM.
HEH. YEAH. GOOD CALL.
WE MET, RIGHT? IN THE PAIN REALMS?
FRIEDA

SOOOO, DON'T TAKE THIS THE WRONG WAY--
--BUT HAVE YOU FED TONIGHT?

I'M STUFFED, THANKS FOR ASKING. WHAT ABOUT YOU?
AND WHO EATS BABY SWEETCORN?
WELL, IN ACTUAL FACT, THE ARCHANGEL MICHAEL.
EARLS WHITE FLOUR
BABY SWEET

IT'S A VERY LONG STORY.

MISS ZIM'ET!

I'VE FINISHED.

WELL, SEE YOU AROUND.
YEAH. SURE.

I DO NOT KNOW *MANY* BAD WORDS, BUT I CALLED MY BROTHER WHO DRIVES A TAXI.
THERE ARE *PLENTY* IN THERE NOW.
THANKS, SABAH.

LET ME ASK YOU SOMETHING. YOU'RE SEEING ME AS A TALL *HISPANIC* GUY, RIGHT?
YES.
WELL THANK *FUCK* FOR THAT.
WOW CHIPS

GOTTA GO.

CARROTS DON'T PEEL *THEMSELVES*.

THERE WERE SOME BOXES TO TAKE OUT TO THE DUMPSTER.
NORMALLY HE ONLY OPENED THE BACK DOOR IN DAYLIGHT, BUT TONIGHT HE FELT THE NEED FOR SOME COOL AIR ON HIS FACE.

HE THREW THE LETTER FROM THE HOSPITAL AWAY, TOO.
HE'D TELL HIS WIFE IN HIS OWN WORDS HOW LONG HE HAD TO SPEND WITH HER.

HIS LYMPH SYSTEM WAS INFECTED, THE LETTER SAID.
THEY COULD REMOVE THE ORIGINAL CANCER, BUT IT WOULDN'T DO ANY GOOD. HE'D DIE ANYWAY.

ON AN IMPULSE HE TRIED TO CURSE. BUT THE WORDS HAD GONE FROM HIS MOUTH AND HIS MIND.
THE ONLY ONE HE HAD LEFT WAS "BLOODY."

SO HE REPEATED "BLOODY" LIKE A MANTRA, AND HE SMOKED A SECOND CIGARETTE.

SMOKE DEVILS DANCED AROUND HIM IN THE SODIUM GLARE OF A SECURITY LIGHT.
AND AT MIDNIGHT--
--SHE RETURNED FOR THE FINAL TIME.

SABAH.
IT'S GOING TO BE A *DIFFICULT* BIRTH. I WANT YOU TO COME WITH ME.

HE WAS A COWARD. BUT HE WAS ALSO A MAN WHO TRIED HARD TO DO GOOD.
TO COME *WHERE*, MISS ZIM'ET?

AND PERHAPS ON SOME LEVEL HE THOUGHT--MISTAKENLY--THAT HE HAD NOTHING LEFT TO LOSE.
TO THE PLACE WHERE I *LIVE*.
IT'S NOT FAR.
BUT THE SHOP--

YOU LOCK THE DOOR AND PUT THE *SIGN* UP. THE SHOP WILL BE FINE.
MISS ZIM'ET, I AM NOT A DOCTOR. YOU REALLY THINK I CAN *HELP*?

OH YES.

BUT THE VASTNESS OF THE NIGHT WAS SITTING ON HIM LIKE A WEIGHT, AND HE SAID NOTHING.

THIS IS THE CINEMA THAT BURNED DOWN.

DON'T WORRY. THIS ISN'T WHERE WE *LIVE.*

IT'S JUST OUR FRONT *DOOR.*

MISS ZIM'ET--
THIS... THIS *PLACE* WE ARE GOING TO--

YOU'RE WITH *ME*, SABAH. BELIEVE ME, NOTHING'S GOING TO TOUCH YOU.

BUT IT'S PROBABLY BEST IF YOU DON'T LET GO OF MY *HAND*.

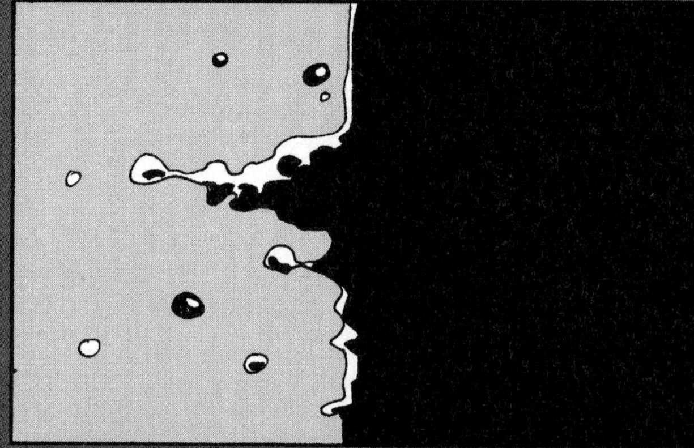

WE SHOULD WALK QUICKLY.
SHE'S HURTING, AND SHE'S *LONELY*. I SHOULDN'T HAVE LEFT HER FOR SO LONG.
WHO IS YOUR *FRIEND*, ZIME'ETNU?
AREN'T YOU GOING TO *INTRODUCE* ME?
AS YOU KNOW, MY *DIET* IS VERY SPECIALIZED.
YOU'D SCARCELY NOTICE I'D *FED*.

GOD IS JUST. HE DOES NOT SEND TO HELL THOSE WHO DON'T DESERVE IT.
SO THE ONLY PRAYER THAT CAME TO THE MAN WAS "TO HIS WILL I SUBMIT."

HE IS MY SISTER'S.
TOUCH HIM, CRUS, AND THE ONLY TEARS YOU'LL BE DRINKING WILL BE YOUR OWN.

I ASK NO MORE THAN IS MY RIGHT.
LUCIFER GAVE US NO RIGHTS. ONLY THIS ISLAND.
IF YOU THINK YOU CAN TAKE HIM FROM ME, DO SO.

HIS TEARS WOULD BE THIN AND TASTELESS IN ANY EVENT.
I DOUBT HE HAS THE CAPACITY TO SUFFER MUCH.

SHE TOOK HIS HAND AGAIN, AND DREW HIM TO HIS FEET. HE NOTICED FOR THE FIRST TIME HOW STRONG HER GRIP WAS.

TOO STRONG FOR HIM TO BREAK.

THERE WERE SOUNDS ON THE WIND LIKE PLEADING VOICES, IN NO LANGUAGE HE KNEW.

SMELLS OF PERFUME AND CARRION, EACH TOO STRONG FOR THE OTHER TO DROWN IT OUT.

FROM INSIDE THERE WAS THE SOUND OF SOMETHING HUGE, THRASHING IN AGONY.
MERCIFULLY, IT WAS TOO DARK FOR HIM TO SEE.
STAY HERE.
SAID THE WOMAN. OR THE THING THAT WORE A WOMAN'S SHAPE.
AND SHE WENT INSIDE.
"TO HIS WILL I SUBMIT. TO HIS WILL I SUBMIT. TO HIS WILL I SUBMIT." AGAIN AND AGAIN HE PRAYED, TRYING TO MEAN IT.
TRYING TO FIND A CORNER IN HIS TERROR TO REBUILD HIS DEVOTION ON.
AND THEN SHE CAME UNTO HIM AGAIN.
SABAH.
THE BABY IS TRAPPED BETWEEN BEING AND NOT-BEING.
THE SPIRITS OF THIS PLACE DEMAND AN OFFERING. I HOPE YOU UNDERSTAND.

BUT I...I HAVE NOT STOLEN, OR LIED, OR *KILLED* ANYONE!
I HAVE NOT *DESERVED* THIS!
AND THAT'S ABOUT AS RELEVANT AS *SALVATION* IS.
AN OFFERING, SABAH. WHAT WILL YOU *GIVE* THEM SO THEY WILL LET MY NEPHEW BE BORN?

THANK YOU, SABAH.

THAT WILL MAKE A *LOVELY* OFFERING.

AND THE THING THAT LIVED IN THE CAVE REACHED INTO HIM WITH A TOUCH SO GENTLE IT REMINDED HIM OF HIS WIFE'S TOUCH.

INTO HIM AND THROUGH HIM AND AROUND HIS LIVER, HIS SPLEEN, HIS LUNGS.

WITHDRAWING AT LAST WITH A HANDFUL OF GRAINY DARKNESS, LIKE THE SHADOW OF A SOUL.

ZIM'ET WENT AGAIN INTO THE CAVE, AND AFTER A TIME HE HEARD A CRY. THE CRY OF A NEWBORN CHILD.

IN SPITE OF HIMSELF HE CRAWLED TO THE THRESHOLD.

IT WAS HIDEOUS BEYOND IMAGINING. BUT IN A HOARSE VOICE HE BLESSED IT.

ITS MOTHER, ALTHOUGH SHE HAD NO FACE AS SUCH, SMILED BACK AT HIM.

OTHERS CAME THEN, BEARING GIFTS OF THEIR OWN. HE WAS INTRODUCED TO THEM, BUT MERCIFUL SHADOW HAD FALLEN ACROSS HIS SIGHT.

HE DIDN'T TRULY SEE THEM.

AFTERWARDS SHE TOOK HIM BACK TO THE GATE.

THE WIND HAD FALLEN. THE WHOLE WORLD WAS BENT IN REVERENT SILENCE.

THE SAME AS ALWAYS.

HIS HEART SWELLED WITH LOVE FOR HER.

WITH THE SUDDEN DIZZYING LIGHTNESS THAT COMES WHEN YOU PUT A BURDEN DOWN AFTER CARRYING IT A GREAT WAY.

AND THE SUN CAME UP.

AND THE WORLD BEGAN AGAIN.

REST IN PEACE
ELAINE

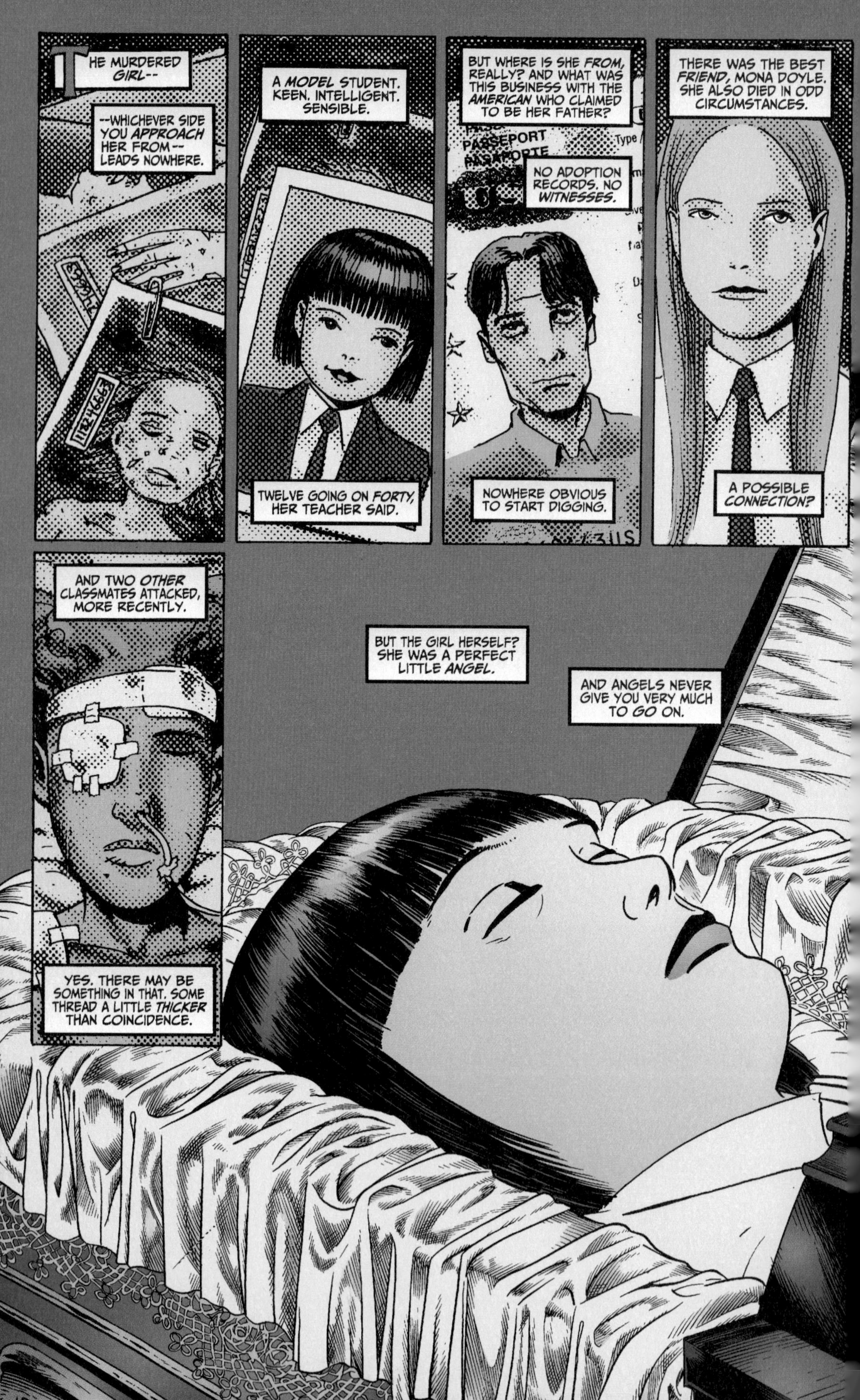
THE MURDERED GIRL--
--WHICHEVER SIDE YOU APPROACH HER FROM-- LEADS NOWHERE.
A MODEL STUDENT. KEEN. INTELLIGENT. SENSIBLE.
TWELVE GOING ON FORTY, HER TEACHER SAID.
BUT WHERE IS SHE FROM, REALLY? AND WHAT WAS THIS BUSINESS WITH THE AMERICAN WHO CLAIMED TO BE HER FATHER?
PASSPORT
NO ADOPTION RECORDS. NO WITNESSES.
NOWHERE OBVIOUS TO START DIGGING.
THERE WAS THE BEST FRIEND, MONA DOYLE. SHE ALSO DIED IN ODD CIRCUMSTANCES.
A POSSIBLE CONNECTION?
AND TWO OTHER CLASSMATES ATTACKED, MORE RECENTLY.
YES. THERE MAY BE SOMETHING IN THAT. SOME THREAD A LITTLE THICKER THAN COINCIDENCE.
BUT THE GIRL HERSELF? SHE WAS A PERFECT LITTLE ANGEL.
AND ANGELS NEVER GIVE YOU VERY MUCH TO GO ON.

WHICH IS WHY I'M HERE TODAY.
LOOKING FOR DEVILS.
COME TO JUDGMENT
PART ONE OF TWO
Based on characters created by
GAIMAN, KEITH & DRINGENBERG
MIKE CAREY writer
PETER GROSS & RYAN KELLY artists
COMICRAFT letters
DANIEL VOZZO colors & separations
CHRISTOPHER MOELLER cover painter
MARIAH HUEHNER assistant editor
SHELLY BOND editor
THE PRIEST TAKES HIS TEXT FROM MARK 10:14. "SUFFER THE LITTLE CHILDREN TO COME UNTO ME."
THE DEFAULT OPTION.

THE MAN WITH THE SCARRED FOREHEAD. I'M SURE I *KNOW* HIM.
NOT FAMILY. HARDLY FRIEND. HIS COUNTENANCE BESPEAKS SOMETHING LIKE *GUILT*.
HE SPEAKS TO THE TALL MAN. BRIEFLY.
THE UGLY CHILDREN *FRET* AND FIGHT. THEY HAVE NOTHING OF THE FAVOR OF THEIR FATHER.
WHEN THEY'VE GONE I COME OUT OF *HIDING*.
MY DUTY IS TO THAT WHICH DOES *NOT* DIE, BUT STILL--
--I FEEL I OWE HER THIS, AT LEAST.
BEFORE GOD, I WILL SEE *JUSTICE* DONE ON HIM THAT KILLED THEE.
OR PASS *MYSELF* BEYOND THE GATES OF THE WORLD.
THESE PLACES *ANGER* ME. SO MANY CROSSES.
SO LITTLE REAL *BELIEF*.

THE FIORENZE HOTEL, LAS VEGAS.
JEEEEESUS!
THIS IS ALL STILL *HERE?*
WHAT'S THE *MATTER* WITH YOU PEOPLE?
MISS PRESTO, I'M REALLY *SORRY.* WE DIDN'T KNOW WHAT TO DO.
WHEN YOU MISSED THE SECOND *SET* LAST NIGHT, THE MANAGER CAME TO *LOOK* FOR YOU.

UMM... I'M SORRY, I NEVER SAW THAT MOVIE.
ANYWAY, THE POLICE SAID THEY WANT TO TALK TO YOU ABOUT A MISSING PERSON. A MR. EDDIE BRAKE?

EDDIE'S STILL MISSING? OF COURSE HE IS. IT'S ONLY BEEN A DAY.
THAT PART'S GOOD. GO ON.

WELL, THAT'S IT REALLY. AND THE MANAGER WANTS TO SEE YOU ABOUT LAST NIGHT.
SHALL I TAKE YOUR COAT?
NO!

I'LL TALK TO THE MANAGER AND THE POLICE AFTER I'VE SLEPT--
--IN A SUITE THAT DOESN'T SMELL LIKE A JACKAL'S ARMPIT. OH, AND HEY--

--A BLOND GUY IS GONNA COME BY--WITH TWO LITTLE CURLS LIKE HORNS IN HIS HAIR.
JUST SEND HIM ON UP.

YES, VERY PRETTY. BUT IF YOU'LL EXCUSE THE CLICHÉ--
--OVER MY DEAD BODY.
INSPECTOR DONOGHUE, YOUR SUPERIORS HAVE ALREADY AUTHORIZED THIS. THE CASE IS MINE.
SOLOMON DOUID
DETECTIVE INSPECTOR
IT SODDING WELL IS NOT.
NOT UNTIL I SIGN IT OFF TO YOU.
I DON'T CARE IF GOD AND ALL HIS BLOODY SAINTS HAVE SEEN FIT TO KISS YOUR ARSE.
WHAT ARE YOU, ANYWAY? WHICH JURISDICTION? YOU'RE JUST A BLOODY NAME.
THWICK
IF I WERE TO KILL YOU NOW--HERE IN YOUR OWN OFFICE--
--IT WOULD NEVER BE UTTERED, MY NAME. OR WRITTEN IN ANY REPORT.
YES. I AM JUST A NAME.
BUT KEEP THIS IN MIND.
YOU UNDERSTAND?

IS THERE ANY POINT IN ASKING WHY YOU'RE TAKING THIS CASE?

I HAVE DREAMED OF HER.
THAT IS HOW GOD TELLS ME WHAT MY DUTY IS.

YOU'LL FIND THE FAMILY ODD. THEY'RE DEFINITELY HIDING SOMETHING.
AND THAT WAS HARDLY AN ANSWER.

WHEREVER I HAVE SEEN INNOCENCE DEFILED OR DESTROYED I HAVE COME IN JUDGMENT--EVEN AGAINST MY OWN FATHER.
AND YOUR SUMMARY OF THIS CASE AMOUNTED TO NINE WORDS.

PERHAPS I WILL RETURN TO JUDGE YOU, TOO.

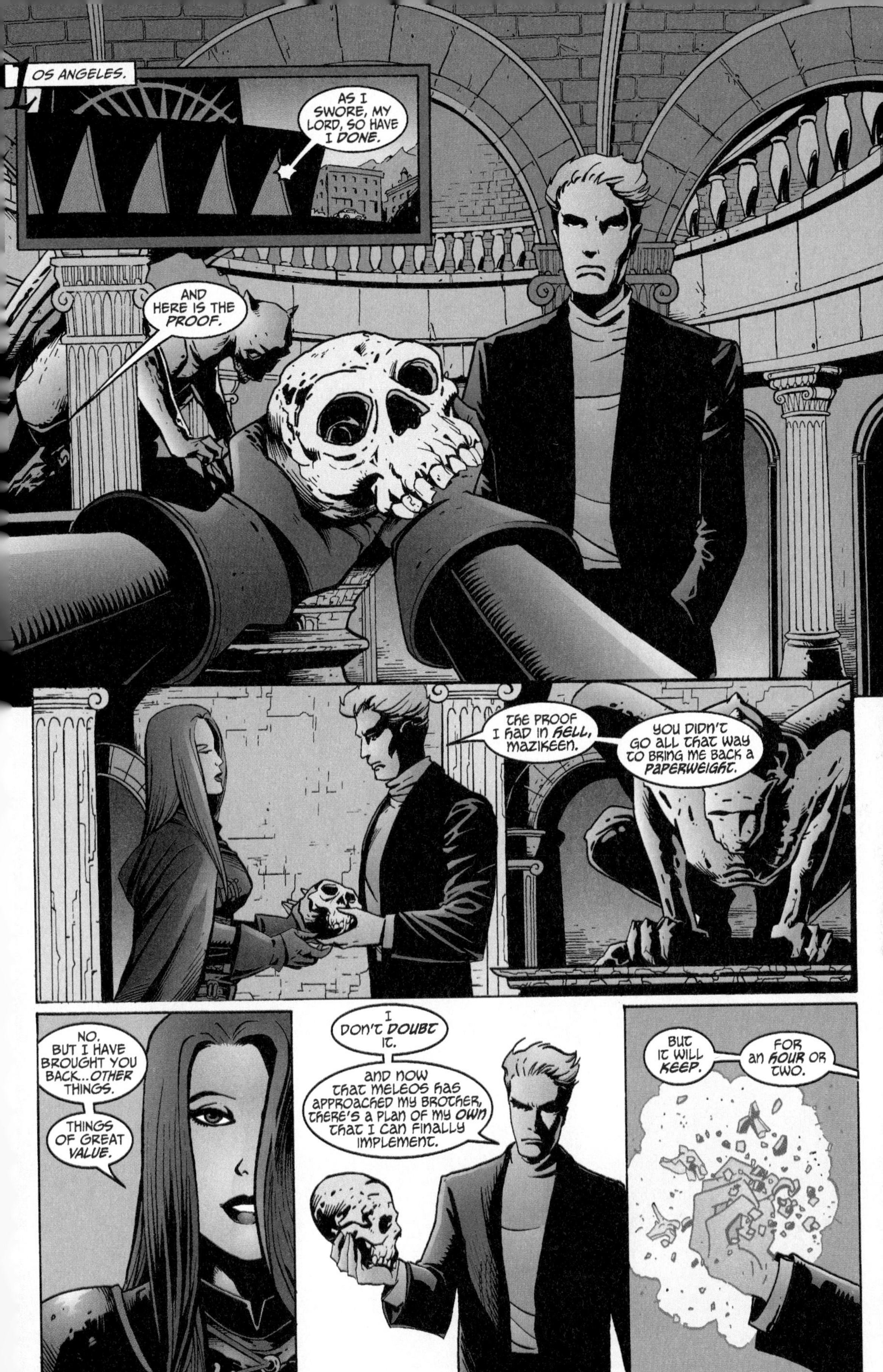
LOS ANGELES.
AS I SWORE, MY LORD, SO HAVE I DONE.
AND HERE IS THE PROOF.
THE PROOF I HAD IN HELL, MAZIKEEN.
YOU DIDN'T GO ALL THAT WAY TO BRING ME BACK A PAPERWEIGHT.
NO. BUT I HAVE BROUGHT YOU BACK...OTHER THINGS.
THINGS OF GREAT VALUE.
I DON'T DOUBT IT.
AND NOW THAT MELEOS HAS APPROACHED MY BROTHER, THERE'S A PLAN OF MY OWN THAT I CAN FINALLY IMPLEMENT.
BUT IT WILL KEEP.
FOR AN HOUR OR TWO.

YOU'RE GOING AWAY AGAIN.
YES. BUT NOT FAR.
AND NOT FOR LONG?
YOU'RE a SOLDIER, MAZIKEEN.
YOU UNDERSTAND HARDSHIP AND SACRIFICE.
I AM YOUR SOLDIER.
I KNOW.
STAND EASY.

KENSAL RISE, NORTH LONDON.
UNUSUAL, INSPECTOR?
IN WHAT WAY?
ANYTHING OUT OF HER NORMAL ROUTINE. IN THE DAYS BEFORE SHE DIED.
A NEW FRIEND OR INTEREST. A CHANGE IN MANNER OR SPEECH.
I DON'T THINK SO. I MEAN, THERE WAS THE NIGHT SHE WENT MISSING--
--BUT THAT WAS MONTHS AGO. BEFORE MATT'S HEART ATTACK.
THERE WASN'T ANYTHING.
WE'VE HAD EVERY BLOODY INSPECTOR UNDER THE SUN HERE ALREADY.
YOU'RE GOING OVER GROUND THAT'S BEEN COVERED TEN TIMES OVER.
WELL, IT MAY BE THAT A DIFFERENT PERSPECTIVE WILL YIELD SOME FRESH INSIGHT.
MRS. BELLOC, WILL YOU SHOW ME HER ROOM?
YES. OF COURSE.

YOUR HUSBAND IS A MAN OF STRONG PASSIONS.
I SUPPOSE HE IS. YES.

THIS IS ELAINE'S ROOM.

IF YOU DON'T MIND, INSPECTOR DOUID, I'LL WAIT DOWNSTAIRS.
IT'S-- VERY HARD FOR ME TO--

PLEASE, FEEL FREE. I'LL CALL YOU IF I NEED YOU.

YOU NEEDN'T HIDE FROM ME.
YOU, AT LEAST, ARE NOT A SUSPECT.

IF YOU THOUGHT I COULD NOT, THERE WAS NO REASON TO STAY HIDDEN.
YOU CAN SEE ME?
I'M DEAD. NO ONE ELSE COULD SEE ME, EXCEPT HER.
BUT YOU SEEMED TO BE LOOKING AT ME, AT THE CEMETERY. I WASN'T SURE.
YOU'RE EASTERMAN. THE MAN WHO CLAIMED TO BE HER FATHER.
I AM HER FATH--
--OKAY, NOT BIOLOGICALLY, BUT MY WIFE WAS HER MOTHER, SO I'M THE CLOSEST SHE HAD.
DO YOU KNOW WHAT THIS IS, MISTER EASTERMAN?
IT'S ELAINE'S GRANDMOTHERS. AN ANGEL DID THAT TO THEM.
WHO ARE YOU?
I AM JUSTICE.
BEGIN BY TELLING ME ABOUT THE ANGEL.

"YOU'RE GOING AWAY AGAIN."
"YES. BUT NOT FAR."
"AND NOT FOR LONG?"
"THERE IS A CAVERN AT THE HEART OF THE WORLD..."
"IS THERE?
"SOMETIMES. IT DEPENDS ON WHAT MOOD THE WORLD IS IN.
"IT IS GUARDED BY THE SVARTALFA-- THE DARK ELVES.
"PROBABLY ENOUGH TO DETER THE COMMON RUCK OF GODS AND MONSTERS.
"BUT TO BE HONEST, I ANTICIPATE NO REAL PROBLEMS AT THIS STAGE.
"WHICH IS CONVENIENT.
"IT MEANS I CAN CONSERVE MY ENERGIES UNTIL I GET TO THE BOTTOM."

GOOD DAY TO YOU, LOKI OF THE JÖTUN.
A GOOD DAY, LUCIFER MORNINGSTAR?
YES. I SUPPOSE IT IS.
NOW.

I HAVE OTHER AVENUES TO EXPLORE.
I COULD NOT EASILY SAY WHY I AM WAITING HERE.

THE DAY WEARS ON. OCCASIONALLY I SEE THEM MOVING INSIDE THE HOUSE.
THEY DO NOT SPEAK TO EACH OTHER. THEY DO NOT GO OUT.

TOWARDS EVENING, MATTHEW BELLOC COMES OUT INTO THE GARDEN.

THINKING HIMSELF UNOBSERVED, HE STANDS BEFORE A TREE, MOTIONLESS, FOR FIFTEEN MINUTES.
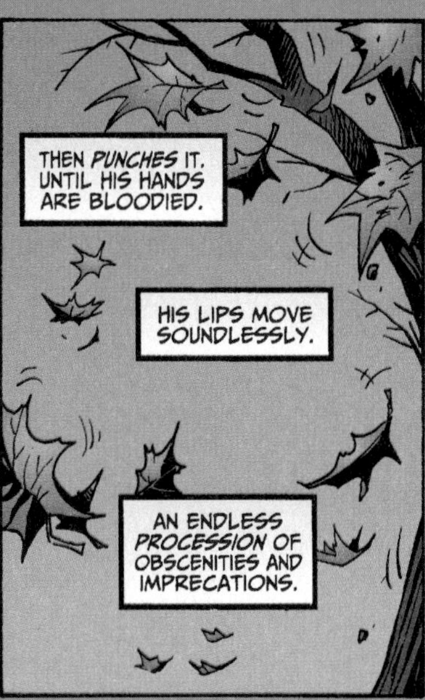
THEN PUNCHES IT. UNTIL HIS HANDS ARE BLOODIED.
HIS LIPS MOVE SOUNDLESSLY.
AN ENDLESS PROCESSION OF OBSCENITIES AND IMPRECATIONS.

THEN THERE IS NOTHING FOR AN HOUR OR MORE.
BUT AT SUNSET, JUST AS I AM ABOUT TO LEAVE--

--I AM FINALLY, AND MOST GENEROUSLY, REWARDED.

YOUR HUSBAND AND I HAVE BUSINESS TO DISCUSS IN PRIVATE.
YOU CAN WAIT OVER BY THE STEPS.
NO. I WILL NOT.
IF I REMOVE THE BOWL, THE VENOM WILL DRIP INTO HIS EYES.
THE PAIN IS TERRIBLE. YOU CANNOT ASK THIS OF ME.
OH YES.
THE VENOM.
OVER THERE. BY THE STEPS, WOMAN.
THIS WON'T TAKE LONG.

YOU KNOW WHY I'VE COME, LOKI.
I BELIEVE I CAN GUESS.
BUT WHAT CAN YOU GIVE ME IN EXCHANGE? THAT'S THE QUESTION.
I NEED THE SHIP FOR A SINGLE VOYAGE. LEND IT TO ME--
--AND I'LL COME BACK HERE ON THE DAY OF RAGNAROK AND FREE YOU.
AND CARRY ME UP ONTO THE DECK? AND HOLD ME HIGH SO I CAN SEE THE DEATHS OF THE AESIR?
YOU HAVE MY WORD.
GO TO MY BROTHER, WHO IS NAMED BERGELMIR.
TELL HIM I SWORE ON OUR FATHER'S BONES THAT YOU COULD HAVE THE SHIP.
THE ALL-FATHER IS GOING TO BE HUGELY PISSED OFF ABOUT HIS SNAKE, LIGHTBRINGER.
PROBABLY.
IF I WERE YOU, I'D KEEP SCREAMING FROM TIME TO TIME.
HE MAY NEVER NOTICE THE DIFFERENCE.

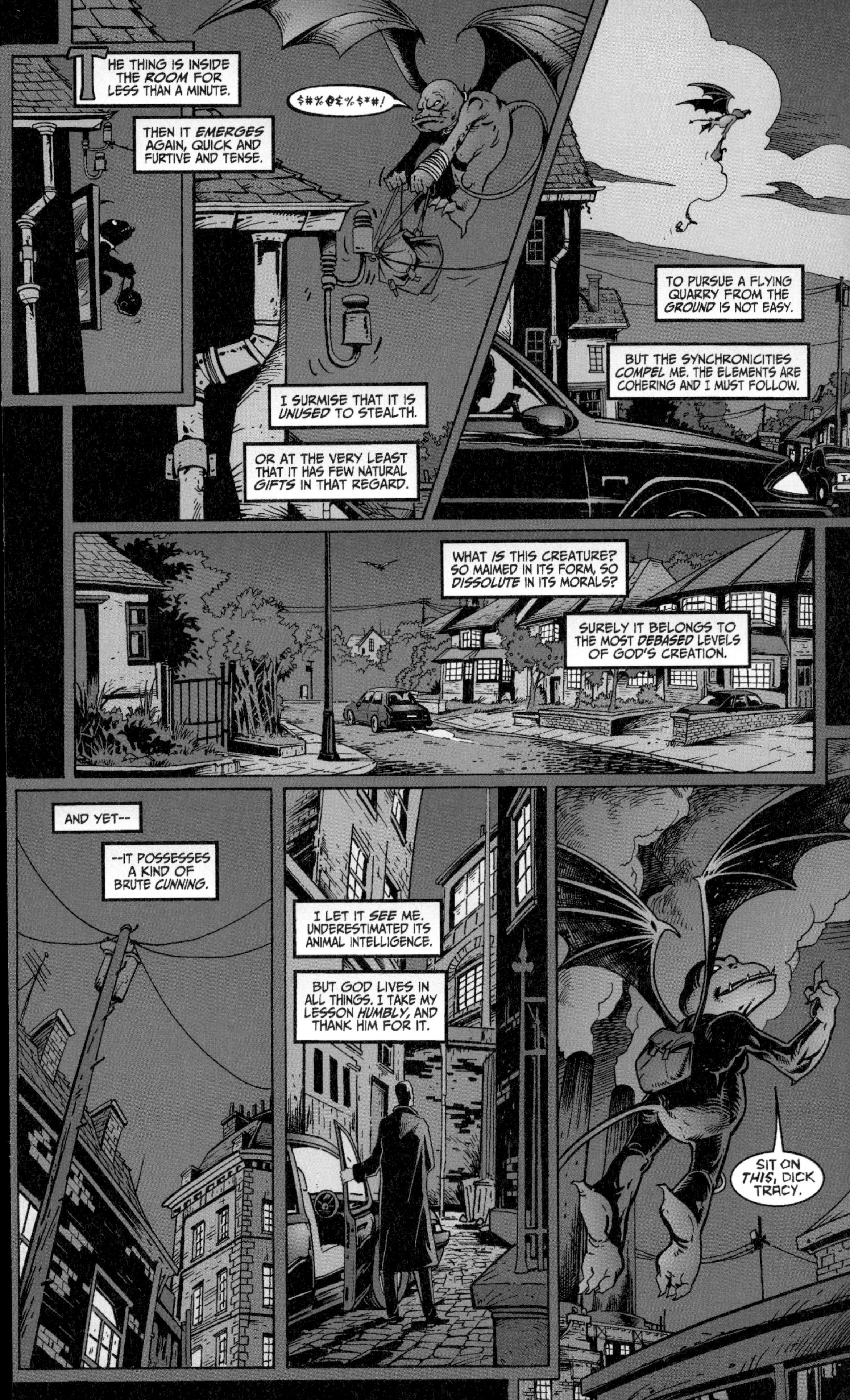
THE THING IS INSIDE THE *ROOM* FOR LESS THAN A MINUTE.
THEN IT *EMERGES* AGAIN, QUICK AND FURTIVE AND TENSE.
$#%@$%$*#!
I SURMISE THAT IT IS *UNUSED* TO STEALTH.
OR AT THE VERY LEAST THAT IT HAS FEW NATURAL *GIFTS* IN THAT REGARD.
TO PURSUE A FLYING QUARRY FROM THE *GROUND* IS NOT EASY.
BUT THE SYNCHRONICITIES *COMPEL* ME. THE ELEMENTS ARE COHERING AND I MUST FOLLOW.
WHAT *IS* THIS CREATURE? SO MAIMED IN ITS FORM, SO *DISSOLUTE* IN ITS MORALS?
SURELY IT BELONGS TO THE MOST *DEBASED* LEVELS OF GOD'S CREATION.
AND YET--
--IT POSSESSES A KIND OF BRUTE *CUNNING*.
I LET IT *SEE* ME. UNDERESTIMATED ITS ANIMAL INTELLIGENCE.
BUT GOD LIVES IN ALL THINGS. I TAKE MY LESSON *HUMBLY*, AND THANK HIM FOR IT.
SIT ON *THIS*, DICK TRACY.

HEY.
HEY YOURSELF.
WHAT KEPT YOU?

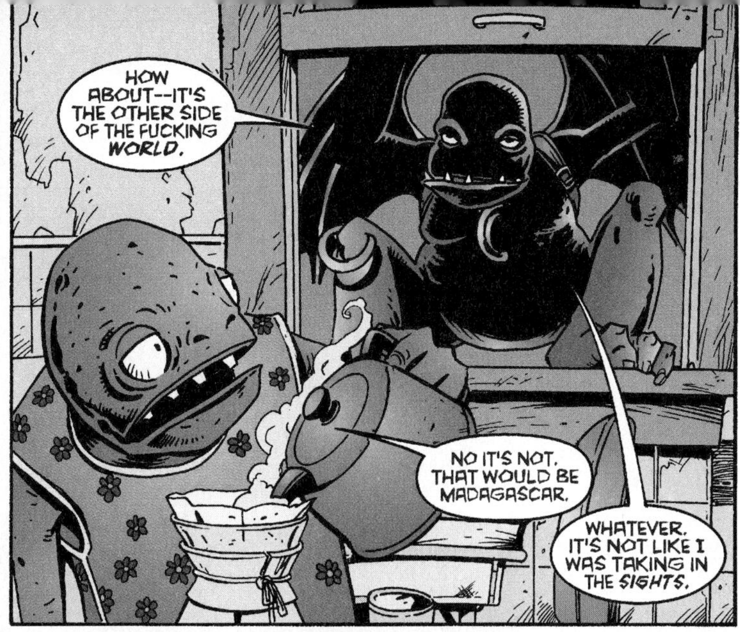
HOW ABOUT--IT'S THE OTHER SIDE OF THE FUCKING WORLD.
NO IT'S NOT. THAT WOULD BE MADAGASCAR.
WHATEVER. IT'S NOT LIKE I WAS TAKING IN THE SIGHTS.

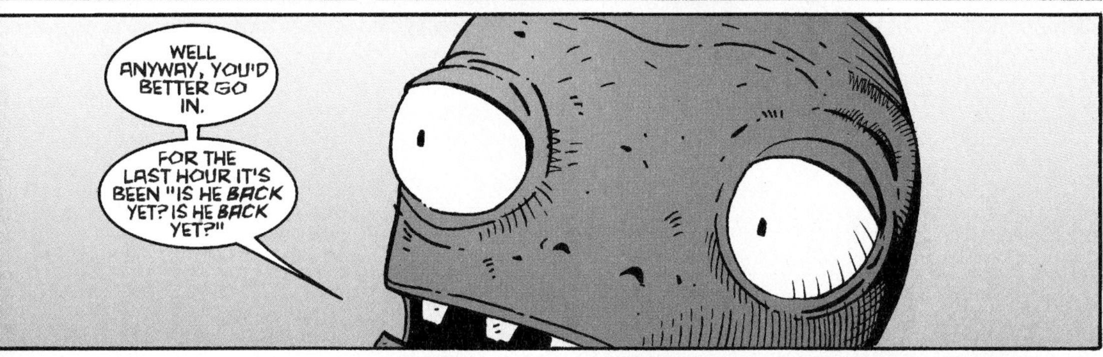
WELL ANYWAY, YOU'D BETTER GO IN.
FOR THE LAST HOUR IT'S BEEN "IS HE BACK YET? IS HE BACK YET?"

THIS WHOLE SITUATION HAS GONE SPECTACULARLY TOO FAR.
YEAH. IF YOU'RE THE VOICE OF MODERATION, IT MUST HAVE.

OKAY, YOU CAN RELAX.
IT'S MISTER ILLEGAL ENTRY.

GAUDIUM! I AM RELIEVED TO SEE YOU.
YEAH. I'M SURE.
AND YOU WERE SUCCESSFUL?
IF YOU MEAN "HAVE YOU COME BACK WITH A BAGFUL OF CRABBY OLD LADIES"--
--THEN YEAH, I GUESS I DID OKAY.
I WILL TAKE THE JEWEL.
DOWN, ROVER.
YOU DON'T PAY MY WAGES.
YOU MAY GIVE THE BEAD TO MELEOS, GAUDIUM.
IT IS NECESSARY. LUCIFER CANNOT PROCEED WITHOUT IT.
WELL, SEE, I'VE BEEN MEANING TO TALK TO YOU ABOUT--
CRASH

NICE GOING, LITTLE BROTHER.
I THOUGHT I LOST THIS SCHMUCK.
NOBODY IN THIS ROOM MOVE.
I AM SOLOMON, THE SON OF DAVID. AND I AM INVESTIGATING A MURDER.

IN ALL THE WORLDS, IN ALL THE AGES OF MAN, THERE WAS NOTHING LIKE HER.
PRECIOUS MONSTER. ANGEL CHILD.
ALL INNOCENCE SHOULD BE PROTECTED.
ALL WHO HARM INNOCENTS SHOULD BE PUNISHED.
IN HER DIARY SHE WROTE "SEE YOU SOON, MONA. LOVE AND KISSES." HER HEART BOTH FULL AND EMPTY.
GOD LET ME SEE THIS. MADE ME FEEL IT.
IT IS WHILE I SLEEP THAT HE SHOWS ME MY DUTY.
AND THEN IN MY WAKING TIME I CRAWL AND GROPE MY WAY TOWARDS JUSTICE.
THE SERAPH, WHO COULD KILL ME WITH A GESTURE, CHOOSES INSTEAD TO CONFESS.
TELLS ME HOW THE ASSASSIN TORE HER BODY. HOW HIS SCHEMING TORE HER SOUL.
SOMETIMES THEY EQUATE CONFESSION WITH ABSOLUTION.
WHATEVER THAT MAY BE.
CELEBRITY SLEUTH
PET

WHAT THE FUCK ARE THEY DOING IN THERE? WASHING EACH OTHER'S HAIR?
YOU'RE GOING TO FIND OUT SOON ENOUGH, LITTLE BROTHER.
HE SAID YOU'RE NEXT.
OH YEAH? WELL HE CAN GO SCREW HIMSELF.
I DON'T EVEN KNOW WHY WE'RE GOING ALONG WITH THIS. WE SHOULD'VE JUST TOSSED HIM OUT THE WINDOW.
WHY ARE WE GOING WITH THIS, ARCHON?
BECAUSE SOLOMON BELIEVES HE SERVES MY FATHER, THE LORD OF HOSTS.
HIS PURSUIT OF JUSTICE IS AN OFFERING-- A PRAYER. I WOULD NOT WISH TO BELITTLE IT.
THE LORD OF HOSTS KICKED YOU OUT. GAVE YOU THE BUM'S RUSH.
YOU THINK PLAYING BALL WITH THIS PSYCHO IS GONNA BUY YOU SOME SORT OF REMISSION?
NO. BUT I DESERVED MY PUNISHMENT, GAUDIUM.
GROTESQUELY ENOUGH, WHAT HOPES I HAVE OF REDEMPTION NOW LIE IN MY BROTHER'S HANDS.

"SO THEY ARE VERY SLENDER HOPES INDEED."
COME TO JUDGMENT
PART TWO OF TWO
MIKE CAREY writer PETER GROSS & RYAN KELLY artists DANIEL VOZZO colors & separations
COMICRAFT letters CHRISTOPHER MOELLER cover painter MARIAH HUEHNER assistant editor SHELLY BOND editor
Based on characters created by GAIMAN, KIETH & DRINGENBERG

THE STAR OF THE MORNING! TCHAH! IT'S A BUG.
BE SILENT, FOOL, AND LET HIM PASS.
I WILL NOT!
I'M LOOKING FOR BERGELMIR, BROTHER OF LOKI.
YOU'RE LOOKING FOR DEATH, LUCIFER. IN JOTUNHEIM, ONLY KIN OF THE GIANTS HAVE THE RIGHT TO--

KLUDD

THERE IS A FOREST A FEW LEAGUES HENCE, LORD. BERGELMIR HAS A CABIN THERE.
I HOPE YOU'LL BEAR NO GRUDGE OVER THE WORDS OF A FOOL.
A GRUDGE? NOT AT ALL. I'M IMPRESSED.
IF YOU'RE ALWAYS SO QUICK TO WEED STUPIDITY OUT OF THE GENE POOL--
--IT'S EASIER TO UNDERSTAND HOW LOKI HAPPENED.

HER BODYGUARD?
YEAH. LOOK, IF YOU'RE DEAF I CAN TALK IN SIGN LANGUAGE.
MICHAEL ASKED ME TO WATCH HER. KEEP HER OUT OF TROUBLE.
AND YET SHE DIED.
LOOK, THAT THING THEY SENT AFTER HER WAS A FRIGGIN' JIN EN MOK. IT GOT PAST ME WEARING HER FATHER'S FACE.
I WAS OUTGUNNED. THAT DOESN'T MEAN I DIDN'T TRY.
PERHAPS NOT. BUT YOU'RE A FALLEN CREATURE. DOUBTLESS IT COMES EASY FOR YOU TO FAIL AND THEN FORGIVE YOURSELF.
EAT SHIT, SHERLOCK!
WHO SET YOU UP AS JUDGE, JURY AND EXECUTIONER?
WHERE DID SHE GO?
WHAT?
THE CREATURE. THE JIN EN MOK.
WHEN THE FIGHT WAS OVER, WHERE DID SHE GO?
WELL, I-- I DUNNO. I DIDN'T SEE.
I GUESS SHE JUST--
I DUNNO.
AND HOW WOULD YOU RATE YOUR OWN PERFORMANCE AS A BODYGUARD?
MEASURED IN USELESS SACKS OF SHIT? A PERFECT TEN.
BUT CESTIS WAS ALL OVER ME. THERE WASN'T ANYTHING I COULD DO.
YOU SEE? YOU HAVE NO NEED OF A JUDGE OR A JURY.
AND AS AN EXECUTIONER I'M REQUIRED ELSEWHERE.
SLAM

I AM FINISHED HERE. *ALL* OF YOU ARE CULPABLE, OR COMPLICIT.
BUT THE *ULTIMATE* GUILT LIES ELSEWHERE.
THERE IS A **PARADOX** HERE, SULEIMAN BIN DAVID. WHATEVER YOU BELIEVE, GOD DID NOT SEND YOU ON THIS ERRAND.
HE **FORBADE** ME TO SAVE HER LIFE.
WHO IS FIT TO EXPOUND HIS WISDOM? NOT *YOU*, FIRST OF HEAVEN, AND NOT I.
IT IS A GLORY TO SERVE, AND A *SIN* TO ASK REASONS.
GET OUT THE *YELLOW PAGES*, SPERA. I'M GONNA SUE THAT GUY'S ASS INTO A GEOSTATIONARY *ORBIT*.
OH, AND SOMEONE SET THE *BATHROOM* ON FIRE.

OTUNHEIM.

I'M LOOKING FOR BERGELMIR OF THE JOTUN.

IS HE *HERE?*

NO.

LOKI HAS OFFERED ME THE USE OF NAGLFAR.
HE SAID THAT BERGELMIR KNOWS WHERE TO FIND IT.
THE SHIP MADE FROM DEAD MEN'S FINGERNAILS? AYE, AYE, BERGELMIR KNOWS OF IT.
AND WHAT BERGELMIR KNOWS, I KNOW. I CAN TAKE YOU WHERE NAGLFAR SLEEPS.
BUT YOU'D HAVE TO DO A FAVOR FOR ME IN RETURN.

HIS ALE, HALF-DRUNK. HIS BOOTS BESIDE THE FIRE.
HE'S NOT GONE FAR, HAS HE, OLD MOTHER?
A FAVOR. AND YOU MUST SWEAR IT.

I SWEAR TO DO WHATEVER YOU ASK OF ME.
UNLESS YOU YOURSELF RELEASE ME FROM MY OATH.

GOOD ENOUGH?
OH, EXCELLENT GOOD, LUCIFER MORNINGSTAR. EXCELLENT GOOD.

LIKE PRIDE.
BEFORE THE FALL.

THIS IS THE PLACE WHERE SHE DIED. OR RATHER--
--THE PLACE WHERE SHE BEGAN TO DIE.
THERE IS BLOOD ON THE OLD STONES.
HER BLOOD. AND THE GREEN ICHOR OF THE THING THAT ATTACKED HER.
CE·DO NOT CROS
CESTIS OF THE DANCING FLESH. WHO BECOMES WHAT SHE CONSUMES. WHO GOD DID NOT MAKE.
SHE WALKED HERE. FIRST ON CLAWED PADS, AND THEN ON NAKED, HUMAN FEET.
THEN THE WINDING TRAIL OF A SNAKE, BUT ONLY FOR TEN YARDS OR SO. AFTER THAT THE FOOTPRINTS RETURN.
THE TRUTH? OR AN ELABORATE LIE? I MUST KNOW.
THEN I CAN JUDGE.

TAKE UP THAT AXE, PRINCE OF THE EASTERN SKY.
IT'S OLD, BUT IT HAS A GOOD EDGE TO IT.

NOW, YOU MUST LOOK ONLY FORWARD. NEITHER TO LEFT, NOR RIGHT, NOR OVER YOUR SHOULDER.
AND TURN NOT YOUR STEPS, BUT WALK ONLY WHERE I DIRECT YOU.

WHEN A LIVING THING COMES WITHIN YOUR SIGHT, YOU MUST KILL IT.
THE FIRST THING YOU SEE THAT LIVES AND MOVES. SWEAR AGAIN, UPON THE AXE.

I'M ALREADY BOUND. BUT I SWEAR AGAIN, UPON THIS AXE. UNLESS YOU RELEASE ME--
WHICH I WILL NOT.
--I'LL DO EXACTLY WHAT YOU'VE ASKED.

THEN WALK ON, TOWARDS THE SETTING SUN.
AND LET'S SEE WHAT CROSSES OUR PATH.

THE BELLOC HOUSE IS IN DARKNESS WHEN I RETURN.
THERE IS A HUNTER'S MOON, BUT THIS IS UNRELIABLE AS AN OMEN.
YESTERDAY I WATCHED MATTHEW BELLOC PUNCH HIS FISTS BLOODY AGAINST THIS TREE. I ASSUMED HE DID NOT SEE ME.
I HAVE ASSUMED TOO MANY THINGS.
A SCATTERING OF BONES. NOT SERIOUSLY HIDDEN, EVEN.
SCORED AND CHEWED, AND STRIPPED SO CLEAN OF FLESH THAT THEY ALMOST SHINE.
THE GLOVE COMPARTMENT IN YOUR CAR WAS THE FIRST PLACE I LOOKED.
THAT'S CALLED GIVING AID AND COMFORT TO THE ENEMY.

SO TELL ME, DETECTIVE.
WHODUNNIT?

THE THING THAT MURDERED ELAINE BELLOC ATTACKED HER *FIRST* IN YOUR SHAPE.
THAT'S WHY HER FRIENDS OPENED THE *DOOR* TO IT.

GOOD. AND THEN?
LATER, IN THE SUBWAY TUNNEL, WHEN IT HAD *KILLED* HER--
--IT TOOK ON SEVERAL *OTHER* SHAPES BEFORE IT FIXED AGAIN, ON HUMAN FORM.

SO YOU'RE SAYING SHE'S STILL SOMEWHERE *AROUND* HERE? IN BORROWED *FLESH?*
THERE IS NO OTHER EXPLANATION.
AMAZING.

NOW WE GET TO MY FAVORITE PART, LITTLE HUNTER.

THE KILL.

THERE. THE *HOLLOW* AT THE FOOT OF THE TREE.
GO INSIDE.

AND KILL THE FIRST THING I *SEE?*
YES! DO IT!
OR SHALL I SAY THAT LUCIFER MORNINGSTAR WAS *FORSWORN?*

NO.
I DON'T THINK YOU'LL BE ABLE TO SAY *THAT.*

KRA-TISCH
SO. "THE FIRST LIVING THING I SEE."
IN SPITE OF THE MIRROR, I'M AFRAID THAT WAS YOU, BERGELMIR.
HOLD! HOLD!

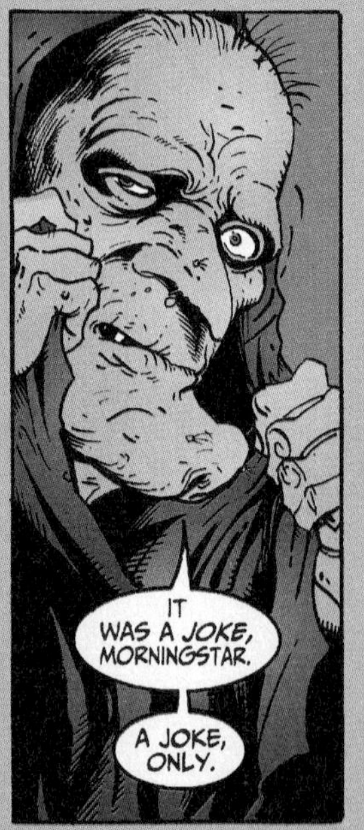
IT WAS A JOKE, MORNINGSTAR.
A JOKE, ONLY.

I'VE SOMETHING OF MY BROTHER'S HUMOR, AFTER ALL.

TAKE ME TO THE SHIP.
OR I'LL SHOW YOU WHAT MAKES ME LAUGH.

"IT'S NOT IN MY NATURE TO *LINGER* TOO LONG AFTER I'VE FED.

"IT'S NOT EVEN *HEALTHY*."

BUT THE CARDS--THE BASANOS --

--WHEN THEY GAVE ME SUBSTANCE AGAIN, THEY SHACKLED ME. OUT OF FEAR, I SUPPOSE.

I AM *BOUND* IN THIS SHAPE. TRAPPED.

I *TRIED* TO CHANGE, DOWN IN THE TUNNEL.

I'VE TRIED SINCE. BUT I KEEP SLIPPING *BACK*.

AND WE EAT *MEMORIES*, AS WELL AS FLESH. THE LONGER I STAY IN HIS SHAPE, THE *STRONGER* THEY BECOME.

I'M TURNING INTO HIM. I'M... THINKING HIS *THOUGHTS*.

SO I'VE *WAITED* FOR YOU TO COME. WITH YOUR BULLETS OF *FAITH* AND YOUR HEART OF FIRE.

I'M GUILTY. PASS *JUDGMENT* ON ME.

TO EXPOSE. TO JUDGE. TO PUNISH. THE CREED BY WHICH I LIVE.
BY WHICH I HAVE LIVED FOR FOUR THOUSAND YEARS.

I AM OLD TO BE LEARNING NUANCES--
WAIT! WHAT ARE YOU DOING?
--BUT THERE ARE NUANCES HERE. DISTURBING ONES.

THE WOMAN--BARBARA BELLOC--HAS LOST SO MUCH.
DON'T TURN YOUR BACK ON ME. I CONFESSED!
DO WHAT YOU CAME FOR!
IF SHE LOSES HER HUSBAND TOO, WHAT WILL THAT DO TO HER?

AND WHAT IS DEATH, TO THIS CREATURE--
I'LL KEEP ON KILLING! I MEAN IT!
I'LL EAT THE WHOLE FUCKING HUMAN RACE!
--COMPARED TO WHAT HAS ALREADY BEEN DONE TO IT?

M...MATT?
CHRIST! GO BACK TO BED, YOU WHINING PIECE OF MEAT. LEAVE ME ALONE.

YOU WERE SHOUTING AGAIN. IS EVERYTHING ALL RIGHT?
IT'S FINE.
EVERYTHING'S FINE.

WHERE WILL YOU *TAKE* HER, LUCIFER? TO THE WALLS OF HEAVEN?
THERE'S NOTHING IN HEAVEN THAT I ***NEED***.
THE JOURNEY I HAVE IN MIND IS A ***LONGER*** ONE--INTO THE MANSIONS OF ***SILENCE***.
AND I WON'T BE GOING ***MYSELF***.
I HAVE A ***CAPTAIN*** AND A ***HELMSMAN*** LINED UP ALREADY.
WELL WHOEVER THEY ARE, I DON'T ENVY THEM *THAT* VOYAGE.
I'M GOING TO NEED THE ***AXE***.
γετυπ λαζψ!
YOU HEAR ME? SHAKE OFF YOUR ***BLANKETS***, YOU HOAR-HEADED SOTS!

MY COUSINS OF THE THURSES.
I'M AFRAID THEY'RE A TORPID LOT.
BUT IN ANY EVENT, THERE IS THE NAGLFAR.
CAN YOU REALLY BEAR TO LOOK AT HER AND NOT TAKE HER HELM YOURSELF?

THERE ARE TIMES WHEN I PREFER TO WORK THROUGH PROXIES.
SO LONG AS THEY'RE RELIABLE.

IN BRUSSELS THERE IS A PEDOPHILE WHO WAS ARRESTED BUT NEVER CHARGED--
--BECAUSE OF WHAT HE KNEW ABOUT TWO GOVERNMENT MINISTERS.
AS I DICTATE THEIR CONFESSIONS, I THINK ABOUT WHAT MICHAEL SAID TO ME.
IS IT POSSIBLE THAT SOMEONE ELSE COULD HAVE SENT ME A DREAM?
USURPED MY HAND AND MY GUN? POINTED ME AND AIMED ME AT A TARGET OF HIS OWN CHOOSING?
AND TO WHAT END? TO TORMENT THE DEMON WITH PROMISE OF RELEASE?
TO ADD DEPTH AND SAVOR TO HER SUFFERING WITH THE BITTERSWEET LEAVEN OF HOPE?
BUT THAT WOULD MAKE ME AN INSTRUMENT OF VENGEANCE, RATHER THAN JUSTICE.
AND IT PRESUPPOSES A MONSTER WHO LOOKS OUT UPON THE UNIVERSE AND SEES NOTHING BUT A BOX OF TOOLS.
FOLLOWING THAT LINE OF THOUGHT TO ITS END WAS THERAPEUTIC. I SUMMON UP THE DREADFUL PHANTASM IN MY MIND--
--AND WITH GREAT RELIEF, DISMISS IT.

THE CREW OF THE NAGLFAR.
MAZIKEEN DAUGHTER OF LILITH, WAR LEADER OF THE LILIM IN EXILE. THAT FACE SHE WEARS IS NOT HER OWN: THE WOMAN JILL PRESTO GAVE IT TO HER WHEN HER OLD FACE BURNED--A FAVOR WHICH MAZIKEEN IS KEEN TO REPAY AT LENGTH WITH A VARIETY OF IMPLEMENTS.
BERGELMIR THE YOUNGEST AND SMALLEST OF THE GIANTS. HALF-BROTHER OF LOKI, WITH WHOM HE SHARES A CERTAIN WAY OF LOOKING AT THE WORLD. HIS FAULTS ARE HIS VIRTUES: HE'S TOO LAZY TO BE VINDICTIVE AND TOO FICKLE TO BE DANGEROUS.
CAL ALMOST AN ANGEL. LIKE HIS SISTER, ELAINE BELLOC, HE IS THE SEED OF THE ARCH-ANGEL MICHAEL INCUBATED IN A HUMAN MOTHER. BUT THE SEED GREW THWART AND BROKEN: CAL IS LESS HUMAN AND LESS ANGELIC THAN ONE MIGHT HAVE HOPED.
JILL PRESTO A CABARET ARTISTE WHO BECAME THE VESSEL FOR THE BASANOS, THE LIVING TAROT. JILL CARRIES BOTH THEIR CHILD AND THE MARK OF THEIR ANGER IN HER CRIPPLED ARM. UNDER THE BASANOS'S AEGIS, NO HARM CAN COME TO HER UNTIL HER PREGNANCY REACHES ITS TERM.
DAVID EASTERMAN A FORMER ADVERTISING EXECUTIVE, DAVID THOUGHT HE WAS ELAINE BELLOC'S FATHER UNTIL THE ANGEL SANDALPHON DISABUSED HIM AND MURDERED HIM IN QUICK SUCCESSION. HE PERSISTS AS AN EARTH-BOUND GHOST, HIS (PARADOXICALLY) PATERNAL LOVE FOR ELAINE THE ROCK TO WHICH HE CLINGS.
GAUDIUM A CHERUB WHO TOOK THE LUCIFER TICKET AND SO LOST HIS RANK AND INSIGNIA. MICHAEL OFFERED HIM A SECOND CHANCE--TO GUARD ELAINE FROM A MONSTROUS ASSASSIN IN EXCHANGE FOR A FULL PARDON--BUT HE BLEW THAT TOO. GOD SAVE US FROM FALLEN CHERUBS WITH UNFINISHED BUSINESS.
SPERA GAUDIUM'S SISTER. IT WOULD BE WRONG TO HOLD THAT AGAINST HER.

THE PAVILION OF THE LANTERNS. NOW.
I STRUGGLE AGAINST ETERNITY.
AHRRRRR!
THIS IS MY ART. THIS IS MY TRAGEDY.
IT IS NOT POIGNANT. NOT AS SUCH. NOTHING I MAKE IS EVER POIGNANT.
PL-- PLEASE! OH GOD, PLEASE!
IT'S BECAUSE THERE IS NO DEATH HERE. IF THINGS CAN'T DIE, ONE SENSES A FUTILITY AT THE BOTTOM OF THEIR SUFFERING.
ALMOST...A FAILURE.
WHEN THE SHIP COMES, NO DOUBT IT WILL BE DIFFERENT. BUT TO THE EVERLASTING PRESENT OF ART, THERE IS NO SHIP. NOT YET.
AND NO CHILDREN ANYMORE. BECAUSE THE CHILDREN ARE SUBSUMED IN THE WORK.
AND SO I WILL ENDEAVOR TO FORGET--
--THAT YOU ONCE HAD NAMES.

NAGLFAR
PART 1 OF 5 THE MUSTER
MIKE CAREY WRITER
PETER GROSS, RYAN KELLY & DEAN ORMSTON ARTISTS
DANIEL VOZZO COLOR AND SEPARATIONS
COMICRAFT LETTERS
CHRISTOPHER MOELLER COVER PAINTER
MARIAH HUEHNER ASSISTANT EDITOR
SHELLY BOND EDITOR
BASED ON CHARACTERS CREATED BY GAIMAN, KIETH AND DRINGENBERG
HOLD HER STEADY THERE, OAF!
I WANT HER CAULKED AND SEALED BEFORE THE CAPTAIN COMES ABOARD.
BE GENEROUS WITH THAT BRUSH, LAD.
IT SS... SS...
SOAKS IN, AYE. IT TAKES A GREAT DEAL OF TAR TO MAKE DEAD MEN'S FINGERNAILS SEAWORTHY.

IT SOUNDS ABSURD, I KNOW. BUT SINCE THE NAILS GROW AFTER DEATH, A LITTLE OF THE SPIRIT MIGRATES TO EACH OF THEM.
THINK OF IT AS A SHIP PLAITED OUT OF HUMAN SOULS.
BUT WH... WHAT'S IT F... F...FOR?

WHAT'S IT FOR? IT'S FOR GOING INTO BATTLE, YOU DOLT!
THE NAGLFAR IS A WARSHIP.

"IT WAS MY UNCLE HRIMTHURSA WHO MADE IT. WOVE IT, I SHOULD SAY.
"VERY DELICATE FINGERS HE HAD--AND FOR THIS WORK HE NEEDED THEM.

"ON THE DAY OF RAGNAROK, WHEN FIMBULVETR SWALLOWS THE WORLD, THE KIN OF JÖTUN WILL SAIL ON HER TO DISTANT ASGARD--
"--AND THE GODS OF THE AESIR, SQUEEZED BETWEEN ICE AND FIRE, WILL BE CUT DOWN LIKE CREATION'S LAST HARVEST."

OR SO THEY SAY. MYSELF, I'M PLANNING TO BE SOMEWHERE FAR ENOUGH AWAY THAT THE NOISE WON'T REACH ME.
A LITTLE MORE CAULK HERE.
THE MORNINGSTAR HAS A SOUR DISPOSITION--

Lux
"--AND A KEEN EYE FOR OTHER PEOPLE'S IMPERFECTIONS."

I'VE ALREADY CHOSEN MY CREW. BUT SAY THERE WERE A SPACE.
ASSUMING THE NAGLFAR SAILS WITH SUFFICIENT BALLAST--

--WHAT USE ARE YOU?
PLENTY. I CAN DO AERIAL RECON. AND I'M A RABID MANIAC IN A FIGHT.
WHEREAS I'M SNEAKIER THAN HIM AND I DON'T SMELL QUITE SO BAD.

ANYWAY, WHAT THE HELL USE IS HE? HE'S JUST A GODDAMN GHOST.
AND FROM WHAT I HEAR HE WASN'T EVEN UP TO MUCH WHEN HE WAS ALIVE.
I WAS BROUGHT HERE AGAINST MY WILL.

AND I REFUSE TO BE A PARTY TO THIS-- WHATEVER IT IS.

THE GHOST HAS A FUNCTION THAT RELATES TO NAVIGATION.
IT'S SIGNIFICANT ENOUGH TO IGNORE THE ENORMOUS IRRITATION HE PROVOKES.
WHEREAS IN YOUR CASE--

LOOK, I KNOW WHAT THIS IS ABOUT. YOU'RE GOING AFTER THE KID'S SOUL, AND I WANNA BE THERE.
IT'S SORT OF MY JOB.

WHAT ABOUT YOU? YOU'RE HIS SISTER, AREN'T YOU?
HE OWES ME MONEY.
FROM THE LAST TIME WE WENT AFTER HER SOUL.

WELL I SUPPOSE THERE'S NO HARM. EXCEPT TO OUR DIGNITY.
FOLLOW ME.

WE'VE GOT ONE MORE CREWMAN TO COLLECT.

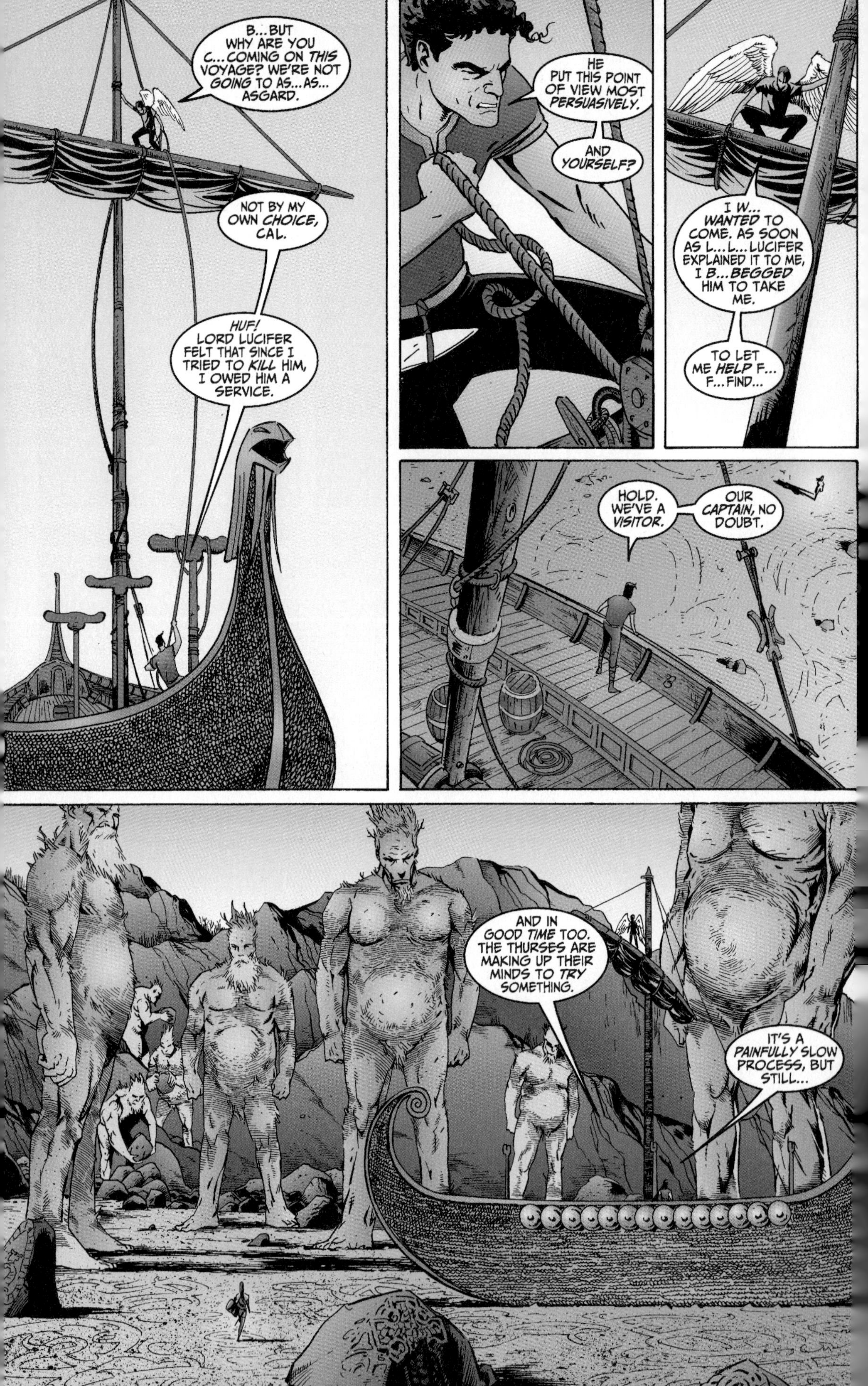
B...BUT WHY ARE YOU C...COMING ON THIS VOYAGE? WE'RE NOT GOING TO AS...AS... ASGARD.
NOT BY MY OWN CHOICE, CAL.
HUF! LORD LUCIFER FELT THAT SINCE I TRIED TO KILL HIM, I OWED HIM A SERVICE.
HE PUT THIS POINT OF VIEW MOST PERSUASIVELY.
AND YOURSELF?
I W... WANTED TO COME. AS SOON AS L...L...LUCIFER EXPLAINED IT TO ME, I B...BEGGED HIM TO TAKE ME.
TO LET ME HELP F... F...FIND...
HOLD. WE'VE A VISITOR.
OUR CAPTAIN, NO DOUBT.
AND IN GOOD TIME TOO. THE THURSES ARE MAKING UP THEIR MINDS TO TRY SOMETHING.
IT'S A PAINFULLY SLOW PROCESS, BUT STILL...

ARE YOU THE *HELSMAN,* BERGELMIR?
THAT I *AM,* MADAME.
A JOB THAT BECAME A THOUSAND TIMES MORE *ATTRACTIVE* THE MOMENT YOU STEPPED ABOARD.
I AM YOUR *CAPTAIN.*
UUF!
LUCIFER SAID YOU'D NEED WATCHING. I PROMISED HIM I'D *SKIN* YOU IF YOU DID LESS THAN YOUR JOB.
AN *EXCELLENT* WOMAN.
I WONDER WHAT HER *BEDPLAY* IS LIKE.
BOY.
Y... YES, C...C... CAPTAIN?
STOW THIS IN THE *DECK HOUSE.* AND THEN SHOW ME THE *WEAPONS.*

LAS VEGAS.
A TRIP?
YOU MEAN A TOUR? YOU BOOKED A TOUR WITHOUT CONSULTING ME?

NO, HOWARD. I MEAN A CRUISE. Y'KNOW, FOR MY HEALTH?
FOR YOUR HEALTH? JILL, PLEASE.
I GIVE THAT SHIT OUT. I DON'T SWALLOW IT.
KING PALOOKA
SKINBOAT LATE SHOW

OKAY. I'VE GOT SOME BUSINESS TO TAKE CARE OF.
PERSONAL STUFF.

LORETTA, HOLD MY CALLS.
WITH BOTH HANDS, HOWARD.
JILL, LISTEN TO ME. AS A FRIEND.
THE POLICE ARE SNIFFING AROUND YOU BECAUSE OF THAT GUY WHO DISAPPEARED. THE FIORENZE ARE PISSED BECAUSE YOU WALKED OUT MID-SEASON.

THIS IS NOT THE TIME TO GO AND CUDDLE YOUR INNER CHILD.

PLUS--AND I DIDN'T WANT TO SAY THIS--YOU'RE UNDER CONTRACT TO DELIVER THE THIRD ALBUM BY JUNE.
SO I'M SORRY, BUT IT'S NO.

YEAH, WELL I'M SORRY TOO, HOWARD. YOU'LL JUST HAVE TO SUE ME.

JILL, DON'T DO THIS. IT'S CAREER SUICIDE.

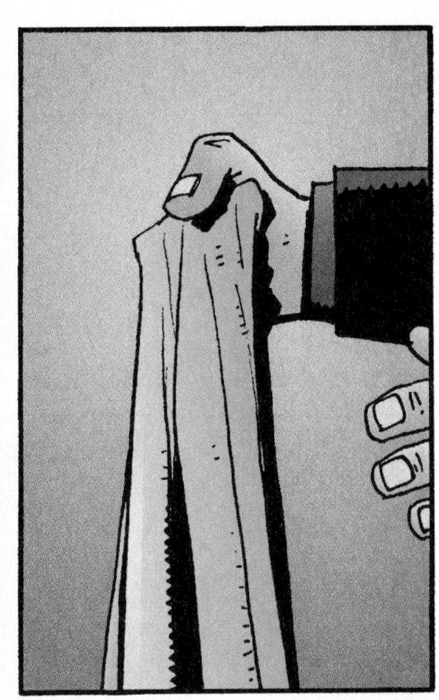

SHIT!
SHIT WITH ICE CREAM!
DON'T STARE AT IT, OKAY?
FUCK! JUST STOP!

I'M GONNA GET THIS FIXED.
I'M GOING TO A PLACE WHERE THEY CAN DEAL WITH STUFF LIKE THIS.

AND THEN I'LL BE BACK, HOWARD. BETTER THAN EVER.
YOU TEAR UP THOSE CONTRACTS AND YOU'LL BE WEEPING BLOOD IN A MONTH OR SO.

OKAY, SO SHE KNOWS HOW TO EXIT.
YOU WANT TO RECLAIM YOUR LOWER JAW AND CALL LEGAL?

CAN I SPEAK A *WORD*, CAPTAIN.
YES.
BUT KEEP IT *BRIEF*.
WE'RE READY TO *SAIL* AS SOON AS THE REST OF THE MUSTER IS ABOARD.
AND I'VE GOT SOMETHING TO *SHOW* YOU. FOR YOUR APPROVAL.
I GAVE SOME THOUGHT TO THE QUESTION OF *OARSMEN*.
WE CAN GET BY *WITHOUT* THEM, OF COURSE, BUT THEY'LL HAVE THEIR USES.
SO--
--I CAME UP WITH *THESE*.
UNLESS YOU'VE ANY OBJECTION...

WHAT *ARE* THEY?
JUST *TWIGS* FROM MY COUSINS' HAIR.
PUT THEM IN THE EARTH AND THEY *QUICKEN*. IT'S HOW GIANTS BREED.

GIANTS?
IT'S JUST A *WORD*. I'M OF THE GIANTS' BLOOD MYSELF, BUT YOU'D HARDLY *KNOW* IT.
UNLESS I WERE TO SHOW YOU MY--

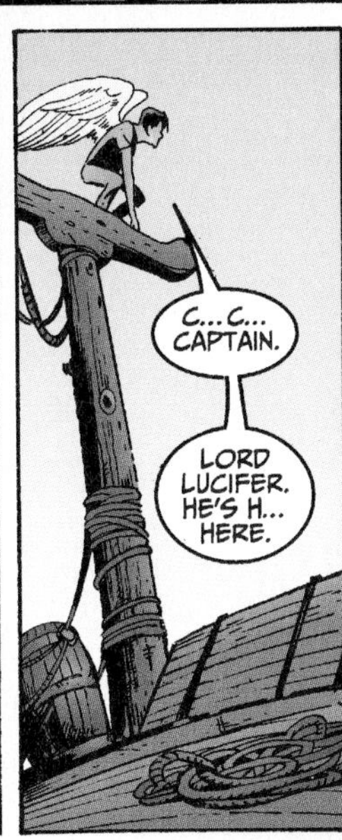
C...C... CAPTAIN.
LORD LUCIFER. HE'S H... HERE.

THAT'S A FINE SPEECH GONE TO *WASTE*.

WHAT CONDITIONS DO YOU NEED TO SET SAIL?
WE CAN SET SAIL NOW.
THE OARSMEN CAN TAKE HER TO THE MOUTH OF THE VALLEY, AND WE'LL CATCH A WIND THERE.

GOOD. HERE IS THE COMPASS, MAZIKEEN. IT WILL POINT TO HER AND HER ALONE.
IT'LL ALSO CURSE AND ARGUE WITH ITSELF A LOT, BUT YOU TUNE THAT OUT AFTER AWHILE.

I CHOSE MOST OF YOU FOR A REASON, AND IT WAS USUALLY THE SAME REASON.
I THOUGHT YOU HAD SOME SLENDER CHANCE OF COMING BACK.

BUT THE MANSIONS ARE AN UNFORGIVING PLACE.
YOU'LL HAVE TO RISE ABOVE YOUR INDIVIDUAL HATREDS AND MISTRUSTS. OTHERWISE YOU'LL DIE.

OR ELSE YOU'LL LIVE, BUT COME BACK UNSUCCESSFUL.
IN WHICH CASE I'LL KILL MOST OF YOU ANYWAY. GOOD LUCK.

PERMISSION TO TAKE HER OUT, CAPTAIN?
YES.
DO IT.

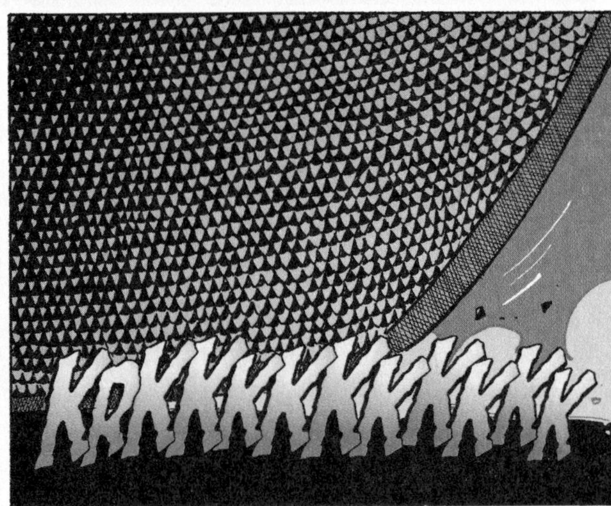

SLOWER ON THE RIGHT! BRING HER HEAD AROUND YARELY!
WE'RE AFLOOD, CAPTAIN.
AND WE'RE STEADY TO THE WEST.

UH... HI. JILL PRESTO. ARE YOU GUYS PART OF AN ACT?
YEAH. KNIFE-THROWING.

HEY!
ARE THOSE THINGS SUPPOSED TO BE THERE?
WHAT ARE THEY DOING?
REGISTERING... UFF...A PROTEST!
THE THURSES HAVE GUARDED THE SHIP FOR A THOUSAND YEARS. AND THEY CAN ONLY KEEP ONE IDEA IN THEIR HEADS AT A TIME.
BROOOOOM
KABOOOOM

IF WE STOP THEY MAY LOSE INTEREST IN US.
THEN WE CAN--
HOLD HER STEADY.
HE SEES US.
LET HIM DEAL WITH IT.
THIS IS WHAT I WAS NAMED FOR.
IN CASE YOU WONDERED.

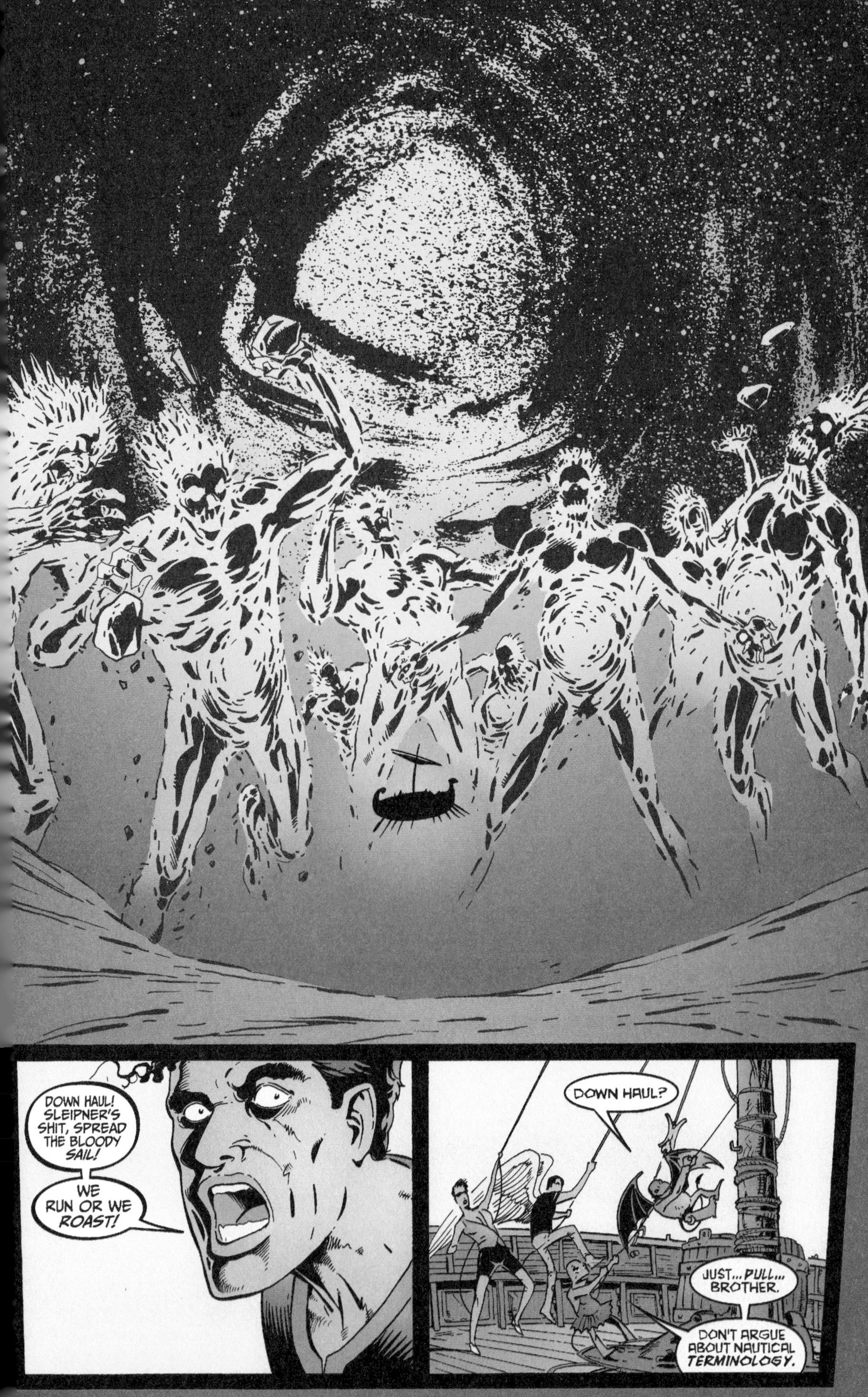
DOWN HAUL! SLEIPNER'S SHIT, SPREAD THE BLOODY SAIL!
WE RUN OR WE ROAST!
DOWN HAUL?
JUST... PULL... BROTHER.
DON'T ARGUE ABOUT NAUTICAL TERMINOLOGY.

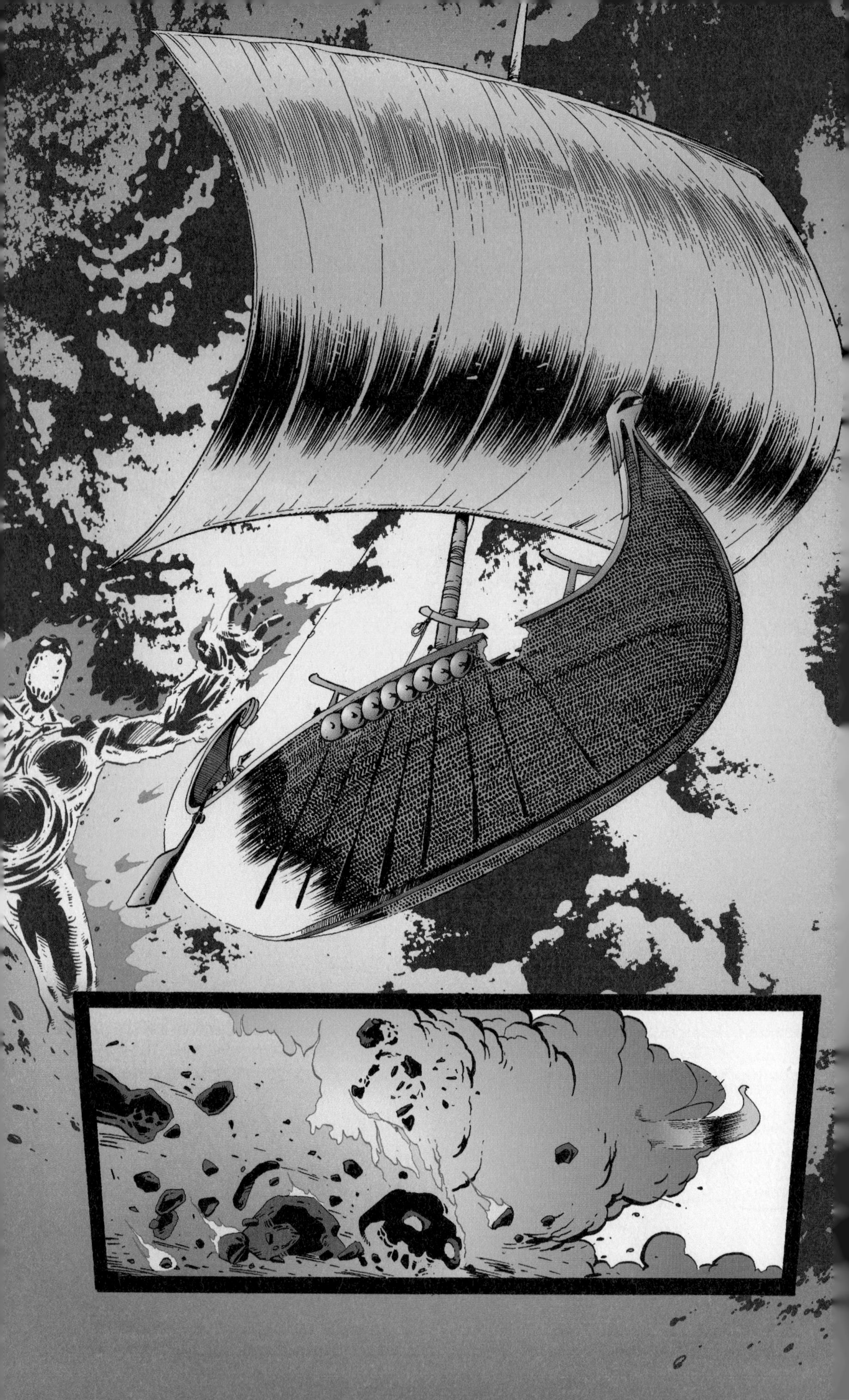

IT'S HARD TO TELL HIS ASSISTANCE FROM HIS *VENGEANCE*, ISN'T IT?
HE DID WHAT HE *NEEDED* TO.

SO, IS THERE A *NAUTICAL* TERM FOR WHAT JUST HAPPENED?
SHUT UP AND PUT THE *SAIL* OUT.

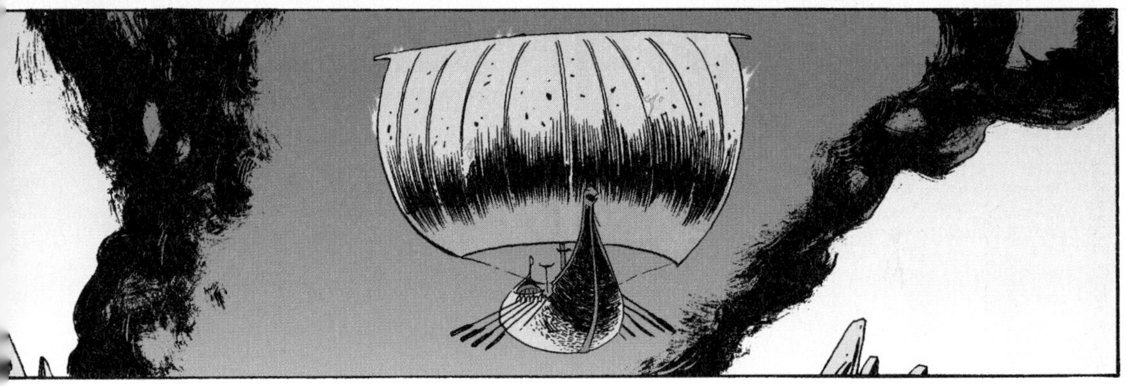

WHERE *EXACTLY* ARE WE GOING?
T...T...TO HEAVEN.
AND THEN ON B...BEYOND. *FAR* BEYOND.

THE MANSIONS OF THE S...S...
SILENCE.

BLEARGHHH!
NO WORSE THAN NAUSEA?
HEY, IT'S BAD ENOUGH.
YOU WERE NOT AFRAID WHEN THE SKY CAUGHT FIRE?
I DIDN'T SAY I WASN'T SCARED. BUT THERE'S LESS AT STAKE FOR ME THAN FOR THE REST OF YOU.
I'M SORT OF PRE-INSURED AGAINST FIRE AND THEFT.

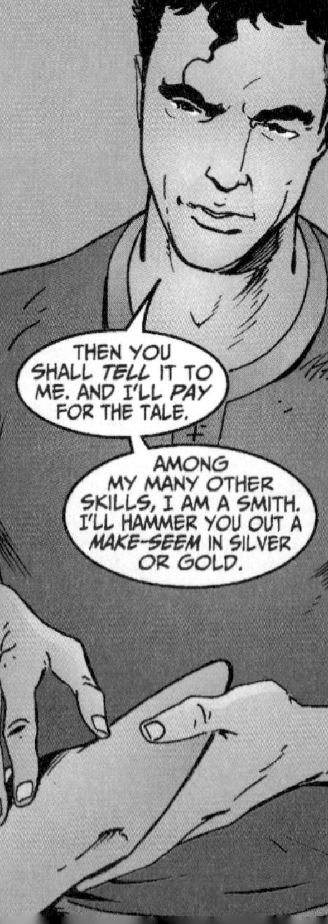

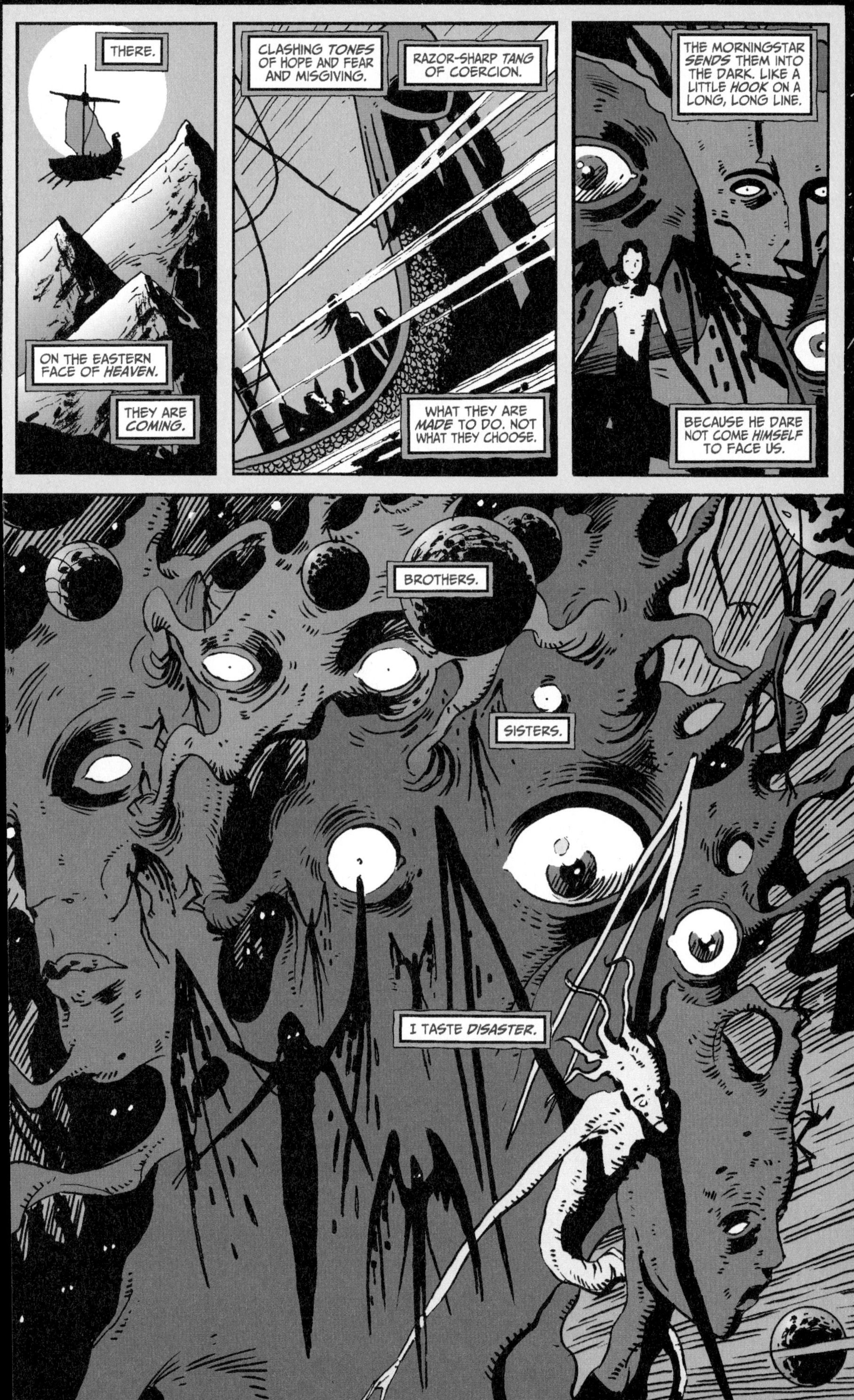

BROTHERS.

SISTERS.

I TASTE *DISASTER.*

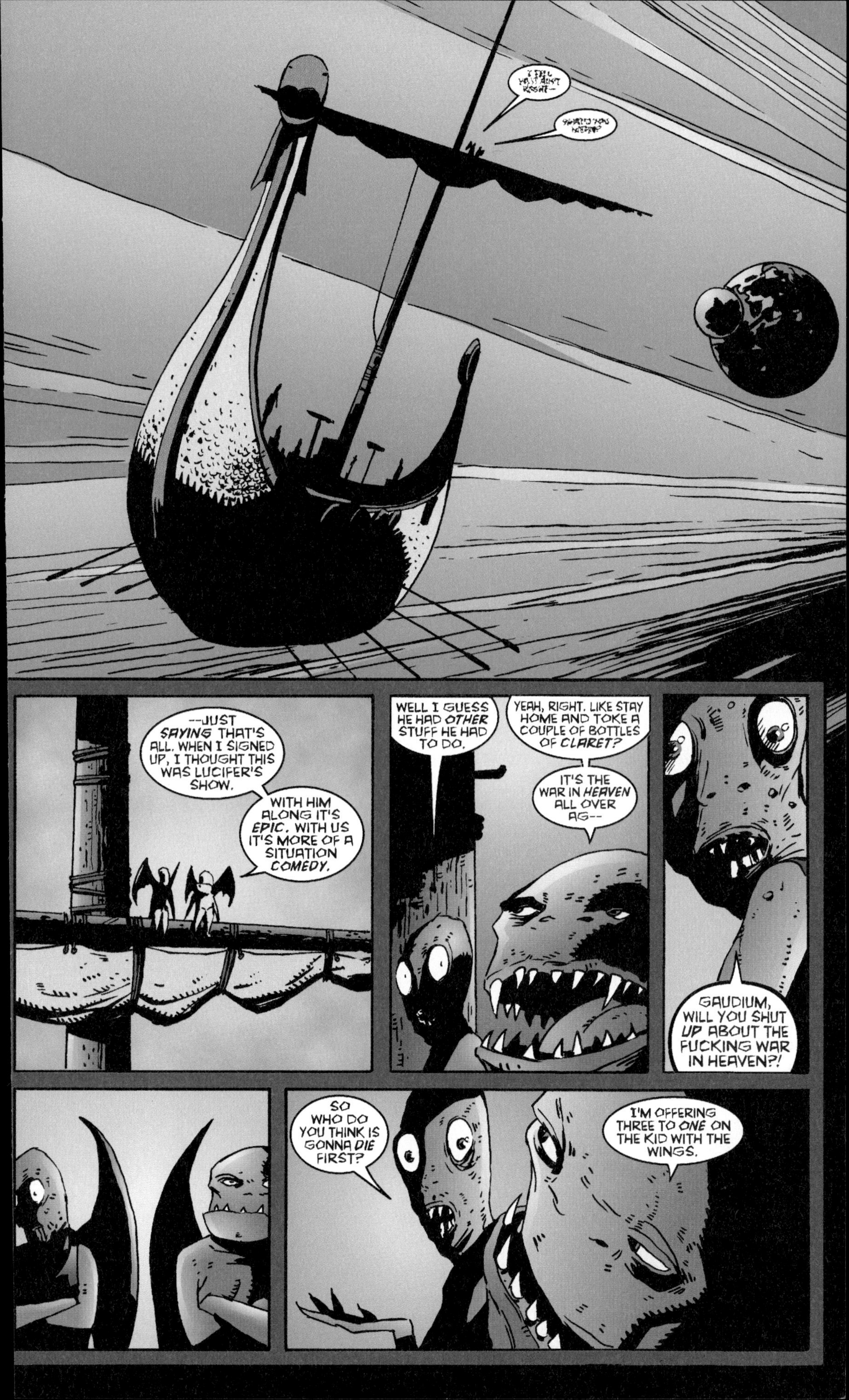

--JUST SAYING THAT'S ALL. WHEN I SIGNED UP, I THOUGHT THIS WAS LUCIFER'S SHOW.
WITH HIM ALONG IT'S EPIC. WITH US IT'S MORE OF A SITUATION COMEDY.

WELL I GUESS HE HAD OTHER STUFF HE HAD TO DO.
YEAH, RIGHT. LIKE STAY HOME AND TOKE A COUPLE OF BOTTLES OF CLARET?
IT'S THE WAR IN HEAVEN ALL OVER AG--

GAUDIUM, WILL YOU SHUT UP ABOUT THE FUCKING WAR IN HEAVEN?!

SO WHO DO YOU THINK IS GONNA DIE FIRST?
I'M OFFERING THREE TO ONE ON THE KID WITH THE WINGS.

WE NEED TO KNOW WHERE WE'RE GOING.
AND THERE'S ONLY ONE WAY OF FINDING OUT.
I KNOW, I KNOW. I'M JUST FRIGHTENED, THAT'S ALL.
COULDN'T SOMEONE ELSE--?
NO. NO ONE ELSE.
THE REST OF THE CREW HAVE OTHER FUNCTIONS. YOU ARE TOTALLY EXPENDABLE EXCEPT FOR THIS.
DO I HAVE TO THREATEN YOU?
NO I GET THE PICTURE.
THANKS FOR YOUR BRUTAL HONESTY.

OH
FU
KKKKHHHHHHHHH!
NAGLFAR
PART 2 OF 5 THE VOYAGE OUT
MIKE CAREY WRITER
PETER GROSS, RYAN KELLY & DEAN ORMSTON ARTISTS
DANIEL VOZZO COLOR AND SEPARATIONS
COMICRAFT LETTERS
CHRISTOPHER MOELLER COVER PAINTER
MARIAH HUEHNER ASSISTANT EDITOR
SHELLY BOND EDITOR
BASED ON CHARACTERS CREATED BY GAIMAN, KIETH AND DRINGENBERG
WELL NOW, LOVEY--
WHAT CAN WE LONG-DEAD LADIES DO FOR THE DEVIL'S HANDMAIDEN?
YOU CAN TELL ME WHERE ELAINE BELLC IS.
IF YOU KNOW.

WHERE OUR LAINIE IS?
SHE DIED, POPPET. IN GIVING YOUR LORD HIS LIFE BACK.
SO WE OWE HIM NO FAVORS. NO FAVORS AT ALL.
BUT HE OWES ONE TO HER. AND HE DECIDED TO PAY.
AYE, OUT OF PURE LOVE, NO DOUBT?
AND NOT BECAUSE OF ANY SCHEMES THAT STILL INCLUDE HER?
HER SPIRIT LIES AHEAD OF YOU. A LONG WAY AWAYS. AND OFF TO PORT.
SPEAK TO US AGAIN, WHEN YOU'RE CLOSER TO.
AND IN THE MEANTIME--
--WE'LL THINK ABOUT WHETHER OR NOT TO TRUST YOU.
ARE YOU ALL R... RIGHT, MISTER EASTERMAN?
I'M DEAD.
YOU WERE THERE, REMEMBER? YOU EVEN HELPED OUT A LITTLE.

YOU'VE A TENDENCY TO FLINCH FROM OUR BOLD CAPTAIN, SWEETING.
I ASSUME YOU'VE CROSSED PATHS BEFORE.
YEAH, SHE WANTS TO KILL ME. ONLY THERE'S SOMETHING INSIDE ME KEEPING ME SAFE. SHE HAS TO WAIT UNTIL I DITCH IT.

WHICH IS WHY I'M HERE.
JUST WISH I KNEW WHERE THE FUCK HERE IS.
WELL, I'VE A SUPERSTITION ABOUT WOMEN'S WISHES. SO HERE NOW--
--YOU'RE FAMILIAR WITH HEAVEN AND HELL, ARE YOU NOT?
I'VE HEARD OF 'EM.
EXCELLENT PLACES BOTH. BUT ESSENTIALLY--IF YOU'LL PARDON THE BANALITY OF THE METAPHOR--TWO FACES OF THE SAME COIN.

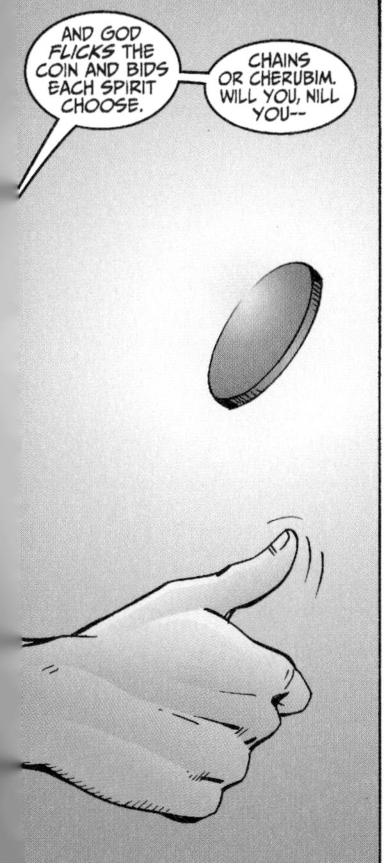
AND GOD FLICKS THE COIN AND BIDS EACH SPIRIT CHOOSE.
CHAINS OR CHERUBIM. WILL YOU, NILL YOU--

BUT THEN THERE ARE THE IRRECONCILABLE DEAD. THOSE THAT SAY NO TO BOTH.
AND OTHER SOULS, FOR WHOM HELL AND HEAVEN OFFER NO FITTING HARBOR.

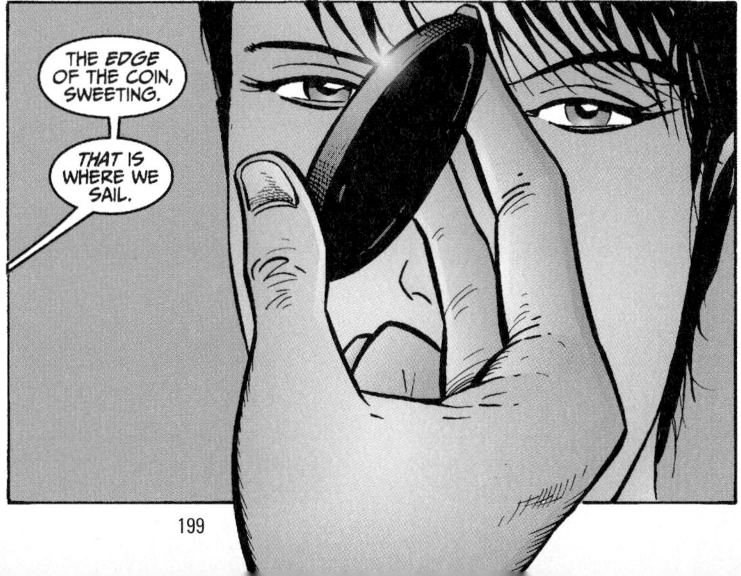
THE EDGE OF THE COIN, SWEETING.
THAT IS WHERE WE SAIL.

THE MUSEUM INSEL, BERLIN.
BROTHER--
--YOUR TASTE FOR IRONY IS BECOMING BOTH OBVIOUS AND OPPRESSIVE.
IRONY? OH, YOU MEAN ANGELS AND HARPS?
AMUSING. I REALLY HADN'T THOUGHT OF IT.
THEN WHY INVITE ME HERE? IS THERE NEWS?
NOT YET. BUT I WANTED YOU TO SEE SOMETHING.
CHRISTIAN HAARNACK MADE THIS IN 1785.
THEN, JUST BEFORE THE ALLIES TOOK BERLIN IN 1945, A SHELL EXPLODED AGAINST THE SOUTH WALL AND MADE THIS CRACK IN THE CASING, HERE.
I ALWAYS THINK OF YOU WHEN I THINK OF HARPS. THEY MAKE A SWEET SOUND WHILE THEIR OWN INTERNAL STRESSES TEAR THEM APART IN SLOW MOTION.
JUST A CRACK, A TENTH OF AN INCH LONG.
AND FIFTY YEARS LATER--
CRASH
--HERE WE ARE.

SO YOU'D HAVE ME DRAW SOME SORT OF LESSON FROM THE DESTRUCTION OF BEAUTY.
DON'T BE RIDICULOUS.
BUT SUPPOSE THE HARP IS A BRIDGE--
--AND THE CRACK'S IN A CENTRAL SUPPORT, A METER BELOW THE SURFACE WHERE IT CAN'T BE SEEN? WHAT THEN?
ARE YOU TRYING TO TEMPT ME, LUCIFER? OUR FATHER HAS A PLAN, AND BOTH DEATH AND LIFE ARE PART OF IT.
WHY SHOULD I INTERVENE TO PREVENT HIS PURPOSE?
BUT YOU DID INTERVENE. WHEN YOU SENT GAUDIUM TO SAVE YOUR DAUGHTER.
THAT WAS DIFFERENT. SHE WAS NOT PART OF THE PATRIMONY OF ADAM.
SHE IS A UNIQUE CASE.
SHE IS YOU WITH A WOMB. UNIQUE DOESN'T EVEN BEGIN TO DESCRIBE WHAT ELAINE IS.
WATCH THE BRIDGE FALL DOWN, AND THEN TELL ME WHERE YOU STAND.

M...M... ME?

WE'LL *ALL* TAKE A TURN, BUT YES.

THIS TIME, IT'S YOU, CAL.

TAKE ONE OF THE *IMPS*, TOO. I WANT TO KNOW EVERYTHING YOU CAN *TELL* ME ABOUT THE TERRAIN UP AHEAD.

BEING WHAT THEY *ARE*, THEY MIGHT SEE SOMETHING YOU'D MISS.

WHAT, LIKE A *LIQUOR* STORE? NEVER MIND. YOU'VE DONE THIS *BEFORE*, RIGHT?

N...NO. TO BE HONEST, THERE AREN'T M...M...*MANY* THINGS I'VE DONE BEFORE.

WELL JUST ZIG WHEN I *ZIG* AND ZAG WHEN I *ZAG*.

NOW THIS IS WHAT WE CALL "BROKEN GROUND."

YOU'RE LIKELY TO GET NASTY *SURPRISES* BECAUSE YOU CAN'T ALWAYS SEE WHAT'S COMING.

ALTHOUGH, HAVING *SAID* THAT--

--THERE'LL ALWAYS BE A FEW THINGS THAT SORT OF JUMP RIGHT *OUT* AT YOU.

M... MIRRORS! THOSE ARE MIRRORS! BUT THEY'RE AS BIG AS M...M... *MOUNTAINS.*

GREAT STUFF. GOOD RECONNAISSANCE STARTS WITH GOOD *DESCRIPTION.*

I'M PUTTING *YOU* IN CHARGE OF THAT.

OH SHIT.

WHATCHA *MAKIN'*, CURLY?
WHAT, LIKE A KIND OF A SORT OF A *SCULPTURE* OR SOMETHING?
IT'S A *GIFT*, LITTLE ONE. FOR THE WOMAN, JILL PRESTO.

NO, A GIFT OF A MORE *PRACTICAL* SORT. BUT PRAY YOU, LET IT BE A *SECRET* TILL IT'S *DONE*.
OH, THAT'S SO *LIKE* YOU. THAT COMPASSION.
FOR SOMEONE SO *HIDEOUSLY* CRIPPLED.

OF COURSE, YOU DO KNOW SHE'S *PREGNANT*, RIGHT?

BERGELMIR.
AYE, CAPTAIN?
GET BACK TO YOUR POST--

--AND STAND ON MY *ORDER*.

HUH! HUF! WE TRIED TO LEAD THEM AWAY, BUT THEY HEADED STRAIGHT FOR THE SHIP.
WHERE'S THE KID? DID HE GET BACK OKAY?
THERE ARE BOWS IN THE DECK HOUSE. BREAK THEM OUT.
CAPTAIN, I AWAIT YOUR ORDERS.
DON'T TAKE YOUR HANDS OFF THAT TILLER.
AND KEEP THE OARSMEN TO A DOUBLE STROKE.
STEER US A WAY THROUGH THEM.

CHOOM
OKAY, MOTHERFUCKERS! I'M ARMED AND DANGEROUS!
THEY JUST FALL APART!
WHAT THE HELL IS THIS?
IT HAS THE STINK OF A DIVERSION.

THE NAGLFAR CARRIES WITH IT EVERY ITEM OF UNFINISHED BUSINESS I COULD THINK OF.
I WANTED TO BE FREE OF ENCUMBRANCES. FREE TO PLAN.

IF YOU WERE EVER TO DIE, THAT WOULD MAKE AS GOOD AN EPITAPH FOR YOU AS ANY.
SARCASM? THAT'S A NEW NOTE FOR YOU, BROTHER.

LUCIFER, I AM GRATEFUL FOR YOUR SEEKING OUT MY DAUGHTER'S SPIRIT. BUT I WOULD HAVE YOU BE DIRECT.
NOT PROWL AROUND ME LIKE AN ANIMAL AFRAID OF THE LIGHT.
WAS I PROWLING? I MERELY ASKED YOU TO STATE YOUR POSITION, THAT'S ALL.

I STAND WHERE I HAVE ALWAYS STOOD.
I WILL NOT FIGHT AGAINST OUR FATHER. AND I WILL NOT HELP YOU BECOME HIM.

SMACK!

BROTHER... DO NOT TEMPT ME TO ANGER.
THERE IS THE SAFETY OF THIS WORLD TO CONSIDER.
I WANT YOU TO BE ANGRY.
HE GAVE US POWER AS GREAT AS HIS OWN--AND THEN WHEN HE WAS DONE WITH WORLD-MAKING, HE FORBADE US TO USE IT.
HE LIED TO ME. TRIED TO EXILE ME FROM THE FACE OF CREATION. AND HE ENGINEERED THE DEATH OF YOUR DAUGHTER.
MUST I REPEAT MYSELF? HE HAS A PLAN.
HAS HE? HE NEVER SHARED IT WITH ANY OF US?
WE HAVE TAKEN IT ON TRUST SINCE THE TIME BEFORE TIME.
BUT YOU STILL HAVE FAITH IN IT? THE GREAT PLAN?
I--YES. COMPLETELY.
BECAUSE I KNOW A PLACE WHERE WE CAN GO AND SEE IT. IF YOU'RE INTERESTED.

WHAT'S--?
WHAT IS THAT?
--THAT--?
OKAY, ELAINE. WHEN A BUNNY RABBIT DIES, HE SORT OF--
GOES UP TO HEAVEN?
NO. BUT A BIT OF HIM STILL LIVES INSIDE YOUR HEAD.
A KNIFE. A KNIFE WITH A SERRATED BLADE AND A SLIP-FREE RUBBER GRIP.
WHY WAS SHE CARRYING IT? TO TRIM HER FINGERNAILS?
UHHHHHHH!

KRESCHH
TISCH
TISCH
TISCH
THEY'RE DYING. I THOUGHT-- I THOUGHT THEY WERE GOING TO ATTACK US.
DO YOU NOT FEEL THAT LIGHT BLEEDING INTO YOUR MIND?
THIS IS A SUICIDE ATTACK.

VERY WELL. I SEE THE TRICK, AND HOW IT'S DONE.

BERGELMIR.
TAKE US UP. AS HIGH AS SHE'LL GO. WE NEED--
THUCK
CURLY? WHAT ARE YOU DOING TO US?
CAN'T--
--CAN'T THINK--
DON'T STRUGGLE, LITTLE ONE.
THERE'S DEATH OR THERE'S ME.

SIT UP SLOWLY, HELMSMAN. AS SLOWLY AS A SHADOW CROSSING A SUNDIAL.
AND EXPLAIN TO ME WHY I SHOULD NOT KILL YOU.
BECAUSE WE ARE STILL ALIVE, CAPTAIN.
NOW THERE'S A REASON THAT SPRINGS TO MIND.
AND OUR SURVIVAL DEPENDED ON YOUR ATTACKING US?
YOU FELT THE FORCE OF THOSE MEMORIES. THOSE LIVES.
THE TIDAL PULL OF THEM. WHIPPING OUR MINDS INTO FROTH AND TATTERS.
I SAY WE STRING 'IM UP. WE HAVE PLENTY OF ROPE.
BE SILENT, IMP.
WHAT WAS HAPPENING THEN?

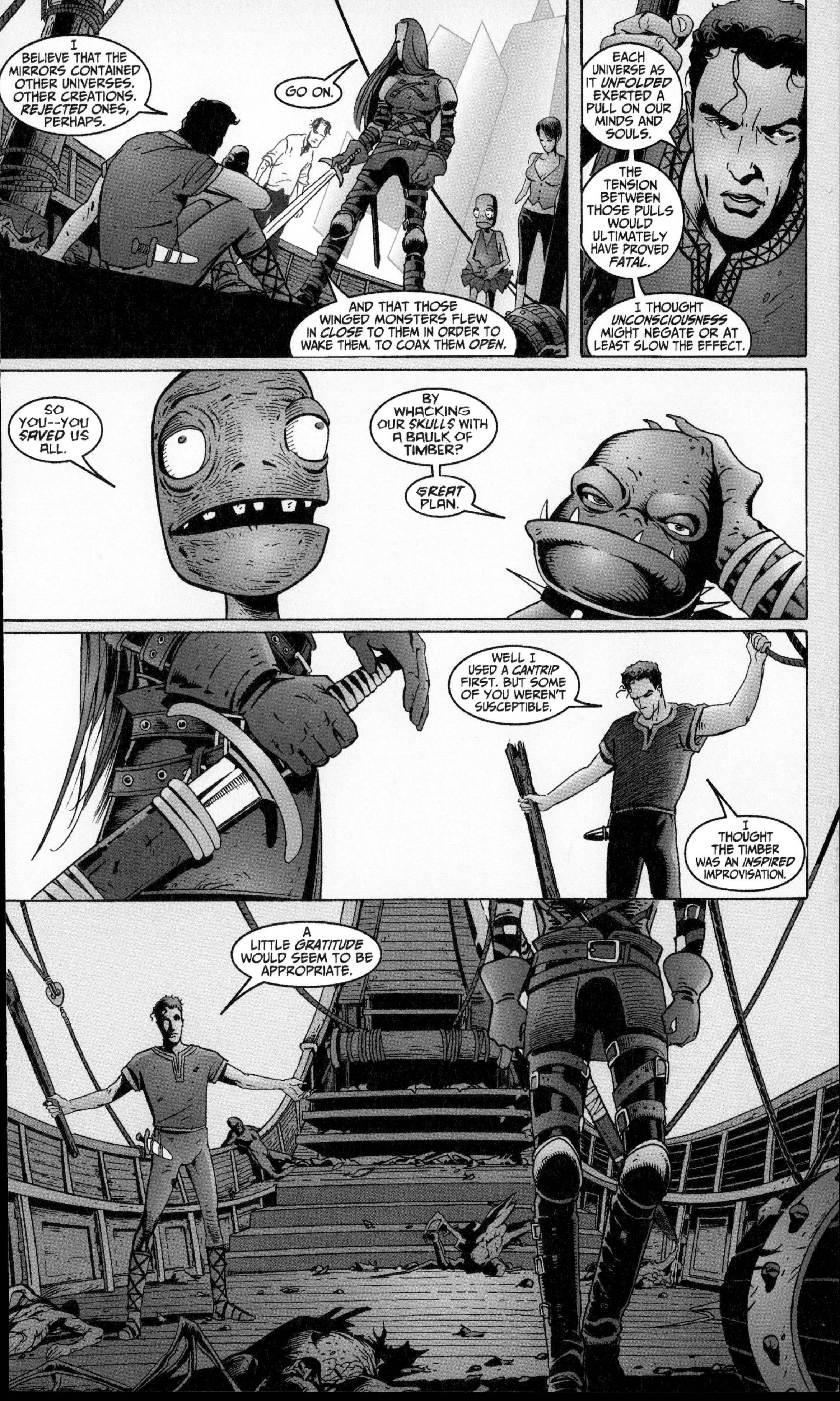
I BELIEVE THAT THE MIRRORS CONTAINED OTHER UNIVERSES. OTHER CREATIONS. REJECTED ONES, PERHAPS.
GO ON.
AND THAT THOSE WINGED MONSTERS FLEW IN CLOSE TO THEM IN ORDER TO WAKE THEM. TO COAX THEM OPEN.
EACH UNIVERSE AS IT UNFOLDED EXERTED A PULL ON OUR MINDS AND SOULS.
THE TENSION BETWEEN THOSE PULLS WOULD ULTIMATELY HAVE PROVED FATAL.
I THOUGHT UNCONSCIOUSNESS MIGHT NEGATE OR AT LEAST SLOW THE EFFECT.
SO YOU--YOU SAVED US ALL.
BY WHACKING OUR SKULLS WITH A BAULK OF TIMBER?
GREAT PLAN.
WELL I USED A CANTRIP FIRST. BUT SOME OF YOU WEREN'T SUSCEPTIBLE.
I THOUGHT THE TIMBER WAS AN INSPIRED IMPROVISATION.
A LITTLE GRATITUDE WOULD SEEM TO BE APPROPRIATE.

--OWE ME A HUNDRED AND FIFTY OF THOSE GREEN DOLLAR THINGS, AND YOU'RE *NOT* GETTING OUT OF IT.
NO I DON'T. CAL'S *MISSING* NOT DEAD.
I DON'T PAY OUT FOR LESS THAN HALF A *CADAVER.*

I USURPED YOUR COMMAND. I BEG YOUR *PARDON* FOR IT.
YOU DID WHAT WAS NECESSARY. WHAT *WORKED.*
BUT NOW WE'VE A CREWMAN LOST AND AN *ENEMY* WHOSE FACE WE HAVEN'T EVEN SEEN.

I THINK THERE'S *WORSE* TO COME.

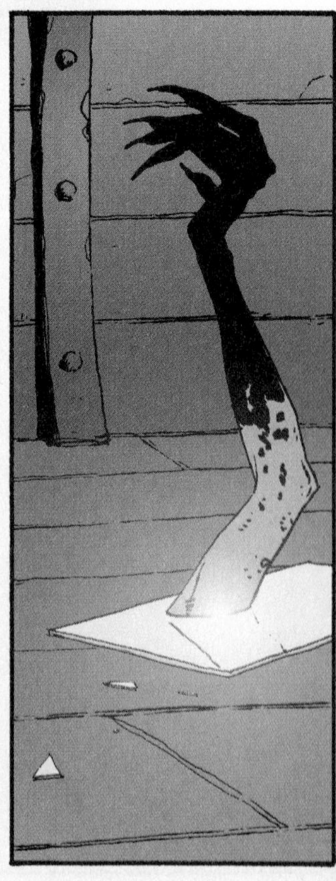

IT IS A CHAIN.
A STRUCTURE THAT IS BOTH ROBUST AND ELEGANT.
EVERY ACTION BIRTHS THE NEXT, SO THAT THERE IS AN INEVITABLE PROGRESS--
--TOWARDS AN END POINT WHICH AT FIRST WOULD HAVE BEEN UNTHINKABLE.
SNIP
I HAVE NOT ENJOYED BEING DEAD. BUT IT HAS EXPOSED ME TO NEW SENSATIONS.
AND IT TURNS OUT TO HAVE ITS PRACTICAL USE, TOO.
BECAUSE, YOU SEE, THEY KNOW NOTHING OF THIS PLACE, OR ITS RULES.
THEY WILL EXPECT IT TO BEHAVE AS IF IT'S REAL.
AND THE TIDES WILL DRAG THEM UNDER--
--WHILE I WATCH.

KRAKOODOOM
HOW DID WE GET INTO THIS FRIGGIN' MESS?
WELL, THIS KID ELAINE GOT FERSCHMUTTERED, AND NOW EVERYONE'S SAYING SHE'S GOD'S GRANDDAUGHTER, AND LUCIFER WANTS US TO FIND HER SOUL SO HE CAN--
I WAS BEING RHETORICAL, FOR FUCK'S SAKE!
HEY.
HEY, LOOK!
IT'S THE KID, CAL.
HE FOUND HIS WAY BACK.
NAGLFAR
PART 3 OF 5 THE WRACK
MIKE CAREY WRITER
PETER GROSS, RYAN KELLY & DEAN ORMSTON ARTISTS
DANIEL VOZZO COLOR AND SEPARATIONS
COMICRAFT LETTERS
CHRISTOPHER MOELLER COVER PAINTER
MARIAH HUEHNER ASSISTANT EDITOR
SHELLY BOND EDITOR
BASED ON CHARACTERS CREATED BY GAIMAN, KIETH AND DRINGENBERG

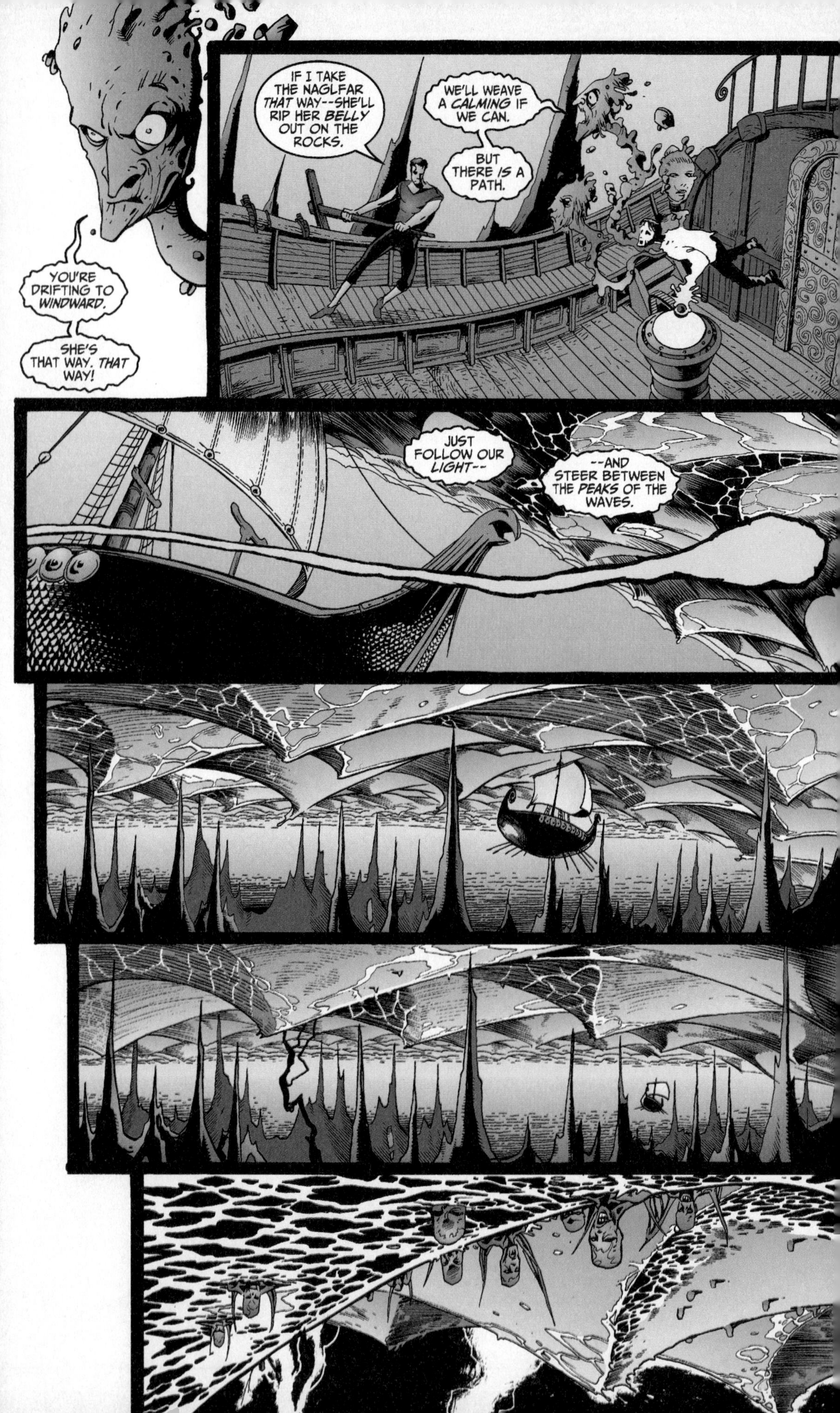
IF I TAKE THE NAGLFAR THAT WAY--SHE'LL RIP HER BELLY OUT ON THE ROCKS.
WE'LL WEAVE A CALMING IF WE CAN.
BUT THERE IS A PATH.
YOU'RE DRIFTING TO WINDWARD.
SHE'S THAT WAY. THAT WAY!
JUST FOLLOW OUR LIGHT--
--AND STEER BETWEEN THE PEAKS OF THE WAVES.

HEY, KID. GLAD YOU MADE IT.
WHAT?
I COULD BE OUT A FEW BUCKS ON A BET, BUT IT'S STILL--
GLEEP!
STOP TRYING TO CONFUSE ME, YOU WINDBLOWN PIECE OF SHIT.
GLEEP!
I WAS HERE ALL THE TIME.
IT WAS YOU THAT GOT LOST.
THUD
CAL LOST HIS STAMMER.
I KNEW THERE WAS SOMETHING.
COULDN'T PUT MY FINGER ON IT...

LUCIFER, WE ARE DIVIDING OUR ENERGIES. THE SEARCH FOR MY DAUGHTER--

--IS OUT OF OUR HANDS RIGHT NOW.

AND THIS OPPORTUNITY MAY NOT REPEAT ITSELF.

WE CAN LOOK OVER OUR FATHER'S SHOULDER FOR ONCE AND SEE WHAT HE'S WORKING TOWARDS. THAT'S WORTH A LITTLE RISK.

COULD YOU GIVE ME A MOMENT?

"AND THAT WE'RE BOTH IN A FAIRLY *SOUR* MOOD."

WELL, THAT'S PASSED.
BUT IT DIDN'T, DID IT? WE STILL HAVE TO COME BACK THIS WAY.
COULDN'T LUCIFER HAVE TOLD US WHAT WE WERE GOING TO FACE?
NO. HE COULDN'T.
HE'S NEVER BEEN HERE.
SAY WHAT NOW?
THE MANSIONS COULD NOT SUSTAIN HIS PRESENCE. THEY'RE TOO FRAGILE.
THAT'S THE ONLY REASON HE DIDN'T COME HIMSELF.
I-- I HAVE THIS TERRIBLE SENSE OF--
I KNOW. LIKE YOU'RE TIED TO THE NOSECONE OF A ROCKET AND YOU LOOK DOWN AND THE ROCKET'S GOT "PROTOTYPE" ALL DOWN THE SIDE OF IT.
EXACTLY.

BUT--
--WHY?
I TOLD YOU, SWEETING. I HATE TO BE IDLE.
AND SYMMETRY ADDS A NEW DIMENSION TO YOUR BEAUTY. FLEX THE FINGERS.
OH MY GOD! IT WORKS!
IT WORKS LIKE IT'S A PART OF ME!
JESUS, CURLY! I CAN'T THINK OF ANYTHING TO SAY.
ANYTHING TO DO. THIS IS JUST TOO FUCKING WONDERFUL!
YEAH? WELL I'LL BET YOU COME UP WITH SOMETHING, YOU SCISSOR-LEGGED SLUT.
AND CURLY IS MY PET NAME FOR HIM.

IT WERE AS WELL FOR YOU TO *SPEAK.*
IF YOU SPEAK WE CAN STOP *HURTING* YOU.
WE ARE YOUR *COUSINS.* EMBRACE US, AND BE *ONE* WITH US.
WE ARE THE *ANGELIC DEAD.* THE REMNANTS OF THE FORCE THAT FOUGHT IN *HEAVEN* WHEN THE MORNINGSTAR REBELLED.
PL... PLEASE. PLEASE. IT'S M... MY *SISTER.*
HUSH NOW. HE IS SMALL AND *BROKEN* AND AFRAID.
HE HAS HELD BACK HIS KNOWLEDGE OUT OF *FEAR.* BUT WHAT *MORE* HAS HE TO FEAR NOW?
WE'RE LOOKING FOR THE GH... GH... *GHOST* OF MY SISTER.

WARM.

SOMETHING'S LIVING INSIDE THIS ROCK. DO YOU MIND IF I CATCH UP WITH YOU?
WE'LL WAIT. BUT MAKE IT QUICK.

SHE IS A DEMON.
YES, A FORMIDABLE ONE.
AND YOU'D REALLY SET HER TO GUARD US WHILE WE'RE HELPLESS?

RRRUUMMBLE!
WELL, SHE'S CERTAINLY UP TO THE JOB. PHYSICALLY CAPABLE, I MEAN.
AND IT'S GOOD THAT SHE'LL HAVE A FULL STOMACH.

BUT I STILL DON'T UNDERSTAND. HOW CAN THIS THING SHOW US OUR FATHER'S THOUGHTS?
AND WHY IS IT HIDDEN HERE, IN THE REALMS OF PAIN?

YOU NEVER CHANGE, DO YOU, MICHAEL? ALWAYS THIRSTY FOR KNOWLEDGE--
--ALWAYS AFRAID THAT SOMEONE'S SPAT IN THE CUP.

WELL MAKE UP YOUR MIND, ONE WAY OR THE OTHER.
THIS IS ONE TIME WHERE PLAYING IT SAFE WON'T BE AN OPTION.

I SMELL DEATH IN THERE. BUT IT'S A FEW WEEKS OLD.
THE FORMER OWNER, SCORIA. THIS WAS HIS TOY.
AND NOW HIS TOMB. HE TRIED TO RAPE HIS WIFE, MAZIKEEN OF THE LILIM, WITH PREDICTABLE RESULTS.

AFRAID, BROTHER?
OF WHAT? THAT RAMSHACKLE MECHANISM? THIS SAD SOULLESS PLACE?
THERE'S NOTHING HERE TO FEAR.

WELL, THERE'S ALWAYS THE TRUTH.

"--OR DO YOU SEE THAT AS SOMETHING TO BE *EMBRACED?*"

THIS IS *CRAZY!* SOMEONE PROBABLY SAW US COME IN HERE.

IT MATTERS NOT WHAT THEY *SEE* OR WHAT THEY *GUESS.*

LET THEM *ENVY* US.

ALARUM OMNES! ALL OF YOU, ON DECK!
THERE'S SOMETHING AHEAD OF US!
WHATEVER IT IS, I'M GOING TO KILL IT WITH MY BARE FUCKING HAND.
FEAR NOT, SWEETING. IF WE MUST WAIT, WE'LL GO TO OUR BANQUET WITH A KEENER APPETITE.
STILL, THE LAD SOUNDS UNHAPPY. BEST FIND OUT WHY.

HOW FAR DOES IT STRETCH?
TO THE LIMITS OF VISION. AND THAT'S NOT ALL.
LOOK TO STARBOARD.
WE'VE PICKED UP AN ESCORT.
OH MY GOD! IT'S THOSE SKELETON THINGS--BUT WE BEAT THEM BEFORE.
WE WEREN'T TRAPPED UP AGAINST A WALL OF THORNS BEFORE.
THIS IS WHAT THEY'VE BEEN WAITING FOR.
WHUMP

BACK OFF, FOR CHRISSAKES.
IT'S NOT LIKELY TO BE A FRIGGIN' FRUIT BASKET.
HOLY CRAP.
IT'S HIM. I MEAN, IT'S YOU, CAL. FUCK!
THAT'S--
--ABSURD.
THEY'RE COMING IN.
GIRD YOURSELVES.

WHAT IS THIS PLACE? IT FEELS LIKE A SHRINE.
IT SHOULD.
THESE ARE THE THOUGHTS OF YAHWEH. MY FATHER.
THE ARTIFICER SCORIA DRILLED INTO HIS MIND WITH ALCHEMICAL ENGINES, AND STORED THE RUNOFF HERE.
THE THOUGHTS OF GOD. AMAZING. MIND IF I--
YEAH, I GUESS YOU DO.
YOU'RE WATCHING OUR BACKS, REMEMBER, UNTIL WE'VE GOT WHAT WE NEED.
AFTER THAT YOU CAN DO WHAT YOU LIKE.

COMING IN?
OR DO YOU HAVE TO BE HOME BEFORE MIDNIGHT?

BECAUSE I RETAIN A SENSE OF DUTY TO SOMETHING BEYOND MYSELF. YOU THINK OF ME AS A FOOL.
THERE ARE NO GROUNDS ON WHICH WE CAN EVER MEET, LUCIFER.

SO WE MUST BE CONTENT TO PITY EACH OTHER FROM A DISTANCE.

I THINK HE WON THAT ONE.
JUST KEEP YOUR MIND ON YOUR JOB, ZIM'ET.
I DON'T WANT ANYTHING TO GET NEAR US.

IS THAT USUALLY A PROBLEM?

ELEGANTLY DONE. BUT IT WON'T HELP.
THEY MEAN TO IMMOBILIZE US.
RAM THE THORNS, BERGELMIR.
BUT WE DON'T KNOW HOW THICK THEY ARE. OR WHAT'S ON THE OTHER--
IT DOESN'T MATTER.
WE'VE GOT NOWHERE ELSE TO GO.

SO--
WHAT ARE
YOU?
A
DOPPELGANGER?
A GHOST? AN ACID
FLASHBACK?
SHUT UP,
YOU STINKY LITTLE
BASTARD.
OR
I'LL GUT YOU
MYSELF.
I'M CAL!
MY NAME IS
CAL! FUCK
YOU ALL!
YOU
GUYS ARE ALL
OVER THE
PLACE, AREN'T
YOU?
BUT
I'VE WORKED
CABARET. I
CAN DEAL.

AH, THE PITY OF IT.
DO NOT THINK I AM UNMOVED, MY SONS.
KKKRRAKKKKKKKKK
I HAVE LIVED THESE LIVES AGAIN AND AGAIN.
I HAVE ENDURED THESE FUTILE QUESTS AND ESCALATING SACRIFICES. THE TURMOIL THAT DROWNS OUT LOVE AND HOPE AND MEANING--
--UNTIL THE HEART STOPS, AND THE LAST BREATH DIES IN THE LAST DRY THROAT.
IT IS A TRAGEDY.
ALL OF IT.

BUT THE PATTERNS PERSIST, TOO...
...PERSIST AND REPEAT THEMSELVES.
INFINITY ANSWERS INFINITY. LIKE MIRRORS FACING EACH OTHER ACROSS A NARROW HALLWAY.
I HAVE MADE WELL.
AND I MADE BEST WHEN I MADE YOU.
NOW COME INTO THE LIGHT--
--WHERE I CAN SEE YOU BOTH.

MICHAEL DEMIURGOS--SPARK THAT EXPANDS FOREVER--OCEAN OF POWER WITH NO SHORE--
--AND SAMAEL--MY SWEET, SAVAGE SAMAEL, WHO BRINGS THE LIGHT WHERE I HAVE TOLD IT TO SHINE--
--HOW I LOVE YOU, MY SONS. HOW I SWELL WITH PRIDE FOR YOU.
YOU MUST NOT TRY TO SPEAK, OR TO MOVE.
SPEECH AND ACTION ARE ALIKE IMPOSSIBLE. AND THERE IS NOTHING TO SAY, OR DO, IN ANY CASE.

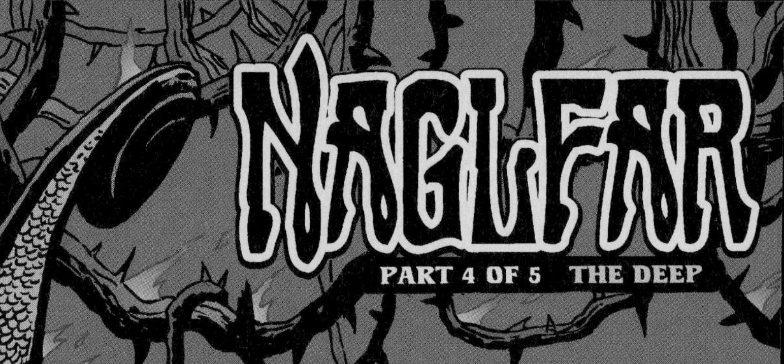
NAGLFAR
PART 4 OF 5 THE DEEP
THE SHIP?
THE SHIP HAS MISCARRIED.
AND YOUR DAUGHTER, MICHAEL-- THE ONLY CAUSE IN CREATION THAT COULD HAVE MADE YOU AND YOUR BROTHER ACT IN CONCERT--

--SHE HANGS IN THE PAVILION OF THE LANTERNS. SET THERE TO BE BOTH WORM AND HOOK.

THE THRONES ARE CAST DOWN, AND THE DOMINIONS HUMBLED.

MIKE CAREY WRITER
PETER GROSS, RYAN KELLY & DEAN ORMSTON ARTISTS
DANIEL VOZZO COLOR AND SEPARATIONS
COMICRAFT LETTERS
CHRISTOPHER MOELLER COVER PAINTER
MARIAH HUEHNER ASSISTANT EDITOR
SHELLY BOND EDITOR
BASED ON CHARACTERS CREATED BY
GAIMAN, KIETH AND DRINGENBERG
THE KEYS TURN IN THE HEARTS OF MEN AND OF ANGELS.
ALL THINGS STAND AS I DETERMINED IN THE MORNING OF THE WORLDS.
FOR YOU ARE THE KING OF CONTRIVANCE AND MANIPULATION, MY SAMAEL. BUT IN THAT, AS IN ALL THINGS--
--YOU LEARNED FROM YOUR FATHER.

DON'T TRY TO MOVE.
MMNUH?
YOU'RE HURT.
WHAT? DON'T BE STUPID.
I CAN'T BE HURT AS LONG AS I'M CARRYING--

I CAN PLEAD GUILTY TO THE *FIRST*, CAPTAIN.
BUT I MAY HAVE TO *DISAPPOINT* YOU ON THE SECOND.

I'M NOT REAL.
I'M NOT ME.

OH JEEZ. THIS GOT FUCKED UP REALLY FAST, DIDN'T IT?
IT WAS THAT WAY TO BEGIN WITH, JILL.
IT'S UNLIKELY TO END WELL FOR ANY OF US.
I WAS HOPING-- Y'KNOW, THAT YOU'D GET TO FINISH THAT SPEECH ABOUT YOUR TRUE VOCATION...
...WITH YOUR VOICE REALLY, REALLY MUFFLED.
HA! YOU SEE, SWEETING, I AM AS SLY AS MY BROTHER, LOKI.
WHEN YOU'VE FOUND ELAINE, YOU MUST COME BACK TO ME--OR ELSE GO UNSATISFIED.
WHO IS HE?
JUST A GOD I MET.
WHAT'S IT TO YOU, JIMINY CRICKET?

WE HEAD THAT WAY. WITH THE FIRE AT OUR BACKS.
IT'S THE LINE THE NAGLFAR WAS ON WHEN SHE FELL.
AND YOU SAY YOU LIVE HERE?
OH YES. MY HOME IS VERY CLOSE BY.
I'LL GUIDE YOU, IF YOU ALLOW IT.
WHEN THE FIRE DIES, THOSE THINGS WILL TRY TO FOLLOW US.
BUT THEY'LL CHECK THE WRECKAGE FIRST.
AND THESE SCRAPINGS AND I WILL SHOW THEM SUCH ENTERTAINMENT AS WE CAN.
WE'LL SEE YOU WHEN WE RETURN, BERGELMIR.
AYE. DOUBTLESS.
DON'T LOOK AT ME LIKE THAT, COUSINS.
IT MAKES ME WANT TO PREACH A SERMON.

FIRST OF ALL, MY SONS, YOU SHOULD KNOW THIS.
THAT I DID NOT NEED YOU.
THE FIRST FLOWER OF LIGHT COULD HAVE BEEN BORN WITHOUT A SEED.
I HAD PLAYED IT THROUGH A THOUSAND TIMES. I KNEW ITS GROWTH AND DECAY TO A NICETY.
AND THERE WAS NO NEED FOR A WEAVER TO SPIN THE LIGHT INTO SUNS.
IT WAS PREGNANT ALREADY WITH THE FORMS WHICH IT WOULD BECOME.
BUT I HAD TO TEACH YOU YOUR SKILLS.
AND THERE WAS NO OTHER SCHOOL.

THEN CAME THE HOST, AND THE SILVER CITY.
AND IF THEY WERE NEEDED, IT WAS ONLY BECAUSE I HAD CREATED YOU.
HOW WOULD YOU LOOK UPON YOURSELVES IF YOU HAD NO PEERS? NO CONTEXT FOR YOUR ACTIONS?
NO MIRRORS INTO WHICH TO GAZE?
AND HOW COULD YOU HEAD-- OR HEAD OFF--
--A REBELLION IF THERE WERE NONE TO FOLLOW YOUR BANNERS?
THERE IS A REASON FOR EVERYTHING I DO.
I ABHOR WASTE.
YES, MICHAEL. THE REBELLION WAS THE POINT. BUT YOU WERE SO SLOW TO ANGER--
--SO RELUCTANT EVEN TO QUESTION THAT I ALMOST DESPAIRED.
WHILE SAMAEL HAS SQUANDERED ETERNITY IN TRYING TO ESCAPE FROM THE PLAN, WHICH OF COURSE FORESAW EVERYTHING HE DID.
UNTIL NOW.

YOU SEE, MY CHILDREN?
IT IS A BUBBLE OF GLASS THAT I BLEW, AND THE CLOSURE MAKES IT PERFECT.
BUT THERE ARE TWO WAYS TO CLOSE THE CIRCLE OF ETERNITY.
AND THE ONLY UNCERTAIN THING, IN ALL THE FROZEN COLONNADES OF CERTAINTY DOWN WHICH I HAVE STARED FOR SO LONG--
--THE ONLY MATTER ON WHICH THERE HAS EVER BEEN THE SMALLEST MOLECULE OF DOUBT--
--HAS BEEN WHICH OF THE TWO I WOULD FINALLY CHOOSE.
NOW YOU KNOW.

OOP!
IT'S ALL RIGHT.
I'VE GOT YOU.

LISTEN, WHAT IS THIS? YOU'RE HANGING AROUND ME LIKE BODY ODOR.
DO I KNOW YOU?
YOU HAVE NEVER SEEN MY FACE. BUT YOU WILL KNOW ME.

IN THE FULLNESS OF TIME--
--YOU ARE TO BE MY MOTHER.

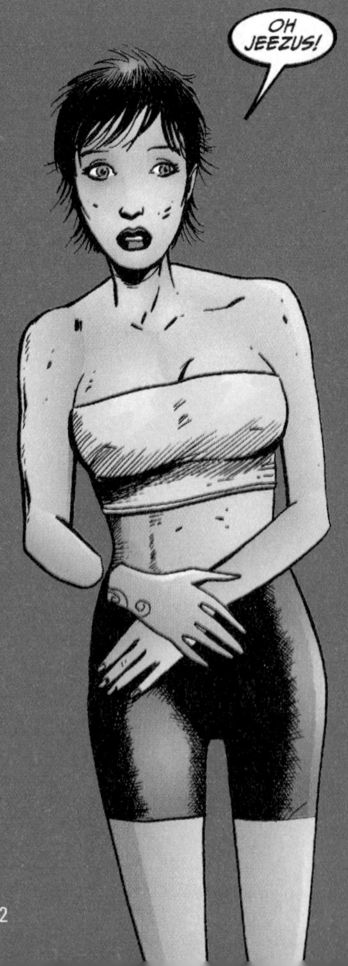
OH JEEZUS!

DO NOT RECOIL FROM ME. THE MAGIC OF THIS PLACE HAS SHEATHED ME IN FLESH.
BUT WE ARE ONE SOUL, MOTHER.
GET THE FUCK AWAY FROM ME!

I WAS RAPED BY A DECK OF FUCKING TAROT CARDS!
I CAME HERE TO GET RID OF YOU-- YOU THINK YOU CAN MELT MY HEART BY CALLING ME "MOM"?

BUT YOU ARE MY LIFE NOW. AND I AM YOURS.
I BREATHE YOUR BREATH. I FEED ON YOUR HEARTBEAT. YOU CANNOT KILL ME.

YOU SEE?
YES. YES, I THINK I--
WE ARE BOUND TOGETHER IN A UNION NONE CAN BREAK.

AMBIVALENCE. CONFUSION. SUSPICION. CONFLICT. UNCERTAINTY.
WHAT?
GO AWAY, BUBBLE OF NOTHING, BEFORE I PRICK YOU.

I LOVE YOU, MOTHER. AND YOU LOVE ME.
LET'S JOIN THE OTHERS NOW, AND SEE--
YOU LITTLE BASTARD!
UUH!
LIKE FATHER LIKE SON, EH? AGAIN WITH THE SLEAZY FUCKING JEDI MIND CONTROL.
WELL LOOK AT THIS, YOU FUCKER.
IT'S A BRUISE. I GOT IT WHEN THE NAGLFAR CRASH-LANDED.
THE SPELL OF PROTECTION? I THINK WE CAN SAFELY SAY IT DOESN'T WORK AROUND HERE.
SO IF YOU MESS WITH MY HEAD AGAIN--
--I'LL RIP YOU OUT OF MY STOMACH WITH MY BARE FUCKING HANDS!

HEY.
DON'T LOOK NOW, BUT WE JUST USED UP OUR LEAD TIME.
WALK ON.
GET AS FAR AWAY FROM ME AS YOU CAN.
HE SAID HE WOULD RELEASE YOU INTO DEATH.
THIS IS THE HOUSE OF THE DEAD.
AND YOU ARE FREE.

YO, MAZI-- WHY DIDN'T YOU DO THAT WAY THE FUCK BACK *THERE*, WHEN WE HAD A SHIP?
IT WAS A LAST *RESORT*.
IT MIGHT EASILY HAVE CHOSEN TO FEED ON *US*.

PLOOF
PLOOF
PLOOF
MICHAEL!
YOU LOOK WIPED. HERE, LET ME GIVE YOU A HAND.
DO NOT... TOUCH ME, DEMON.
DO NOT ADDRESS ME.
ALL MY LIFE I HAVE OBEYED HIM. AND FOR THAT I HAVE HIS PITY?
I MUST BE TORMENTED AND HARRIED INTO FOLLOWING LUCIFER'S EXAMPLE?
WELL IT IS ENOUGH!

THERE.

I WANTED TO BE SURE I HADN'T *MISSED* ANYTHING.

AH... AH...AH... AH!
I SEE THEM. HUSH NOW.
I SET YOU UP SO HIGH TO TEMPT THIEVES, NOT WARN ME OF THEM.
MY GREETINGS TO YOU, TRAVELERS.
WHAT IS IT THAT YOU SEEK?
THE SPIRIT OF A HUMAN CHILD.
THERE ARE MANY THOUSANDS OF SPIRITS HERE. I USE THEM FOR DECORATION, AS YOU CAN SEE.
TO FIND ONE AMONG SO MANY WOULD BE HARD.
DO YOU OBJECT TO OUR LOOKING?
OH YES, MAZIKEEN, DAUGHTER OF OPHUR.
TSUKI-YOMI OBJECTS MOST STRENUOUSLY.

I CAN'T TAKE YOU ANY FURTHER. I NEED TO BE SOMEWHERE ELSE.
I'LL BE FINE. LUCIFER--
--SOMETHING'S HAPPENED, HASN'T IT? SOMETHING BIG?
IT COULD BE REALLY USEFUL FOR ME TO BE AHEAD OF THE GAME ON THIS ONE.
IT'S REALLY A FAMILY MATTER.
YOU MEAN IT ONLY CONCERNS--
I MEAN IT'S NOT SOMETHING I'M PREPARED TO DISCUSS.
BUT IF YOU WANT SOME ADVICE, ZIM'ET, I'D SAY TO CHOOSE A DIRECTION THAT LEADS AWAY FROM THE SILVER CITY.
SET OFF NOW, AND KEEP MOVING UNTIL THE STARS START TO DIM.

"Because on the *face* of it--
"--this changes *everything*."
YOU INTEND TO STAND IN THE *WAY* OF OUR SEARCH?
I AM *DETERMINED* ON IT.
IT WAS THE PROJECT I *SET* MYSELF, ONCE I ACCEPTED THE FACT OF MY *DEATH*.
IN THE ORDINARY WAY OF THINGS, GODS PASS *GENTLY* AND WITHOUT PAIN INTO NON-EXISTENCE.
BUT LUCIFER HAD *DISPOSAL* OF MY FATE.
AND SINCE HE DENIED ME THAT PEACE, IT SEEMED FITTING TO DENY *HIM* SOMETHING IN RETURN.
THE LINK BETWEEN HER SPIRIT AND HIS IS VERY *STRONG*.
I KNEW THAT HE WOULD *SEARCH* FOR HER. NOT IN HIS OWN PERSON, OF COURSE. HE CANNOT *COME* HERE.
BUT HE WOULD SEND PROXIES AND I WOULD FRUSTRATE THEM. AS MANY TIMES AS--
WELL YOU'RE *DEAD* ALREADY--
--AT LEAST THIS WILL COME AS NO *SURPRISE*.
AH.

I SHOULD HAVE WARNED YOU, DAUGHTER OF OPHUR. ALL THINGS IN MY GARDEN HAVE BEEN FASHIONED BY MY HANDS.
I TOOK ESPECIAL CARE WITH THE LAWS OF CAUSALITY.
I KNEW YOU WERE COMING. SO AGAIN, I HAVE BEEN VERY CLEVER AND ARTFUL--
--BUT IT IS NOT POIGNANT.
PAIN IS MY MEDIUM, AS PERHAPS YOU GUESSED.
YOU'RE ALL MOST WELCOME HERE.

BUT IT IS THE ONE THING I CANNOT SEE. THE THING I BREAK EVEN BY TOUCHING IT.

RANDOMNESS.

NAGLFAR

CONCLUSION: FULL FATHOM FIVE

MIKE CAREY WRITER
PETER GROSS, RYAN KELLY & DEAN ORMSTON ARTISTS
DANIEL VOZZO COLOR AND SEPARATIONS
COMICRAFT LETTERS
CHRISTOPHER MOELLER COVER PAINTER
MARIAH HUEHNER ASSISTANT EDITOR
SHELLY BOND SENIOR EDITOR
BASED ON CHARACTERS CREATED BY GAIMAN, KIETH AND DRINGENBERG

WHERE IS MY DAUGHTER? WHAT HAVE YOU DONE WITH HER?
YOU NEVER HAD A DAUGHTER. ONLY THE ILLUSION OF ONE.
AND NOW YOU WILL LOSE EVEN THAT, DAVID EASTERMAN.
YOU! YOU'RE DEAD!
YOU'RE A DEAD MAN!
NO. I HAVE EXPLAINED THIS.

I AM A DEAD GOD.
AND THIS IS MY HEAVEN.
YOU THREE--YOU DO NOT INTEREST ME.
TWO OF YOU HAVE NO FLESH, AND THE THIRD IS ALREADY DEAD.
CONFUSION. FEAR. DESSSP...
DESPAIR. YES. WHY NOT?
WHUMP
WHUMP
I'LL TELL YOU WHY NOT.
THWUCK!

YOU'VE GOT HOLES IN YOUR OMNIPOTENCE I COULD DRIVE A FLYING SHIP THROUGH.
AND I'VE GOT SOMETHING TO LIVE FOR AGAIN--
--REALLY
GREAT
SEX.
YOU ARE DISRESPECTFUL, JILL PRESTO.
BUT YOU ARE ALSO IRRELEVANT.
NOT TO ME.

"I HAVE FACED YOU BEFORE--
"--AND SWALLOWED INSULTS AT YOUR HANDS."
BUT TODAY I AM IN A DIFFERENT HUMOR.
STEP ASIDE OR YOU WILL SURELY DIE.
ARCHON, WE HAVE OUR ORDERS. NOBODY ENTERS THE PRESENCE WITHOUT YOUR FATHER'S SUMMONS.
NOT EVEN YOU.
THEN BE AT PEACE. YOU DIE IN FULFILLMENT OF YOUR DUTY.
THAT WAS MY AMBITION ONCE.
I HAVE LEARNED HARD LESSONS SINCE.

"I HAVE SEEN THE LIGHT."

YOU...
...MAY NOT...
...TOUCH HER.
WHY? BECAUSE SHE'S THE VESSEL YOU SAIL IN?
SHE IS OUR... MOTHER.
WE ARE TO BE... BORN...FROM HER FLESH.
WELL, I HAVE HEARD THAT THE DEVIL LAUGHS--
FWOOOSH
--WHEN WE MAKE PLANS.

IF YOU HAD COME INTO YOUR HERITAGE--
--AND IF WE HAD MET ON SOME OTHER GROUND-- IT MIGHT HAVE BEEN DIFFERENT.
SHIT...
THERE MIGHT HAVE BEEN MORE OF GRANDEUR TO THIS--
--AND LESS OF PATHOS.
BUT HAVE NO FEAR.
ART WILL TRANSFORM YOU INTO SOMETHING MEANINGFUL.

MICHAEL, PLEASE. THINK OF WHAT YOU'RE DOING. THE ENTIRE HOST WILL RALLY TO THIS PLACE.
YOU WILL CONDEMN THEM TO DEATH, BECAUSE WHILE THEY ARE ALIVE THEY WILL DEFEND THE THRONE AND THE PRESENCE.
I HAVE NO WISH TO KILL ANY OF YOU, URIEL. BUT I INTEND TO SPEAK WITH MY FATHER.
WE WILL BOTH OF US DO WHAT WE MUST.
ARCHON, STAY YOUR HAND!
THERE IS NO NEED FOR THIS! LOOK!
LOOK!
HIS DOOR STANDS OPEN!

WHAT'S THIS ABOUT?
WE MOURN OUR DEAD, COUSIN.
THOSE WHO DIED THE FINAL DEATH WHEN WE ATTACKED THE SHIP.

AND WHICH WAY DID THE SHIP GO?

ONWARDS. INWARDS. WHO CAN SAY? BUT IT SEEMS I SHOULD KNOW YOU, COUSIN.
WERE YOU THERE WHEN WE FOUGHT THE REBEL LUCIFER?

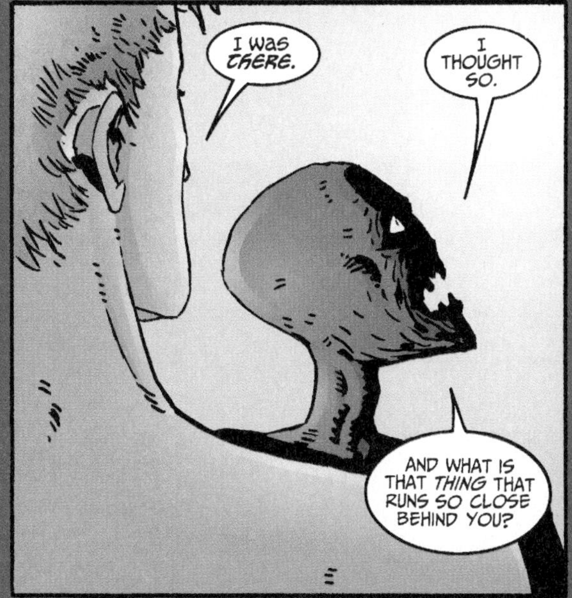

I WAS THERE.
I THOUGHT SO.
AND WHAT IS THAT THING THAT RUNS SO CLOSE BEHIND YOU?

THAT'S THE END OF THE WORLD.
THANKS FOR YOUR TIME.

THE EYE OF A NEEDLE HAS AN SYMBOLIC FORCE.
THERE IS, FOR EXAMPLE, A SCRIPTURAL TEXT IN WHICH IT IS MADE TO REPRESENT THE GATE OF HEAVEN.
A VERY AMUSING CONCEIT.
AND THEN, OF COURSE, THERE IS THE HEAD OF THE NEEDLE.
THAT, TOO, HAS A THEOLOGICAL SIGNIFICANCE.
FOR ON THE HEAD OF A NEEDLE--
--ANGELS CAN BE MADE TO DANCE.

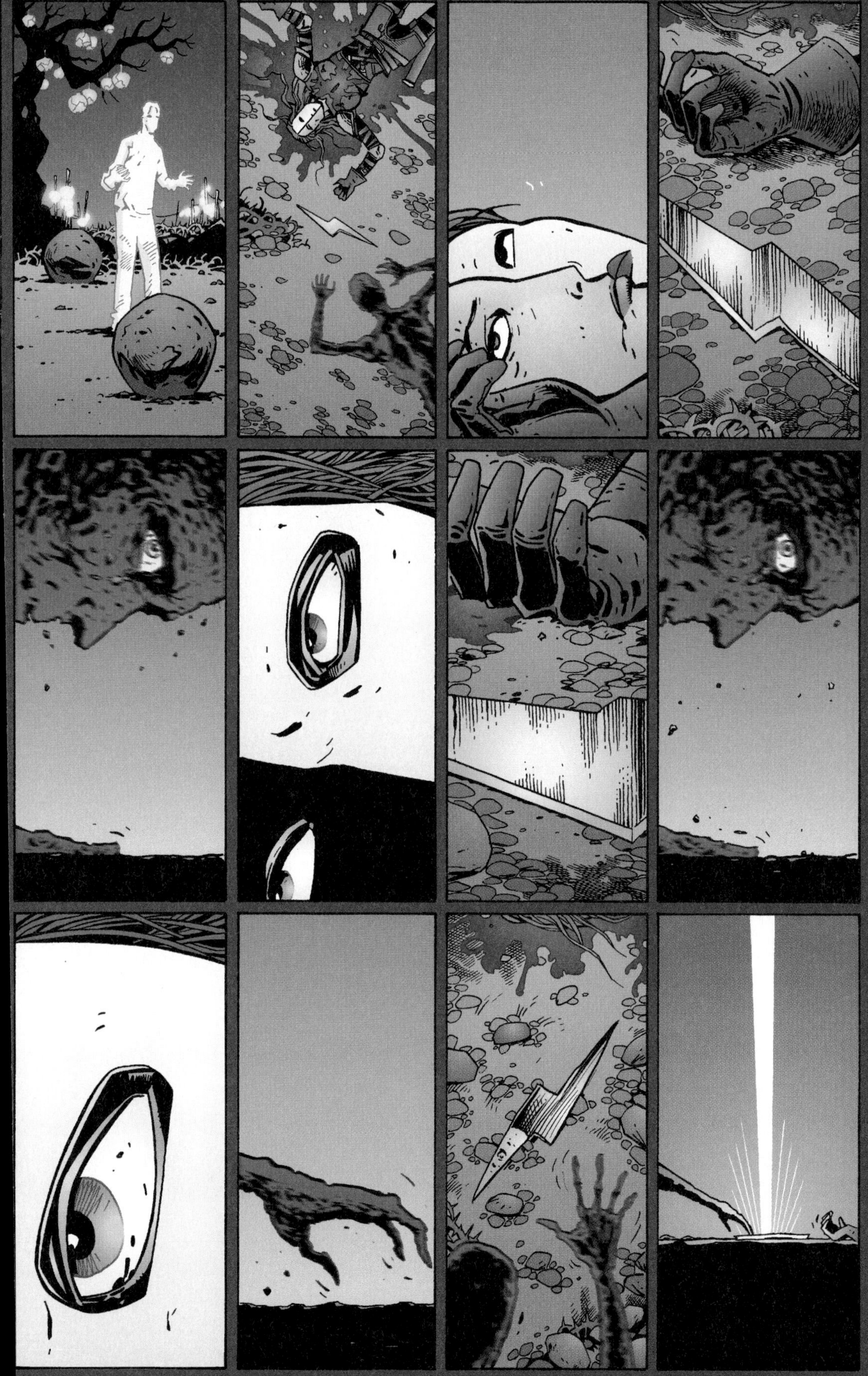

STILL WATCHING?
NO. BUT I CAN HEAR YOU, FOR A MOMENT OR TWO MORE.
WAS THERE ANYTHING YOU WISHED TO SAY TO ME, MY SON?

WHAT WOULD BE THE POINT?
WE'RE NOT CAPABLE OF LEARNING FROM EACH OTHER.

GOOD... MORROW TO YOU... LUCIFER MORNINGSTAR.
YOU FIND ME... AT SOMETHING OF A DISADVANTAGE.
I CAN SEE THAT, BERGELMIR.

I DON'T HAVE TIME TO CUT YOU DOWN.
THIS IS GOING TO HURT.

LAY ON.
IT WOULD BE DEMEANING... TO DIE WHERE NO WOMEN... COULD WEEP ON MY GRAVE.

WHAT IS THIS?
A PIECE OF SOMEWHERE ELSE, SHINING IN MY GARDEN?

IS THERE A MEANING TO THIS, SPAWN OF THE BASANOS?
SPEAK.
GUUUUH!
A... B...BEAC... BEACON...

BUT THERE IS NOBODY TO--

UKKHH!

HEY, LOOK! NORMAL SERVICE HAS BEEN RESUMED!
WELL THANK FUCK FOR THAT.
THE SHIP! BERGELMIR BROUGHT THE SHIP.

OH. IT'S YOU.
BUT I THOUGHT YOU COULDN'T--

THE RULES OF ENGAGEMENT HAVE CHANGED.

THOUSANDS--
--THOUSANDS OF SOULS--
THEN LET'S DO THIS THE EASY WAY, MAZIKEEN.
COME TO ME, ELAINE BELLOC.
NOW.

BERGELMIR IS ALREADY ON BOARD.
COME NOW IF YOU'RE COMING AT ALL.
YOU HEARD THE MAN--
--LET'S GET THE FUCK OUT OF HERE.

MOTHER--
PLEASE--
IT'S YOUR CHOICE.
I SWORE NOT TO HARM HIM. I SAID NOTHING ABOUT RUNNING A RESCUE SERVICE.
THEN LET THE LITTLE FUCKER BLEED.

"THROUGH THE LAND OF THE GODDAMN *GIANTS*-- OUT THE WRONG SIDE OF *HEAVEN*--

"--DOING THE OWL AND THE *PUSSYCAT* ROUTINE WITH ANGELS AND GHOSTS AND GODS AND FUCK KNOWS WHAT *ELSE*.

"I MEAN, I GOT WHAT I *WANTED*. I'M NOT COMPLAINING.

"BUT IT WAS A HELL OF A LONG WAY TO COME FOR AN *ABORTION*."

THOSE ARE HIS HANDS! FOR *GOD'S* SAKE, BE CAREFUL!

ARE YOU TALKING ABOUT ANY *PARTICULAR* GOD, OR ARE YOU JUST MOUTHING OFF?

GUUUH!

CRAZY WORLD.

WHERE DO DEAD ANGELS GET GALVANIZED SIX-INCHES?

LUCIFER, WHAT HAVE YOU *DONE?*

WHAT I *HAD* TO DO. THE MANSIONS OF SILENCE WERE A FRAGILE STRUCTURE.

THEY WERE NEVER *MEANT* TO SUPPORT MY PRESENCE.

WHAT SHOULD WE DO, URIEL?
WHAT CAN WE DO? ONLY WAIT?
WHEN MICHAEL COMES FORTH AGAIN, WE WILL CLOSE THE DOORS.

NOW READY YOURSELVES, SERAPHS.
BUT DO NOTHING TO ANGER HIM.

IS YOUR BUSINESS HERE DONE, ARCHON?
WHAT? YES. OF COURSE IT IS.
AS IS YOUR OWN, URIEL.

THE PRIMUM MOBILE IS EMPTY. GOD HAS DEPARTED THIS PLACE.
FOREVER.
The End

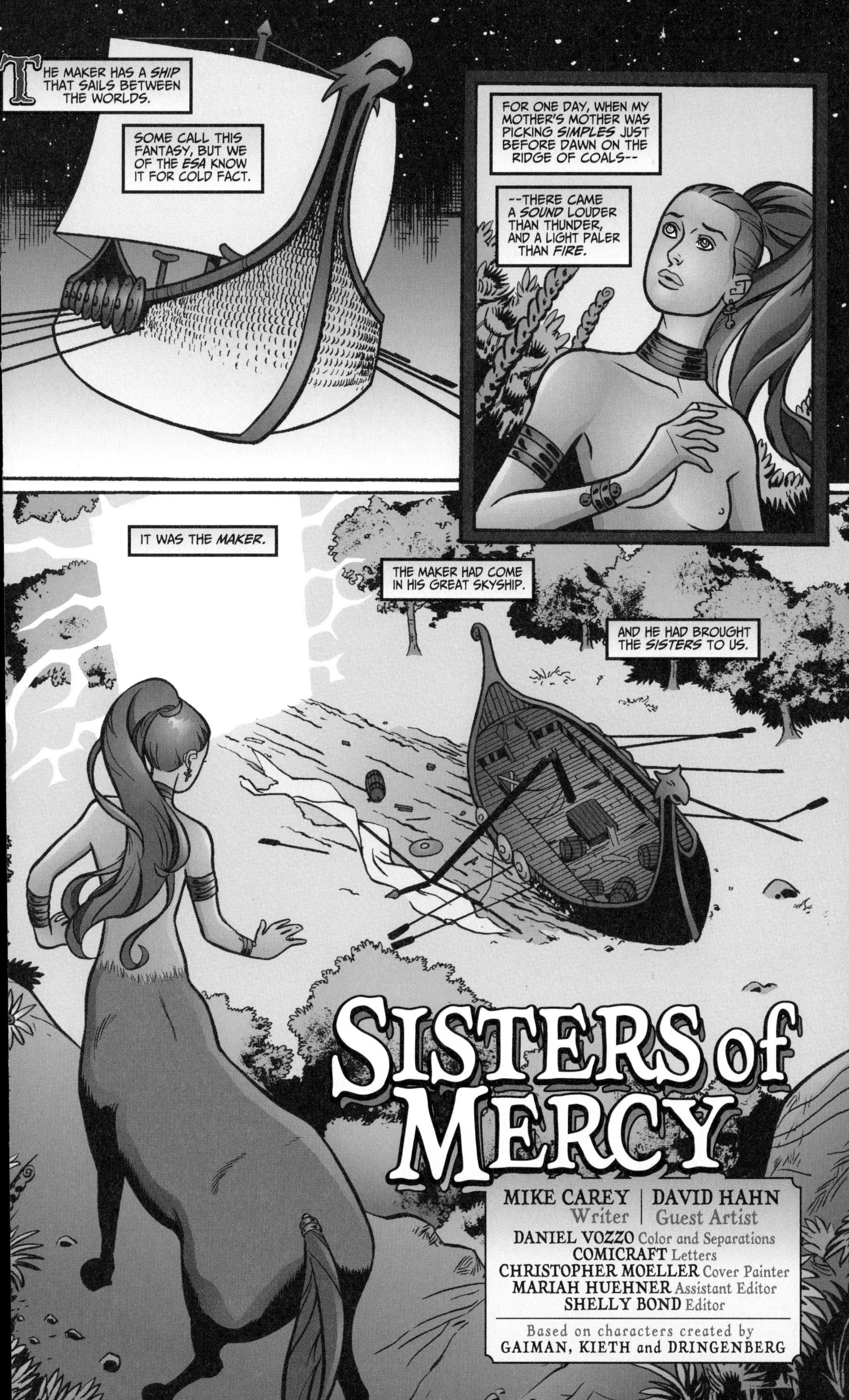
THE MAKER HAS A SHIP THAT SAILS BETWEEN THE WORLDS.
SOME CALL THIS FANTASY, BUT WE OF THE ESA KNOW IT FOR COLD FACT.
FOR ONE DAY, WHEN MY MOTHER'S MOTHER WAS PICKING SIMPLES JUST BEFORE DAWN ON THE RIDGE OF COALS--
--THERE CAME A SOUND LOUDER THAN THUNDER, AND A LIGHT PALER THAN FIRE.
IT WAS THE MAKER.
THE MAKER HAD COME IN HIS GREAT SKYSHIP.
AND HE HAD BROUGHT THE SISTERS TO US.
SISTERS of MERCY
MIKE CAREY Writer
DAVID HAHN Guest Artist
DANIEL VOZZO Color and Separations
COMICRAFT Letters
CHRISTOPHER MOELLER Cover Painter
MARIAH HUEHNER Assistant Editor
SHELLY BOND Editor
Based on characters created by
GAIMAN, KIETH and DRINGENBERG

WELL THAT WAS A WHOLE FESTERING HEAP OF FUN.
WE SHOULD DO THIS EVERY YEAR.
OUR BUSINESS WITH EACH OTHER SEEMS TO BE CONCLUDED.
BERGELMIR, THE NAGLFAR IS YOURS AGAIN. THANKS FOR THE LOAN.
YOU'VE DONE A TERRIBLE THING, MORNINGSTAR.
I STILL BELIEVE THAT YOU'LL BE BROUGHT TO PAY FOR IT, ONE WAY OR ANOTHER.
WELL, BELIEF IS MEANT TO BE A GREAT CONSOLATION.
TAKE IT WITH YOU WHEN YOU GO.
SO HEY, DID YOU HAPPEN TO SEE WHERE MICHAEL WENT?
YOU KNOW, WHEN YOU GUYS WERE DONE WITH... WHATEVER?
TO THE SILVER CITY.
BUT I'D GIVE HIM SOME ROOM TO SULK IN, IF I WERE YOU.

THAT'S THE TROUBLE WITH QUESTS.
EVEN IF THEY'RE SUCCESSFUL--
--THEY ALWAYS END IN AN ANTICLIMAX.
EARRRRRGHHHHH!
IT'S OKAY, MONA. WE'RE SAFE NOW.
AHUH! AHUH! AHUH!
EVERYTHING'S GOING TO BE ALL RIGHT.
EVERYTHING'S GOING TO BE FINE.

YOU SAVED US ALL.
I SAVED YOU.
I OWED YOU A LIFE. I DISLIKE HAVING THAT HANGING OVER ME.
YOU HAVE A NUMBER OF OPTIONS, ELAINE. I CAN GIVE YOU BACK THE BODY THAT YOU HAD.
OR YOU CAN BE BORN INTO A NEW ONE--AND START AGAIN WITH NO MEMORY OF ALL THIS.
HOW LONG HAVE I BEEN DEAD?
A LITTLE MORE THAN A MONTH.
THEN THERE'S ALREADY BEEN-- A FUNERAL AND EVERYTHING?
OF COURSE.
I'D LIKE TO THINK ABOUT IT FOR A WHILE...
...IF YOU DON'T MIND.

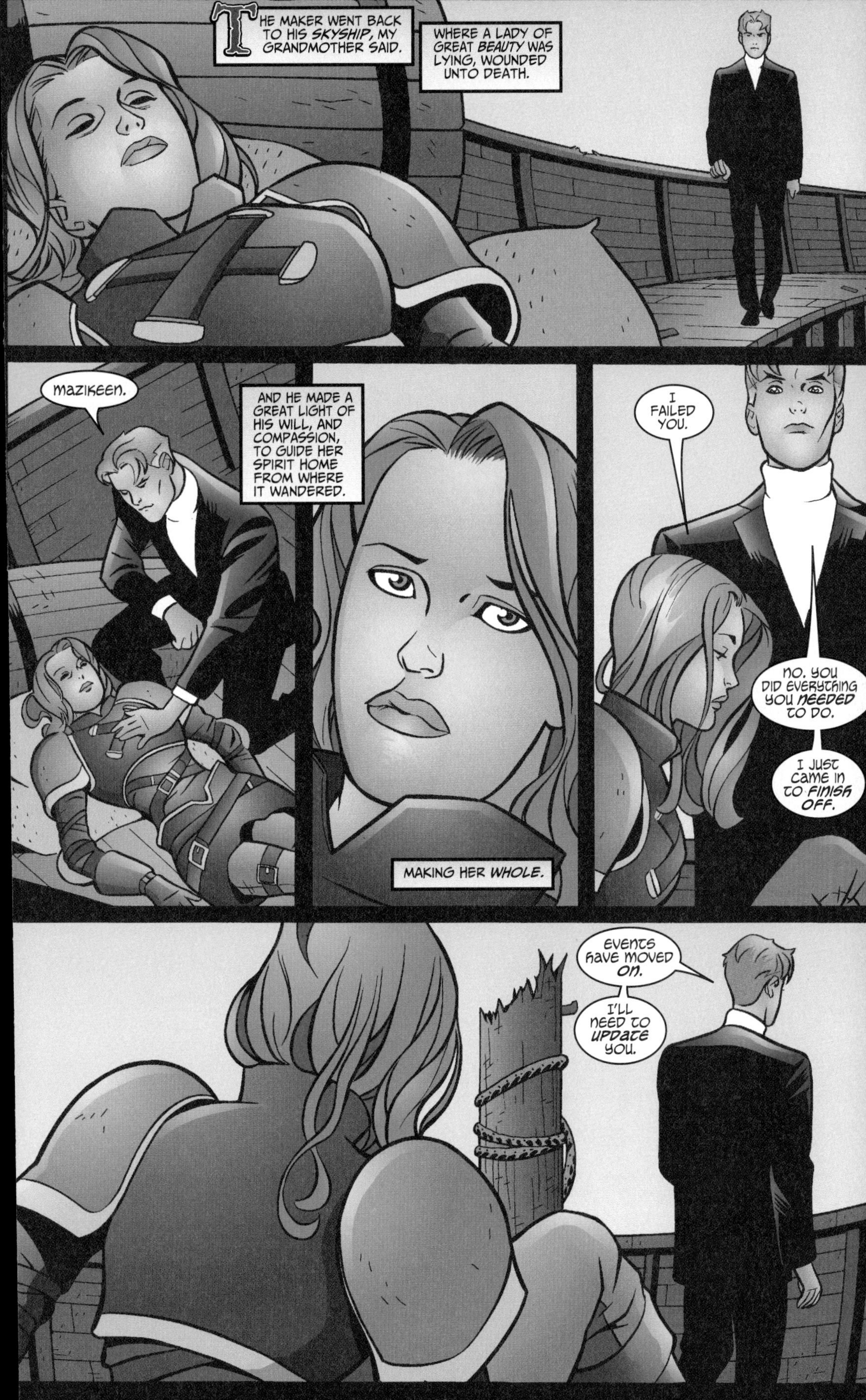
THE MAKER WENT BACK TO HIS SKYSHIP, MY GRANDMOTHER SAID.
WHERE A LADY OF GREAT BEAUTY WAS LYING, WOUNDED UNTO DEATH.
MAZIKEEN.
AND HE MADE A GREAT LIGHT OF HIS WILL, AND COMPASSION, TO GUIDE HER SPIRIT HOME FROM WHERE IT WANDERED.
MAKING HER WHOLE.
I FAILED YOU.
NO. YOU DID EVERYTHING YOU NEEDED TO DO.
I JUST CAME IN TO FINISH OFF.
EVENTS HAVE MOVED ON.
I'LL NEED TO UPDATE YOU.

I DON'T SEE WHAT'S TO THINK ABOUT, ELAINE.
DON'T YOU?
WE CAN BE ALIVE AGAIN! WE CAN BE REAL!
I MEAN, IT'S OKAY FOR YOU. YOU CAN GO OFF TO HEAVEN AND BE AN ANGEL.
I JUST GET TO BE DEAD. A SORT OF BALLOON WITHOUT A STRING.
IT SUCKS.
IT'S -- I DON'T THINK IT'S THAT EASY, MONA.
ARE YOU READY NOW?
NO. NOT REALLY.
I JUST DON'T KNOW. IF I COME BACK TO LIFE--
--AREN'T PEOPLE GONNA START ASKING QUESTIONS?
LET THEM ASK.
MEMORY IS MORE MALLEABLE THAN YOU THINK.
BUT IF THAT BOTHERS YOU, THEN BEGIN AGAIN. IT'S ALL ONE TO ME.

BUT THEN I WOULDN'T REMEMBER BEING ME.
I CAN'T EVEN REMEMBER WHAT CORN FLAKES TASTE LIKE.
SO I WAS WONDERING--
COULD WE--MAYBE--GO BACK HOME FOR JUST A LITTLE WHILE. LIKE A DAY?
OH YES!
A TRIAL PERIOD?
JUST TO REMIND US WHAT IT WAS LIKE. IT FEELS A LOT LONGER THAN A MONTH.
OH PLEASE PLEASE PLEASE! THAT'D BE SO GREAT!
THIS IS BEGINNING TO IRRITATE ME.
USE THE GATE OVER THERE. YOU HAVE THREE HOURS.
WHAT IF WE'RE LATE?
THE BORROWED FLESH I'M GIVING YOU WILL LAST UNTIL THAT TIME IS UP.
IF YOU'RE LATE--

"--I WON'T COME LOOKING FOR YOU A SECOND TIME."
COME ON, COME ON, COME ON!
KOOLWOR
OH MY GOD! S CLUB 7 HAS TURNED INTO S CLUB 4!
HOW LONG WAS I DEAD, A HUNDRED YEARS?
OLWORTH
I'VE NEVER HEARD OF HALF THESE BANDS. TATU? GIRLS ALOUD?
TATU IS PRETTY GOOD.
TATU
COME ON, MONA.
WE'VE ONLY GOT THREE HOURS.
YOU GO AHEAD. I'M GONNA LISTEN TO SOME OF THIS STUFF.
BUT -- DON'T YOU WANT TO GO HOME?
ARE YOU KIDDING?
I'LL MEET YOU AT THE GATE.
BUT DO YOU EVEN KNOW THE--?
OF COURSE I DO. SEE YA!

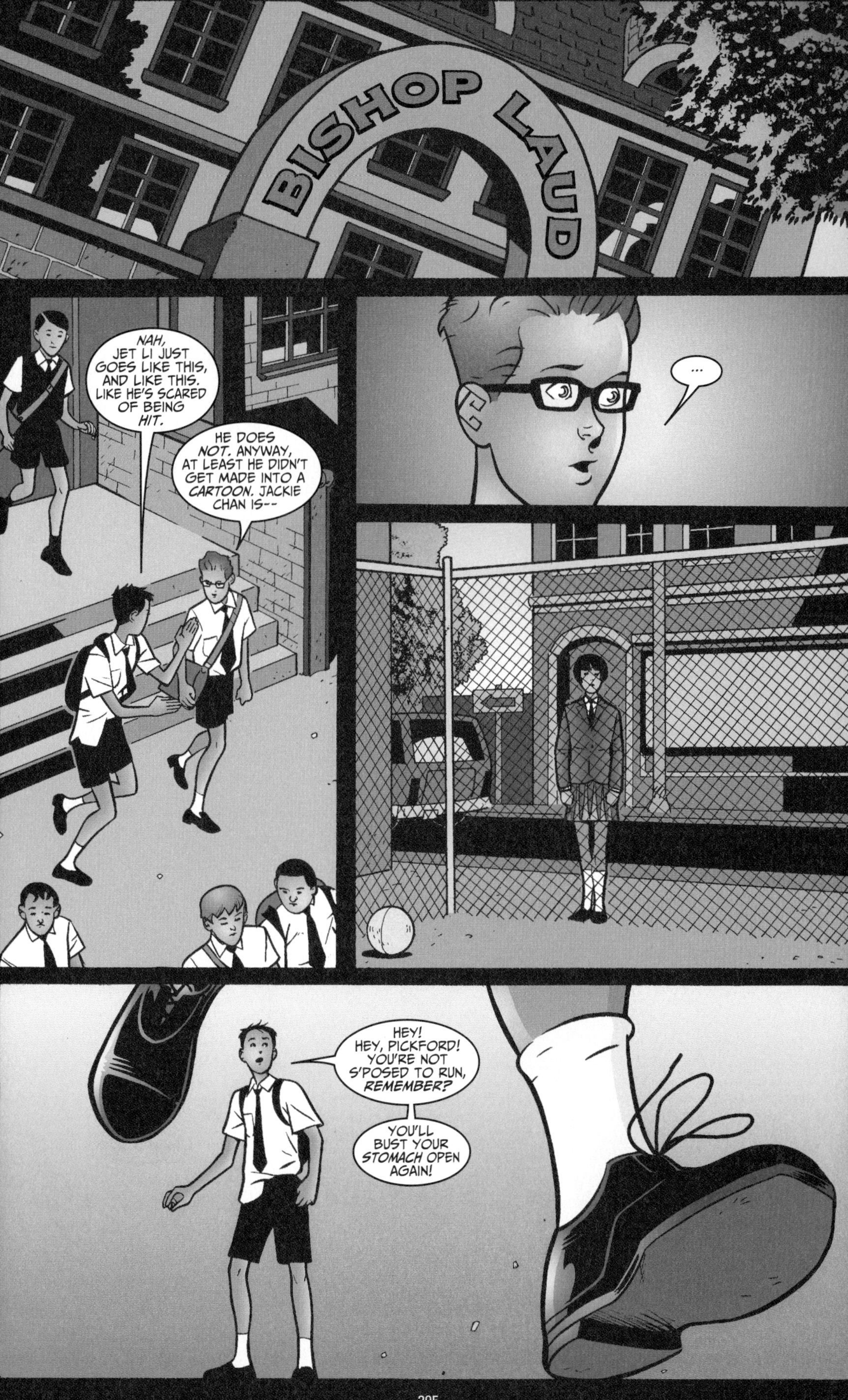
BISHOP LAUD
NAH, JET LI JUST GOES LIKE THIS, AND LIKE THIS. LIKE HE'S SCARED OF BEING HIT.
HE DOES NOT. ANYWAY, AT LEAST HE DIDN'T GET MADE INTO A CARTOON. JACKIE CHAN IS--
...
HEY! HEY, PICKFORD! YOU'RE NOT S'POSED TO RUN, REMEMBER?
YOU'LL BUST YOUR STOMACH OPEN AGAIN!

ELAINE! HUF! HUF!
HI, BARRY!
OH MY GOD, YOU'RE NOT DEAD! YOU'RE NOT DEAD!
IT'S A LONG STORY.
IT'S SO GOOD TO SEE YOU. HOW'VE YOU BEEN? HOW'S SARAH?
UMM... SARAH'S STILL IN THE HOSPITAL.
THEY'VE REINFLATED HER LUNG, BUT SHE'S GOT TO SLEEP IN AN OXYGEN TENT.
OH GOD. THAT'S AWFUL.
BARRY, I MIGHT NOT SEE YOU AGAIN AFTER THIS. SO I WANTED TO SAY THANKS--FOR TRYING TO PROTECT ME.
AND SORRY FOR WHAT--FOR EVERYTHING THAT--
OH, THIS IS HOPELESS.
JUST MOVE OUT OF THE WAY FOR A SECOND.
HSSSSSSSS

ELAINE! THOSE ARE--
I'LL MISS YOU, BARRY. I'LL REALLY MISS YOU.
THOSE ARE WINGS ON YOUR...
ONE FOR YOU.
AND ONE FOR SARAH.
PICKFORD, YOU GOT AN ANGEL.
YEAH.
WHAT'LL YOU SWAP 'ER FOR?

"I'LL BE YOUR ANGEL," BY KIRA. HAH!
I OUGHTA GET THAT ONE FOR ELAINE.
VEEVEEVEEVEEVEEVEE
OW!
STUPID DOOR. IT'S SUPPOSED TO BE AUTOMATIC!
VEEVEEVEEVEEVEEVEE
IT IS AUTOMATIC, MISSIE.
AND RIGHT NOW IT'S AUTOMATICALLY STAYING SHUT.
VEEVEEVEEVEEVEEVEEVEE
GOT 'ER, HARRIET. RESET THE ALARM, YEAH?
COME ON, MISSIE. LET'S TALK.

--OR ARE THERE OCCASIONS WHEN EVEN MURDER IS JUSTIFIED?
YES! FUCKING YES!
ON TODAY'S MORAL MAZE WE'LL ASK THE ARCHBISHOP OF YORK WHAT--
YOU.
I WAS HOPING TO SEE BARBARA.
YOUR MOTHER IS AT WORK.
HHHRRRRRRR...
FIRSTLY, LET ME SAY--
FUCK!
SQUARRRRRRK!

I'M NOT *HIM.*
I KNOW, CESTIS.
I STOLE HIS SHAPE TO KILL YOU. BUT NOW--
NOW YOU CAN'T GET OUT.
AND YOU CAN'T EVEN *HATE* ME, BECAUSE IT'S HIS MIND YOU'RE TRYING TO HATE ME WITH.
I THINK IT WILL STOP *HURTING* SOON.
WHEN THERE'S LESS OF *YOU,* AND MORE OF *HIM.*
OH PLEASE. PLEASE.
I'M WRITING BARBARA A *NOTE.* CAN YOU TELL HER IT'S HERE?
I-- I LOVE YOU, ELAINE.
I'M SORRY. I'M SO *SORRY* I HURT YOU.
IT DOESN'T *MATTER.*
IT PROBABLY WOULD'VE WORKED OUT THE *SAME* IN THE END.

SEVEN CDS, FIVE MARS BARS AND A PACK OF SUGAR-FREE GUM. THAT'S QUITE A HAUL.
OKAY, MISSIE. WHAT'S YOUR *NAME?*
DIANE HORNBY.
PHONE NUMBER?
THERE'S NOBODY *HOME.*

KOOL

THEN WHAT *SCHOOL* ARE YOU FROM? ROUNDHEY?
WE JUST MOVED HERE. I DON'T EVEN *HAVE* A SCHOOL YET.
IS THAT SO?

I NEED TO GO TO THE BATHROOM.
GOOD.
ANYTHING THAT'LL GIVE YOU A SENSE OF *URGENCY* IS FINE WITH ME.
I MEAN -- I'VE GOT THAT SUGAR THING. DIABETES. I NEED MY ASPIRIN.
INSULIN.
KEEP TALKING. THE TRUTH IS *OUT* THERE.
GIVE IT *UP,* KID.
I CAN GET TO THAT *DOOR* BEFORE YOU'RE HALFWAY OUT OF YOUR SEAT.

HEY!
WHAT'RE YOU--?
OH MY GOD!
OH MY SWEET CHRIST!
FINALLY!
MONA, WHAT HAPPENED TO YOUR BODY?
DOESN'T MATTER.
DIDN'T EVEN HURT THIS TIME AROUND.

SO YOU'VE DECIDED?
YES.
IT'S NOT GOING TO WORK.
EITHER WAY.
SO MANY PEOPLE HAVE BEEN HURT. BARRY AND SARAH... MATT AND BARBARA... MISTER EASTERMAN...
IF I GO BACK HOME IT'LL JUST HAPPEN AGAIN. BUT I'VE GOT AN IDEA.
THERE WAS THIS ANGEL I MET IN HELL. HE TALKED WITHOUT SAYING ANYTHING.
DO YOU--?
YES. I KNOW HIM.
WELL HE'S GOT A JOB, HASN'T HE?
HE'S NOT JUST REAL QUIET, HE'S IN CHARGE OF QUIETNESS.

YOU WANT TO BE A GUARDIAN SPIRIT.
YOU DO?
WHAT WOULD YOU GUARD?
EVERYTHING.
I'VE TOLD THE PEOPLE OF THIS WORLD THAT THEY'RE FORBIDDEN TO WORSHIP.
I DON'T WANT TO BE WORSHIPPED.
I'D JUST SORT OF BE UP THERE WATCHING.
OH YEAH. AND MONA WOULD GET TO GUARD SOMETHING, TOO.
I WOULD?
HEY, THAT'D BE COOL.

WHAT D'YOU THINK YOU'D GO FOR?
GOD, I DON'T KNOW.
MAYBE POP MUSIC. OR CHOCOLATE.
I THOUGHT I WAS BEYOND BEING SURPRISED. BUT NO.
THAT'S THE MOST GROTESQUE AND RIDICULOUS SUGGESTION I'VE EVER HEARD.
AND YET PERHAPS --
-- THAT'S ONE OF ITS STRENGTHS.
IF YOU'RE GOING TO HAVE GODS, YOU MIGHT AS WELL HAVE FARCICAL GODS THAT COMMAND NO RESPECT...
...THAT BRING THE VERY CONCEPT INTO DISREPUTE.

OVER TO YOU, MONA.
WAIT, WAIT! I DIDN'T THINK!
UMM...
HOW ABOUT -- HEDGEHOGS? THEY'RE SMALL AND THEY GET RUN OVER A LOT.
SOMEONE SHOULD LOOK OUT FOR THEM.
VERY WELL. YOU ARE THE TUTELARY SPIRITS OF THIS WORLD.
THOUGH NONE WILL NAME OR BLESS YOU, EVEN IN THEIR THOUGHTS.
MONA DOYLE, I SET YOU OVER HEDGEHOGS.
ELAINE BELLOC, I SET YOU OVER EVERYTHING EXCEPT HEDGEHOGS.
KEEP THE NOISE DOWN TO A REASONABLE LEVEL. AND IN CASE YOU SHOULD BE TEMPTED TO LOOK OVER MY SHOULDER --
-- DON'T.

SO THEY WERE BORN TO US. THE SISTERS WHOSE MERCY ENFOLDS US FROM SUNRISE TO SUNRISE.
IF OTHERS GRIEVED FOR THEIR LOSS, WE DID NOT KNOW OF IT.
AND IF OTHERS KNEW THEIR BOUNTY BEFORE WE DID, WE DO NOT BEGRUDGE OR ENVY.
HEYA! I HAVE TOLD IT TO YOU, MY DEAR ONE, AS MY MOTHER TOLD IT TO ME.
KEEP IT SILENT IN YOUR HEART--
--UNTIL YOU TELL IT, TOO.

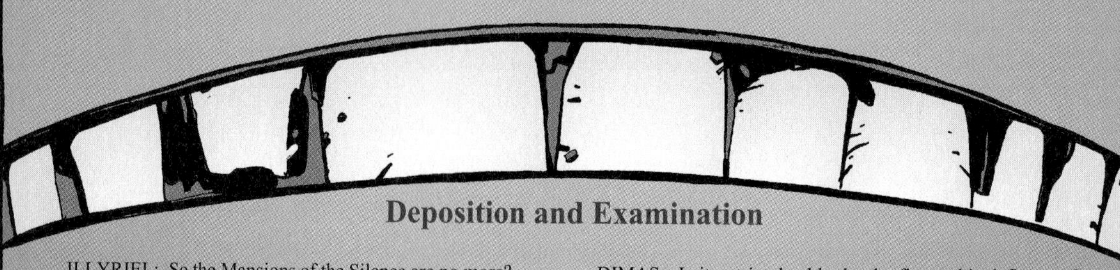

Deposition and Examination

ILLYRIEL: So the Mansions of the Silence are no more?

URIEL: Lucifer Morningstar destroyed them. He wished to retrieve the spirit of the child, Elaine Belloc – but the Mansions were too fragile to endure his footsteps. They crumbled, and a billion, billion souls were cast into the ultimate dark.

CASERA: That is monstrous.

THUMIEL: But it is in keeping with his earlier actions. Ever he has behaved without shame or conscience, and since he left Hell he is worse, not better.

ILLYRIEL: The place he built, in an Earthly city. Does it still stand?

URIEL: It is called Lux. And yes, it still stands. Or rather it stands again. When the demon Mazikeen and the human woman Beatrice Wechsler fought the Jin en Mok there, it was destroyed. But Lucifer rebuilt it as a cathedral without doors – a monument to his own arrogance and self-love. It is where he placed his gate, that is now a thousand gates. His gate that links all places in our creation to his own, and to each other.

DIMAS: Is it not intolerable that he flaunts his defiance of God in this way?

CASERA: It is… unfortunate. But God Himself expressed no opinion on the matter. Indeed He gave Lucifer the letter of passage that allowed the gate to be opened. And when Amenadiel led the Host in war against Lucifer, they were repulsed.

ILLYRIEL: By which you mean…?

CASERA: That if God's will had gone with them, they would surely have triumphed.

URIEL: It is debateable.

THUMIEL: No, it is beyond debate. If we could not know for sure what Yahweh willed when He was with us, then we will scarcely know it now, when He is gone from us, and from the worlds He made.

DIMAS: You are weeping, Thumiel. It little avails to weep.

THUMIEL: The throne is empty, and we are orphans. What shall avail us now?

(silence, which lengthens)

GREECE. THE PELOPONNESE.
KLEON, THIS IS MADNESS.
MADNESS!
PERHAPS IT WAS WOLVES?
A HUNDRED SHEEP IN ONE NIGHT? DON'T BE ABSURD!
LOOK -- THIS WAS DONE WITH A CLUB. OR THE BUTT OF A RIFLE.
NINETY-EIGHT SHEEP.
WHAT?
DID YOU SPEAK TO ME?
I SAID NOTHING.
IT WAS I WHO SPOKE.
I SAID THERE WERE ONLY NINETY-EIGHT SHEEP.
A HAPPY CHANCE, THEN--
--THAT THE TWO OF YOU CAME TO COUNT THEM.

KLUD
WAKE, GARAMAS. WAKE AND SPEAK TO ME.
I HAVE PREPARED YOUR BREAKFAST.
LITTLE BROTHER--
-- I DID NOT LOOK TO RISE SO EARLY.
BROTHERS IN ARMS

WHAT HAS HAPPENED, GYGES, THAT YOU RISK MY IRE IN THIS WAY?
YAHWEH. YAHWEH IS *GONE*, BROTHER.
YAHWEH?
WHICH ONE IS *HE?*
CHOMF
THE GOD OF THE *COVENANT.* THE GOD OF THE CREATION.
AH. AND HE IS DEAD?
THAT SEEMS UNLIKELY.
HE IS NOT *DEAD.* BUT HE HAS DEPARTED.
AND WITHOUT THE ORDER ESTABLISHED BY THE *GODS,* OUR OWN POSITION BECOMES DIFFICULT.
IT BECOMES *UNTENABLE.* BUT THERE ARE *OLDER* ORDERS.
LET US GRAFT OURSELVES ONTO ONE OF THEM.

ELSEWHERE. LOS ANGELES.
NUUUUUH!
NO! NO! NO!

BEATRICE.

JESUS, LOVER. DID YOU COME OR DID YOU SLIP A DISK?

I'M SORRY, I--
THIS WAS A BAD IDEA. I'M SORRY.

HEY, I'M NOT OFFENDED.
IN FACT, LET ME GUESS.

YOU'RE BASICALLY STRAIGHT, BUT YOU'VE GOT A CRUSH ON SOME WOMAN YOU KNOW --
--AND YOU THOUGHT SLEEPING WITH A CALL GIRL WOULD GET IT OUT OF YOUR SYSTEM. AM I RIGHT?

LOOK, I DON'T MIND, DARLIN'. I GET LOTS LIKE THAT.
AND A DOLLAR IS A DOLLAR, Y'KNOW?

STUPID. STUPID AND PATHETIC.
I WOULDN'T HAVE DONE THIS IF I WAS THINKING STRAIGHT.
I MEAN, GOD, IT'S BEEN TWO YEARS SINCE I EVEN SAW HER. SINCE LUX REOPENED AS A CATHEDRAL.
EXCUSE ME. SORRY.
WHATEVER MAZ IS DOING, IT'S A SAFE BET SHE'S NOT THINKING ABOUT ME.
AND NOW -- NOW WHAT? VISIONS? HALLUCINATIONS?
TWO MONSTERS IN A FIELD, EATING DEAD SHEEP.
THERE'S SOMETHING WRONG WITH MY MIND.
I'VE GOT TO SEE SOMEONE. STRAIGHTEN MYSELF--
...
BLOOD.
NOW WHERE THE FUCK DID THAT COME FROM?

LUCIFER'S COSMOS.

EDOM PLAIN.

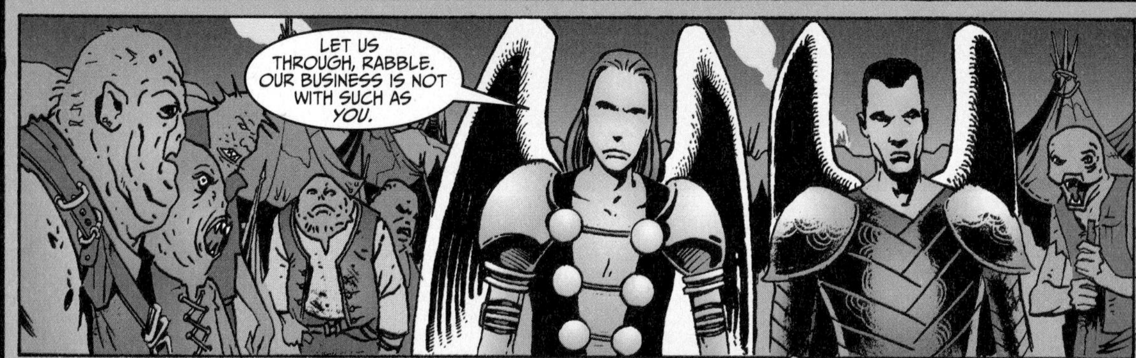

THE DREAMING.

LET US *IN*, DREAM.

IF WE HAVE TO *FORCE* YOUR HOSPITALITY, IT WILL BE THE WORSE FOR YOU.

BE *QUICK*, GARAMAS.

THEY ARE HARD TO *HOLD*.

AHRRR!

MY LORD SHAPER IS NOT AT *HOME*.

OTHERWISE YOU WOULD NEVER HAVE *LIVED* TO REACH HIS DOOR.

WHO'S DOWN THERE?

WHAT'S ALL THAT *RACKET?*

I AM *DUPLICITY*, OF THE ENDLESS. THIS IS MY BROTHER, *DECEIT*.

YOU MUST LET US IN. WE COME ON *FAMILY* BUSINESS.

DUPLICITY AND DECEIT ARE THE SAME THING.
AND YOU'RE THE TITAN BROTHERS, GYGES AND GARAMAS.
IS THERE SOME KIND OF RIOT GOING ON, LOOSH?
'COS NO ONE INVITED ME.
IT'S ALL UNDER CONTROL, MERVYN.
SOME IMPOSTORS WERE TRYING TO GAIN ENTRY.
BUT LORD MORPHEUS LEFT THE CASTLE WITH INSTRUCTIONS TO DEFEND ITSELF--
"--SO I IMAGINE THEY'LL WANT TO BE ON THEIR WAY."
WHAT ABOUT THE THRESHOLD, BROTHER? DESIRE'S DOOR IS USUALLY--
NO.
I HAVE A MIND TO TRY SOMETHING A LITTLE MORE AMBITIOUS.
IF THE ABSENCE OF YAHWEH IS THE ROOT OF OUR PROBLEM--
--THEN WHY NOT BECOME HIM?

FIAT LUX.
THAT'S A BLASPHEMY.
POSSIBLY. IT'S HARD TO BE SURE THESE DAYS,

WHERE'S MICHAEL? STILL SULKING?

I TOLD YOU, URIEL. THIS IS FUTILE.
MICHAEL HAS WITHDRAWN FROM US.
HE SITS AT THE FOOT OF THE PRIMUM MOBILE AND WILL SPEAK TO NO ONE.

THAT IS WHY WE CAME, MORNINGSTAR. WE WONDERED IF THE HOLY NAME GAVE YOU ANY REASONS FOR HIS LEAVING.
OR ANY INDICATION AS TO WHEN--

HE'S BURNED HIS BRIDGES BEHIND HIM.
CLOSED THE CIRCLE OF ETERNITY-- FOM THE OUTSIDE.

AS TO THE REASON, IT WAS ALWAYS HIS PLAN TO LEAVE--
--ONCE HE HAD CHOSEN A SUCCESSOR.
AND THAT WOULD BE YOU?

THAT WOULD BE BOTH OF US. MYSELF AND MY NOBLE BROTHER.
YOU SEE, EACH OF US SUPPLIES SOMETHING THAT THE OTHER LACKS.

THAT'S ABSURD.
IT'S ALSO IRRELEVANT. NEITHER OF US WANTS THE JOB.
BUT OTHERS WILL.

YAHWEH IS -- WAS -- THE DETERMINANT OF THIS REALITY. THIS CREATION.
NOW THAT HE'S GONE, EVERY GOD, DEMON AND TOOTH FAIRY WILL WANT TO STEP INTO HIS SHOES.

UNLESS YOU PREEMPT THEM.

HOW DO WE BECOME YAHWEH, GARAMAS?
WE USURP THE SPACE THAT HE HAS LEFT EMPTY.
I SEE NO GREAT DIFFICULTY IN THIS.
TO BEGIN WITH, WE TRACE THE EDGES OF THAT SPACE.
WE DETERMINE ITS SIZE, ITS CONTOURS.THE POINTS AT WHICH IT TOUCHES THAT WHICH IT IS NOT.
FOR EXAMPLE, TO BE A GOD REQUIRES A BELIEF IN THE VALUE OF REWARD AND PUNISHMENT.
OBSERVE.
ROBERTS SHOES
YOU. YOU HAVE OBEYED THE SIGN.
YOU WILL ENJOY LONG LIFE AND PLENTY, AND YOU WILL BEAR A HUNDRED CHILDREN.
BUT THE REST OF YOU -- YOU HAVE STOLEN AND FORNICATED.
AND IN YOUR HEARTS YOU HAVE WISHED FOR YOUR FRIENDS TO FAIL.

YOU ARE LOATHSOME IN OUR SIGHT.
THAT WAS EASY ENOUGH.
THAT WAS ONLY A BEGINNING.
OH, JESUS.
THERE IS A SEQUEL.
WHICH COMES BEFORE.

YOU'RE TWELVE MINUTES LATE.
I'M SORRY, LEANNE. I STARTED TO LEAK ON THE FREEWAY.
HAD TO GO BACK HOME AND CHANGE, YOU KNOW?
BEATRICE. WHAT THE HELL, GIRL?
WHAT, YOU DON'T PACK A SPARE TOWEL IN YOUR PURSE?

WELL STAN ISN'T IN YET EITHER, SO I'LL PUT YOU DOWN AS SIX O'CLOCK.
THANKS, LEE.
HEY, EVERY TIME'S A CELEBRATION, RIGHT? MEANS YOU'RE NOT PREGNANT.

DON'T FEEL A LOT LIKE CELEBRATING.
STIGMATA? NOSE BLEED?
OR THAT PROSTITUTE COULD'VE MAYBE--

HEY, CAN I GET SOME DRINKS ON LANE EIGHT?
UH... SURE.
LET ME TAKE YOUR ORDER.

OOH, IT'S ALL IN THE WRIST ACTION.
I'LL SHOW YOU SOME WRIST ACTION, SHITBIRD.
SALLY'S BOW
SATURDAY BOWLING
KA-LANG
LEAGUE
HAPPY HOUR
WHAT THE F-- ?
OULFF!
AAAAA!

WHUMF
THIS ONE?
YES. AN OLD IMAGE, BUT CLEAR.
NOW!
THE ANGLE IS A LITTLE STEEP, THOUGH.
FROM OVER HERE, THEN?
DO IT NOW!
CRASH
YES, THERE WOULD BE BETTER.
L... LEANNE?
STANLEY?
OH MY GOD.
BOWL
SALLY'S BOW
SALLY'S BO

WE HAVE COME A LONG WAY.
FIVE THOUSAND YEARS. PERHAPS A LITTLE MORE.
THESE ARE ONE OF THE PEOPLES THAT WILL WORSHIP HIM.
AND THERE, ON THE HORIZON, ARE THEIR ENEMIES. PURSUING THEM.
BUT THESE WILL BE THOUGHT OF AS DEEDS PERFORMED BY HIM.
AND THUS WE PLANT OUR OWN SEEDS IN THE GARDEN HE HAS MADE.
NOW WE WILL GIVE THEM A PLURAL NAME - ELOHIM - FOR THEIR SINGLE GOD.

MIRACLES ARE THE VERY *COINING* OF BELIEF.
LIKE GOLD, THAT KEEPS ITS PRICE NO MATTER *WHOSE* FACE IT BEARS.
SO *QUICK*, BROTHER. SO QUICK AND SO SLY.
THE QUICKER THE *BETTER*.
ONCE *THIS* IS DONE, I CAN GO BACK TO SLEEP.

OPEN BOWL 24 HOUR
GRILL HELP WANTED
ATM INSIDE

"HOW MANY VOICES?" THE POLICE GUY WANTS TO KNOW.

SO I LIE.

NATURALLY I LIE.

POLICE LINE • DO NOT CROSS

BECAUSE THE TRUTH IS TOO FUCKING SCARY TO LOOK AT RIGHT NOW.

TWO. YEAH, JUST -- JUST TWO.

AND YOU DIDN'T SEE ANYONE?

THE WHOLE PLACE WAS COMING APART. PEOPLE WERE -- WERE JUST FLYING THROUGH THE AIR.

I DON'T KNOW WHAT I SAW.

I MEAN, WHAT AM I SUPPOSED TO SAY?

THAT THERE WAS A THIRD VOICE?

WELL, LOOK. THEY'RE GONNA TAKE YOU TO THE HOSPITAL NOW - GET THOSE CUTS LOOKED AT.

WE'LL TALK SOME MORE LATER ON.

BECAUSE THERE WAS, RIGHT AT THE END THERE.

"PREACHING TO THE HOST..."
"THAT WAS A NOVEL EXPERIENCE."
YOU THINK THE OTHER POWERS ARE MOBILIZING?
THEY'D BE INSANE NOT TO. THEY'LL NEVER HAVE A BETTER CHANCE TO TAKE CONTROL.
THE ONLY QUESTION IS WHO'LL BE FIRST TO--
THAT LEAVES US WITH NO QUESTIONS AT ALL, THEN.
AH.
GYGES AND GARAMAS. THE CHILDREN OF CHAOS.
I'D HAVE EXPECTED THE COMIC INTERLUDE TO COME FURTHER DOWN THE BILL.

I DIDN'T INVITE YOU HERE, SO--
--IS THERE ANYTHING YOU WANTED TO SAY BEFORE SENTENCE IS PASSED?
YES, MORNINGSTAR. THERE IS.
WE ARE BORROWING YOUR GATEWAY.
WE HAVE NEED OF IT.
I'M SURE THERE ARE NUANCES I'M MISSING HERE. BUT TO BE HONEST--
--I DON'T REALLY CARE.

WHEN YAHWEH WAS LORD OF ALL, THEN YOUR FIRES WERE TO BE FEARED.
AYE.
BUT NOW WE ARE LORDS OF ALL.
WE HAVE STEPPED INTO YOUR FATHER'S SPACE, MORNINGSTAR. AND YOUR FATHER IS THE LIGHT YOU SHINE BY.
SO YOU HAVE NO POWER AGAINST US.
THERE IS NOTHING FURTHER TO DETAIN US HERE, BROTHER. THE GATE IS OPEN.
LET US TAKE OUR PLACE IN HEAVEN.

LUX.
FAREWELL, MORNINGSTAR. YOU MUST COME AND WORSHIP US SOON.
IF YOU ARE SUITABLY HUMBLE, WE WILL RECEIVE YOU GRACIOUSLY.
MAZIKEEN.
NO.
STAY HERE. GUARD THE GATE UNTIL I RETURN.
AND IF YOU DON'T?
THEN TAKE THE LILIM TO THE SILVER CITY, AND HOLD IT FOR AS LONG AS YOU CAN.
IF I DON'T JOIN YOU THERE, YOU CAN MOURN ME AT YOUR LEISURE.

ANGELS OF THE HOST, BEHOLD --
-- THE NEW FACES OF YAHWEH!
BROTHER? THIS IS NOT THE SILVER CITY.
THAT IS OBVIOUS.
THIS IS EFFRUL, IN THE HINTERLAND BEHIND HELL.
THE MORNINGSTAR HAS TRICKED US.
HOW? WE HAVE TAKEN HIS FATHER'S PLACE!
HIS FLAMES CANNOT BURN US! HIS POWER CANNOT WORK ON US!
BUT MY WILL IS STILL MY OWN.

DO YOU THINK WE NEED YOUR GATES TO RISE TO HEAVEN, LIGHTBRINGER?
NO. I'M SURE YOU DON'T.
BUT FROM THE BORDERS OF HELL, IT'S A LONG WALK.
DID YOU KNOW EFFRUL? I LEFT HIS BONES HERE AFTER I KILLED HIM.
AND THE LOCAL GENTRY TURNED HIS SKULL INTO A BOUNDARY MARKER.
WHAT I KILLED, I CAN BRING BACK.
THAT'S ALSO A MATTER OF WILL.
AAAURRGHHH!!!

VERMINOUS ANGEL! HAVE YOU NOT REALIZED YET THAT WE ARE GOD?
YES.
I HAVE.
BUT YOU HAVEN'T. NOT FULLY.
POWER LIKE THAT TAKES TIME TO BED IN.
SPLAT
"THE INTERIM IS MINE."

NOTHING. NO CONCUSSION, CERTAINLY. NO WOUNDS, EITHER.
THE BLOOD CHECKS OUT AS YOURS, BUT I'M DAMNED IF I KNOW WHERE IT CAME FROM.
SHE SOUNDS DISAPPOINTED. I SAY THANKS ANYWAY.
THEN -- BECAUSE I'VE GOT NOTHING TO LOSE -- I GO FOR BROKE.
IS THERE A BACK WAY OUT OF HERE?
MS. WECHSLER, YOU'RE A WITNESS TO A MULTIPLE HOMICIDE--
--AND THE LAPD WILL WANT MY BLOOD IF YOU WALK OUT OF HERE WITHOUT TALKING TO THEM FIRST.
I DIDN'T SEE ANYTHING.
ON THE OTHER HAND, THEY DON'T PAY ME TO BE A SECURITY GUARD.
IF YOU TAKE THE WRONG DOOR OUT OF THE CAN, THERE'S NO TELLING WHERE YOU'LL END UP.
I FEEL SO WEIRD. LIKE ALL OF THIS ALREADY HAPPENED TO ME ONCE.
LIKE I'M RUNNING, AND I'M HIDING, AND I ALREADY KNOW HOW IT TURNS OUT.

IT TURNS OUT BADLY.
GOT A PHOBIC TYPE DOWN IN PRE-OP, AMINA.
CAN YOU HOLD HIS HAND FOR ME?
IN A MINUTE. LET ME DEAL WITH THIS MEDICARE STUFF.
IT MUST RETURN ALONG THE SAME PATH.
WHAT?
HER BLOOD IS THE GUIDE. YOU UNDERSTAND?
HELLO? WHO'S THERE?
YES. BLOOD. I UNDERSTAND.
DO IT. DO IT NOW.
UUUUUF!
PFOOM

THE SILVER CITY.
THE TEMPTATION TO USE THOSE SPEARS WILL BE VERY STRONG.
FOR YOUR OWN SAKE, RESIST IT --
-- AND TELL MICHAEL I'M HERE TO SEE HIM.
L... LUCIFER, UNDER GOD'S INTERDICTION YOU CANNOT SET FOOT HERE.
ALL THE SAME, HERE I AM.
DO YOU REALLY NEED TO PURSUE THESE FORMALITIES TO THE POINT WHERE I KILL YOU?
ISN'T THERE ONE OF YOU WHO KNOWS HOW TO THINK?
SERAPHS.
STAND DOWN.

URIEL.
LUCIFER MORNINGSTAR.
IS THIS PROVOCATION OR AN OVERTURE OF PEACE?
IT'S NEITHER. I NEED TO SPEAK WITH MY BROTHER. I COULD EXPLAIN --
-- BUT BY THE TIME I'M FINISHED THE SILVER CITY WILL BE A PALE GREY SLAGHEAP.
THEN... PASS.
BUT AS I TOLD YOU, MICHAEL SPEAKS TO NO ONE.
HE'LL SPEAK TO ME.

FIVE...
BILLION...
YEAAAAAAARG!!!
KILL LUCIFER! EAT LUCIFER! SHIT LUCIFER!
NUUUUUUH!
TAKE HEART, BROTHER. NOW THAT WE -- ARE GOD --
-- DEATH CAN HAVE NO -- HOLD ON US.
GAAAAAAAAH!

WHAT HAVE YOU *DONE* TO HIM, BROTHER GARAMAS?
I HAVE TURNED HIS *BLOOD* TO MOLTEN LEAD.
GROW YOURSELF SOME FLESH -- YOU LOOK *GROTESQUE*.

SEE. WITH A THOUGHT I AM *WHOLE* AGAIN.
LET US GO ON TO *HEAVEN*, AND BE ENTHRONED.

A *MOMENT*, GYGES. IT BEHOOVES US TO BE CAREFUL.
CAREFUL? ARE WE NOT *GOD?*
AYE, WE ARE GOD, BUT STILL --

I CAME HERE TO BE ALONE, LUCIFER. WILL YOU RESPECT MY WISHES?
OR DO YOU PREFER TO BE CAST OUT OF HEAVEN ALL OVER AGAIN?
THE TITANS HAVE WALKED OUTSIDE OF TIME, AND USURPED OUR FATHER'S POWER.
THE TITANS ARE A JOKE IN POOR TASTE.
NONETHELESS, THEY'RE COMING HERE NOW TO ASSERT THEIR RULE. I WASN'T ABLE TO STOP THEM.
I CARE NOT. I SERVED OUR FATHER FAITHFULLY, AND MY REWARD WAS TO BE CHASTISED FOR NOT BEING YOU.
SO -- IF YOU ARE TO BE HIS SUCCESSOR, THIS PROBLEM IS YOURS.
YOU'RE VERY GENEROUS, BROTHER.
AM I?
I THOUGHT WE MIGHT ACTUALLY COME TO BLOWS OVER THIS.

BUT SINCE YOU'RE HAPPY TO WAIVE YOUR BIRTHRIGHT--
--AND SINCE NOBODY ELSE IS LIKELY TO PRESS A CLAIM AGAINST ME--
LUCIFER!
I DID NOT MEAN--
-- THEN WITHOUT UNDUE FORMALITY I TAKE MY PLACE IN PRIMUM MOBILE.
I AM SAMAEL, THE SON OF YAHWEH.
GOD OF THIS CREATION, AND OF THE OTHER.

LOS ANGELES.
THE CAB DRIVER IS THE PROTECTIVE TYPE.
I MEAN, CRAZY PEOPLE HANG OUT HERE. YOU WANNA BE CAREFUL.
THANKS. KEEP THE CHANGE.
AND GOD HELP ME, PROTECTION'S WHAT I'M LOOKING FOR.
PROTECTION, AND-- IF I'M HONEST-- SOMETHING ELSE.
CALIFORNIA
HER FUCKED UP FACE. HER SMELL OF SWEAT AND SPICED WINE.
HER ARMS, STRONGER THAN A MAN'S ARMS.
STRIKE TWO PRAY THAT HE WILL COME AGAIN
MAZIKEEN. ARE YOU STILL ALIVE?
ARE YOU IN THERE?
OR DID HE BUILD THIS TO BE YOUR TOMB?

COME OUT, LITTLE ANGELS. YOU ARE GYGES' SERVANTS NOW.
COME OUT AND SING HYMNS TO ME.
BROTHER. I HAVE CONSIDERED.
RETURN TO ME, AND I WILL EXPOUND MY THOUGHTS.
I WILL BE BACK PRESENTLY. THINK OF SOME RHYMES FOR MY NAME.
I WILL HAVE MY HYMNS.
WHAT HAVE YOU DECIDED, BROTHER GARAMAS?
THIS: THAT WHEN CONFRONTING THE MORNINGSTAR FACE-TO-FACE, AS WE INTEND TO DO--
--IT IS BEST TO STAB HIM ALSO IN THE BACK.
WE WILL WEAVE A DUINUM.
A DOUBLE OF LUCIFER WHOSE TOUCH WILL NEGATE AND CONSUME HIM.

AN EXCELLENT PLAN!
BUT... FROM WHAT WILL WE WEAVE IT?
FROM MEMORIES.
THERE MUST BE MORTALS WHO HAVE BEEN TOUCHED BY THE LIGHTBRINGER, WHO HAVE SEEN HIM AND SPOKEN WITH HIM.
WE WILL COMB THEIR MINDS, AND TAKE FROM THEM WHAT WE NEED.
IT IS BUT SLENDER PICKINGS. GLIMPSES AND GUESSES.
HE HAS HELD HIMSELF ALOOF.
OR THEY HAVE SHRUNK FROM HIM, INSTINCTIVELY, SENSING WHAT HE IS.
BUT SEE -- HERE IS ONE.
A MORTAL WOMAN WHO HAS STOOD NEXT TO HIM, AND FLINCHED NOT.
LET US EXAMINE HER MORE CLOSELY.

THIS ONE?
YES. AN OLD IMAGE, BUT CLEAR.
THE ANGLE IS A LITTLE STEEP, THOUGH.
FROM OVER HERE, THEN?
YES. THERE WOULD BE BETTER.
BUT SOFT YOU NOW, BROTHER.
SHE HAS ENOUGH MEMORIES OF HIM, AND TO SPARE.
BUT WHY SIFT THROUGH THE MOMENTS OF HER PAST, ONE BY ONE--
--AND TAKE AN AGE ABOUT IT--
--WHEN THERE IS A BETTER AND A SIMPLER WAY?

BROTHER, THIS IS NOT WHAT I INTENDED.
AND I WILL NOT ALLOW IT.
IS THERE A PROBLEM, MICHAEL?
YOU SAID YOU DIDN'T CARE.
STILL, THIS -- DISPLAY OFFENDS ME.
AS YOU WISH IT TO.
ONCE BEFORE YOU ROUSED ME TO ANGER AS A MEANS OF MANIPULATING ME. BUT HAVE A CARE.
WHEN ONCE I START TO DESTROY, I MAY NOT STOP WITH YOU.
AH, AND NOW WE SEE IT. UNDER THE SHOW OF VIRTUE.
THE HURT PRIDE. THE SCREAM OF SELF. THE NURTURED GRIEVANCES.
YOUR SINS. NOT MINE.
BROTHER, IF YOU CAN FIND NO MIRROR IN MY FACE--
--THEN WHERE IN ALL THE WORLDS WILL YOU SEE YOURSELF?

LUCIFER, YOU ARE INSANE.
I HAVE WARNED YOU IN THE CLEAREST TERMS.
I TAKE TO WARNINGS AS YOU DO TO THINKING FOR YOURSELF.
I ASSURE YOU. IN ALL THIS DEAD EXPANSE OF -- POINTLESS MATTER -- AND POINTLESS LIVES--
--THERE IS NOTHING -- NOTHING! - THAT I CARE ABOUT ENOUGH TO SPARE IT.
THEN WE'VE GOT NOTHING MORE TO SAY TO EACH OTHER--
--ASSUMING WE EVER DID. ONE FINAL THING, THOUGH...
THERE ARE THREE OF US WHO CAN CONTINUE YAHWEH'S LINE.
THREE OF US WHO CAN STILL POSE A THREAT TO THE TITANS.
USE IT AS A BLINDFOLD.
THEN YOU WON'T HAVE TO SEE WHAT THEY DO TO HER.

DO YOU *HAVE* HER?
NOT QUITE. THIS REQUIRES -- A LITTLE *CONCENTRATION.*
AND I AM, AS USUAL, *PLAGUED* BY DISTRACTIONS.
THERE! HAVE *HOLD* OF HER.
IN THE *PRESENT* MOMENT, WHERE WE MAY LAY OUT ALL HER THOUGHTS MOST EASILY AND *EXAMINE* THEM.
WILL SHE *SUFFICE?*
HER THOUGHTS ARE *CONFUSED.* DISORDERED. BUT SOME IMAGES STAND *OUT.*
NOOOOO!

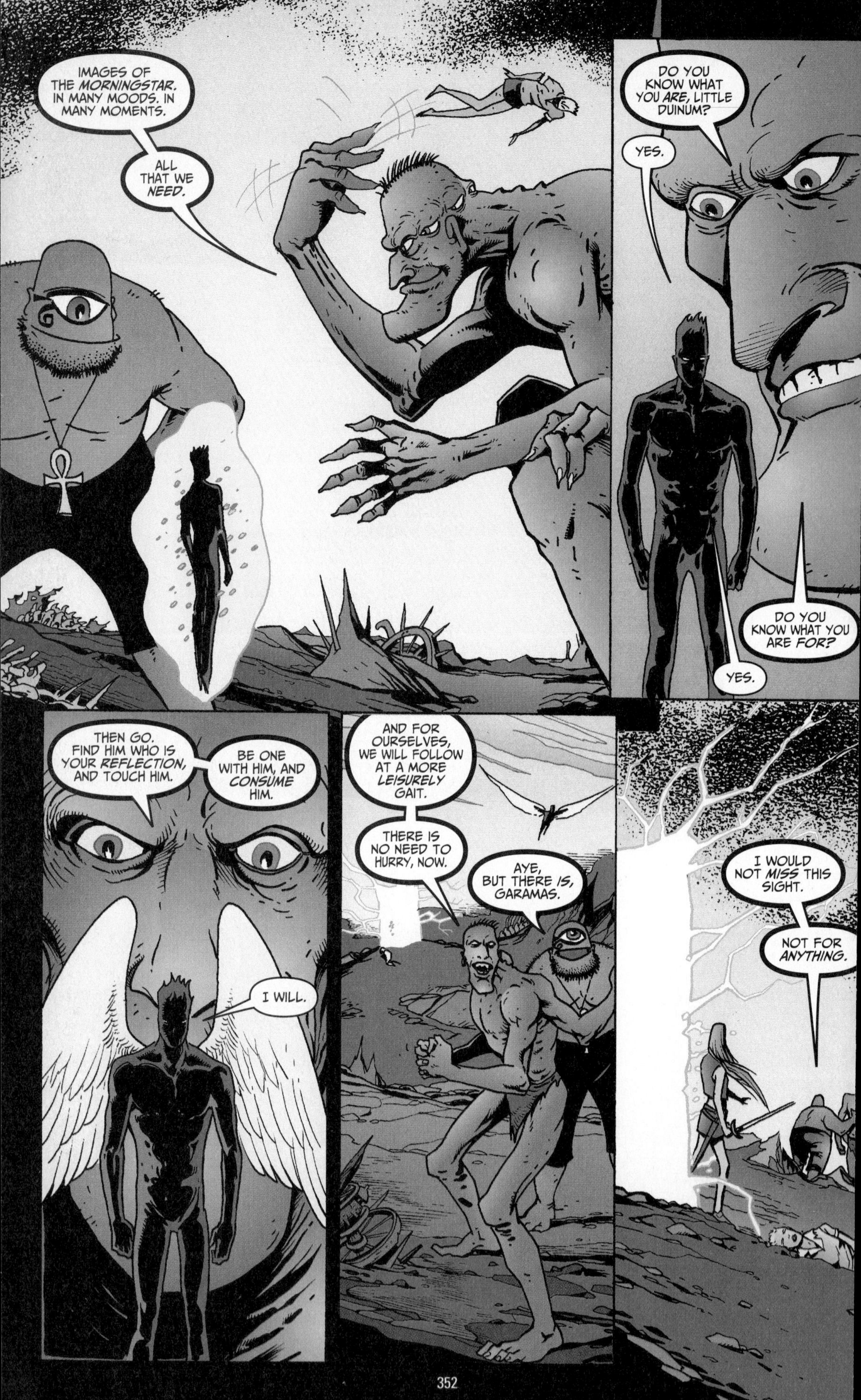

IMAGES OF THE MORNINGSTAR. IN MANY MOODS. IN MANY MOMENTS.
ALL THAT WE NEED.
DO YOU KNOW WHAT YOU ARE, LITTLE DUINUM?
YES.
DO YOU KNOW WHAT YOU ARE FOR?
YES.
THEN GO. FIND HIM WHO IS YOUR REFLECTION, AND TOUCH HIM.
BE ONE WITH HIM, AND CONSUME HIM.
I WILL.
AND FOR OURSELVES, WE WILL FOLLOW AT A MORE LEISURELY GAIT.
THERE IS NO NEED TO HURRY, NOW.
AYE, BUT THERE IS, GARAMAS.
I WOULD NOT MISS THIS SIGHT.
NOT FOR ANYTHING.

CAN'T THINK. CAN'T SEE.
DON'T KNOW IF I'M *DEAD* OR JUST EMPTY.
SOMEONE'S *BREATHING*, SO THE WORLD'S STILL THERE.
SOMETHING'S *MOVING*.
SOMETHING'S MOVING ME.
M... MAZIKEEN? MAZ?
YOU... HOW? WHEN DID YOU --? WHERE ARE YOU *TAKING* ME?
TO HEAVEN.

SO, YOU'VE SPOKEN?
YES. WE'VE SPOKEN.
AND YOU'VE AGREED ON A PLAN?
I'M AFRAID NOT.
MY BROTHER FEELS A LITTLE AMBIVALENT ABOUT THE PROSPECT OF HEAVEN'S SURVIVAL. AND HIS OWN.
YOU'D BETTER TAKE ME TO THE ARMORY.
"WHATEVER'S COMING--
"--I WANT TO BE READY FOR IT."

IT'S FUNNY. I FANTASIZED ABOUT HER HOLDING MY HAND.
MAZ, DON'T! PLEASE DON'T!
ABOUT HER WALKING WITH ME.
I CAN'T -- I CAN'T DEAL WITH THIS.
I CAN'T BE HERE. IT'S JUST WRONG.
BUT IN THE DREAMS I GOT TO KEEP SOME FEELING IN MY WRIST.
OW!
AND WHEN SHE TURNED TO LOOK AT ME, IT WAS DIFFERENT.
THEY MEAN TO KILL HIM.
I WILL NOT ALLOW IT.
THE BUILDINGS ARE SINGING TO EACH OTHER.
ELEGIES. LAMENTS. FUNERAL HYMNS.
I CAN ALMOST MAKE OUT THE WORDS.
I ALMOST KNOW WHO THEY'RE FOR.

BROTHERS IN ARMS

MIKE CAREY Writer PETER GROSS and RYAN KELLY Artists
DANIEL VOZZO Color and Separations CHRISTOPHER MOELLER Cover Painter
COMICRAFT Letters MARIAH HUEHNER Assistant Editor SHELLY BOND Editor
Based on Characters Created by GAIMAN, KIETH and DRINGENBERG

Part Three of Three

NOT A BAD FIT.

IS THERE A *SWORD* THAT GOES WITH THIS?

LUCIFER -- WHY ARE YOU HERE? THE DEFENSE OF HEAVEN IS NO BUSINESS OF YOURS.
YOU'RE RIGHT. IT ISN'T.
I CAME HERE TO TALK TO MY BROTHER -- NO MORE THAN THAT. AND IT'S MYSELF I'M DEFENDING.
THE REST IS JUST A SIDE EFFECT.

STILL, THE HOST WILL ASSIST YOU -- IF I EXPLAIN TO THEM...
...YOUR INTERESTS AND OURS ARE ONE HERE.

NOT REALLY. MICHAEL WOULD HAVE MADE A DIFFERENCE. THE REST OF YOU WILL ONLY MAKE A TARGET.

WE ARE REQUIRED TO FIGHT FOR HEAVEN AND THE HOLY NAME. IT IS WHAT DEFINES US.

YOUR WILLINGNESS TO GROVEL IS WHAT DEFINES YOU.
YOUR SUBORDINATION OF YOURSELVES TO ANOTHER'S WILL.

THAT NOISE! THEY ARE UPON US!
I DON'T THINK SO.
OMNIPRESENCE WILL BE ONE OF THE HARDER TRICKS TO MASTER.

YOU BAG OF WINGS AND WISHBONES.
I TOLD YOU I CAME UNDER TRUCE, AND YOU DREW ON ME.
KILL HER! NEVER MIND ME, KILL HER!
WHAT TRUCE? YOU HEAR THAT YAHWEH IS GONE AND YOU GATHER LIKE KITES!
BUT THE CITY WILL ENDURE! IT WILL ENDURE FOREVER!
IT MIGHT.
YOU WON'T.
PUT UP YOUR WEAPONS, ALL OF YOU.
IF YOU HAVE BUSINESS HERE, DEMON, THEN STATE IT.
ZONAQUEL IS NOT ALONE IN FINDING YOUR PRESENCE HERE UNACCEPTABLE.
What is it, Mazikeen?
THEY HAVE FASHIONED A DEATH FOR YOU.
IT'S COMING HERE NOW --

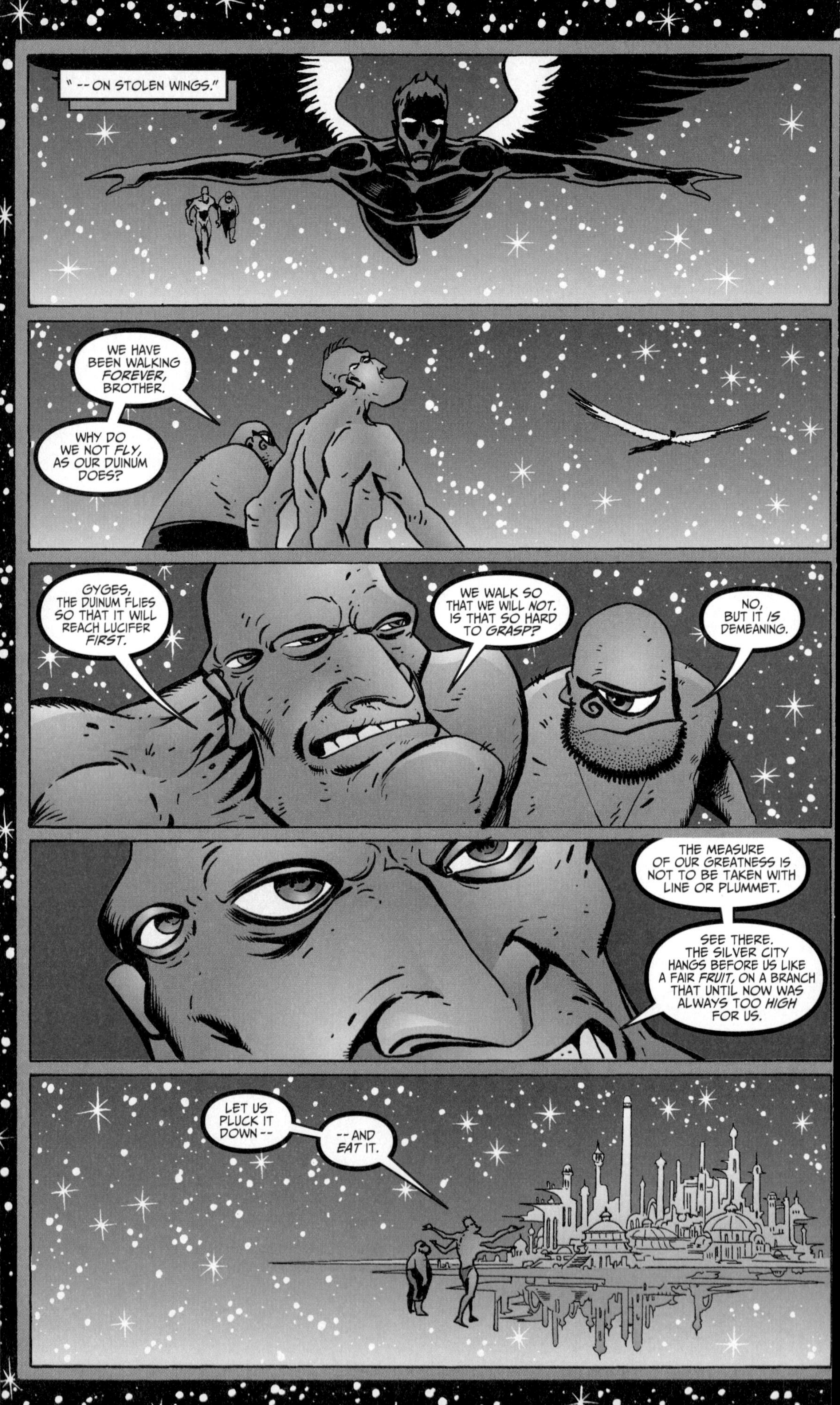
" -- ON STOLEN WINGS."
WE HAVE BEEN WALKING FOREVER, BROTHER.
WHY DO WE NOT FLY, AS OUR DUINUM DOES?
GYGES, THE DUINUM FLIES SO THAT IT WILL REACH LUCIFER FIRST.
WE WALK SO THAT WE WILL NOT. IS THAT SO HARD TO GRASP?
NO, BUT IT IS DEMEANING.
THE MEASURE OF OUR GREATNESS IS NOT TO BE TAKEN WITH LINE OR PLUMMET.
SEE THERE. THE SILVER CITY HANGS BEFORE US LIKE A FAIR FRUIT, ON A BRANCH THAT UNTIL NOW WAS ALWAYS TOO HIGH FOR US.
LET US PLUCK IT DOWN --
-- AND EAT IT.

SO I'M IN HEAVEN. JUST IN THE LITERAL SENSE.
AND THAT'S MY OLD BOSS. AND THE WOMAN I USED TO WAIT TABLES WITH.
AND MY WRIST STILL HURTS WHERE SHE HELD ME SO THIS IS REAL.
SO THE MONSTERS ARE REAL AND THE BLOOD WAS REAL AND ALL I'M THINKING IS WHY IS SHE LOOKING AT HIM LIKE THAT?
I'M LOSING IT *I'M IN HEAVEN* DOES SHE LOVE HIM?
THEY USED HER *MEMORIES* OF ME? YOU'RE SURE?
I SAW IT. A DOUBLE OF YOU, WOVEN FROM BLACK THREADS.
THEY SAID IT WOULD *CONSUME* YOU WHEN YOU TOUCHED IT.
THEN YOU WILL *NOT* TOUCH IT. THE HOST WILL *ENGAGE* IT, WHILE YOU FIGHT THE TITANS.
THEY EXERCISED THEIR WILL AND THEIR POWER DIRECTLY ON HER.
THERE MIGHT BE *ANOTHER* WAY.
AND HE TURNS AND *LOOKS* AT ME. LOOKS ME STRAIGHT IN THE EYE.
BUT IT'S *HER* NAME HE SPEAKS.

DARK ANGEL, BY GOD'S DECREE I BID YOU PAUSE AND --
DOWN HERE, MOCKERY. I'M NOT HIDING FROM YOU.
IF YOU'RE MY DEATH, I'M YOURS.

BUT I EMBRACE THAT DEATH. IT IS MY PURPOSE.
IT IS MY FULFILLMENT.
YOUR FULFILLMENT? SPARE ME.
THIS ALREADY FEELS LIKE MASTURBATION.
I CANNOT BURN. MY ENDING IS PRE-ORDAINED.
WHEN WE BECOME ONE -- WHEN WE CANCEL EACH OTHER OUT -- I WILL FINALLY KNOW --
-- PEACE --?
CLEARLY, TITANS --
-- BEATRICE WECKSLER'S MEMORIES OF ME WERE LESS THAN PERFECT.

THIS IS WHAT IT ALL COMES DOWN TO, THEN.
THIS IS WHAT IT WAS ALL ABOUT.
SHE HOLDS ME TIGHT. TOO TIGHT.
LIKE SHE THINKS I MIGHT RUN.
LIKE SHE DOESN'T UNDERSTAND, OR IT DOESN'T MATTER.
BUT I WOULDN'T.
THAT'S THE SICK THING.
GNOTHE -- YOUR RISING. GNOTHE -- YOUR ROAD. GNOTHE -- YOUR RESTING.
I KNOW WHAT SHE'S GOING TO DO TO ME.
BUT IF I RAN --
-- I'D JUST END UP IN SOME PLACE THAT DOESN'T HAVE HER IN IT.

YOU ARE NOTHING TO US, MORNINGSTAR!
LESS THAN NOTHING!
I SEE. IS THAT WHY YOU TRIED TO KILL ME WITH A TOY --
-- INSTEAD OF FACING ME YOURSELVES?
EARRGHHHHH!
YOU SEE, GYGES? MIGHT IS NOTHING WITHOUT WILL.
WE HAVE BOTH!
WE ARE YAHWEH!
WE HAVE ALL THE VIRTUES HE HAD!
REALLY?

MY APOLOGIES FOR DOUBTING YOU, THEN.
TCHOK
I'M SORRY! I'M SO SORRY! HE MOVED!
HE MOVED WHEN I TRIED TO HIT HIM!
GAAAAAAAAAH!

HE... CANNOT... MOVE...
...IF WE... DO NOT... *ALLOW* HIM TO.
CRASH
NOW I WILL *FINISH* HIM.
DO NOTHING.
IT IS *ALREADY* FINISHED.

"HER BLOOD IS THE GUIDE. IT MUST RETURN ALONG THE SAME PATH. YOU UNDERSTAND?"
"YES. BLOOD I UNDERSTAND."
MAZ. I WAS COMING TO FIND YOU.
THAT'S WHY I WAS THERE -- OUTSIDE LUX...
GNOTHE -- SWIM UPSTREAM TO WHERE YOU WERE SPAWNED.
...BECAUSE YOU TOLD ME ONCE -- I THOUGHT YOU SAID YOU WANTED ME.
AND TAKE THIS WITH YOU.
I LOVE YOU.
I'VE LOVED YOU EVER SINCE --
I KNOW.

I WANT TO STAY AND WATCH.
COME, BROTHER. THE OUTCOME OF THIS IS NOT IN DOUBT.
TO SEE THE MORNINGSTAR THRASH AND SQUIRM AS HE DIES.
THIS, MORE THAN ANYTHING, BRINGS HOME TO ME WHAT I NOW AM.
WHAT YOU ARE NOW, GYGES KOPROGENITOS--
--IS DEAD.

WAS THIS WHAT YOU INTENDED, BROTHER?
TO MOVE ME TO ANGER? TO ROUSE ME FROM MY LETHARGY?
WELL, I AM ROUSED.
BUT NOT MUCH MOVED.
GKKKKKK!

I... HOWEVER...
...AM BECOMING ...ANGRY.
THEN DO IT!
DO IT NOW.
IF THIS CITY WILL NOT ACKNOWLEDGE US --
-- THEN LET IT FALL!

NO! NO, WE MUST BE ONE!
WE MUST BE NOTHING!
EVENTUALLY, PERHAPS.
YOU GO ON AHEAD.
HOW -- HOW DID YOU ACCOMPLISH THIS, LUCIFER?
THEY WERE IMMUNE TO MY POWER.
THEY WERE IMMUNE TO ALL POWER -- EXCEPT THEIR OWN.
BUT THE VIRTUE OF THE TITANS WAS TO TRANSCEND TIME. I TURNED IT BACK ON THEM.
KILLED THEM BEFORE THEY BECAME OMNIPOTENT.
"THE WOMAN WHO THEY TOUCHED WAS THE CONDUIT."
"THE CHANNEL THROUGH WHICH I WAS ABLE TO TOUCH THEM BACK."

STOP.
YOU'RE STILL ALIVE. THE BLOW PASSED THROUGH YOU.
AAARHHHHH! AHUH! AHUH! AHUH!
IT IS OVER?
IT'S OVER.
THEN THERE IS NO LONGER A NEED FOR YOUR PRESENCE HERE.
BEATRICE. I NEED YOUR HELP IN ONE FINAL ACT.
OH GOD! OH GOD!
PASSION IS BLASPHEMY IN THIS HOLY PLACE.
AND I HAVE A GREAT NEED TO BLASPHEME.

WILL YOU TAKE THE *THRONE*, THEN?

NO. BUT NEITHER WILL **YOU**.

I WILL BE MORE **VIGILANT** IN THE FUTURE. YOU WILL NOT BE **NEEDED** AGAIN.

ARROGANCE, TOO. IS THIS CONVERGENCE OR CHIASMUS, MICHAEL?

WILL WE BECOME *TWINS*, OR PASS EACH OTHER GOING IN *OPPOSITE* DIRECTIONS?

EITHER WAY, I FIND YOUR *FAITH* -- AS I FIND MOST FAITH --

-- *GROTESQUELY* MISPLACED.

I WOKE UP FROM A SCARY DREAM.
I THOUGHT HOW DID THE BED GET TURNED AROUND?
I THOUGHT IF IT'S NIGHT THEN HOW COME IT'S SO HOT?
BUT THERE WAS SUNLIGHT ON MY HAND. RIBBON SUNLIGHT. A SWORD BLADE.
AND THIS WASN'T MY BED.
SO MANY SMELLS I DIDN'T RECOGNIZE. SO MANY SOUNDS.
SHOUTS. METAL CLANGING OFF METAL. LIKE A WAR GOING ON JUST OUTSIDE THE WINDOW.
BUT THEY WEREN'T FIGHTING. THEY WERE JUST TRAINING.
A THOUSAND MONSTERS GOING THROUGH THEIR PACES.
IN STRICT OBEDIENCE TO HER COMMANDS.
LIKE ME.
LIKE ME.

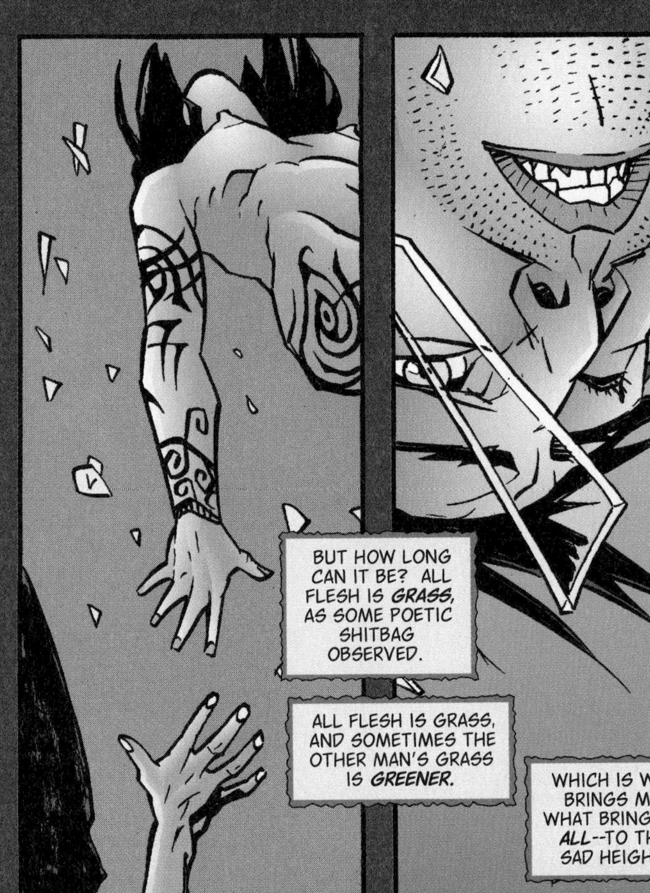

Neutral Ground

Mike Carey-Writer
Ted Naifeh-Guest Artist
Ken Lopez-Lettering
Daniel Vozzo-Colors and Separations
Tara McPherson-Guest Cover Painter
Mariah Huehner-Assistant Editor
Shelly Bond-Editor

Based on characters created by Gaiman, Kieth and Dringenberg

HE'S A CLERK IN A LAW FIRM.
LAW SCHOOL DROPOUT HIMSELF, SO HE'S PATRONIZED BY HIS BOSSES AND DESPISED BY HIS PEERS.

AND IF HIS TRAINING DOES OCCASIONALLY ALLOW HIM TO SPOT A GLITCH--
--AN ANOMALY THAT THE EYE OF THE UNINITIATED WOULD GLOSS OVER--

--WELL, IT'S NOT LIKE ANYONE'S EVER GOING TO THANK HIM.
MISTER FULBRIGHT?
THERE'S SOMETHING HERE THAT--WELL, IT ISN'T QUITE RIGHT.

YOU SEE, THIS IS A FUNDS TRANSFER FROM THE CLIENT ACCOUNT, BUT THERE'S NO CODE OR CASE NUMBER AGAINST IT.
EVERY TRANSFER HAS TO BE IN RESPECT OF A SPECIFIC CASE.

AND IT'S SUCH A LARGE SUM THAT--

JUST PROCESS THE GODDAMN PAPERWORK, SEWELL.
IF WE WANTED YOU TO THINK, WE BE PAYING YOU LIVING WAGE.

AFTER HOURS HE'S GOT ANOTHER LIFE.
ANOTHER HALF-LIFE, RATHER--BECAUSE IT'S AS PRONE TO DECAY AS THE FIRST.
THE GENITAL WARTS
HE LIKES THE FREEDOM OF PUNK ROCK.
THE TORN SHIRTS. THE CURSE WORDS. THE PUBLIC SPITTING.
JOHN FUCKING RUSH MARRIED SONY FUCKING LAIR.
THE CHURCH WAS MADE OF CORPSES AND THE CAKE WAS PUBIC HAIR!
BUT EVEN HERE HE FAILS TO REALIZE--
--THAT CONTEXT IS EVERYTHING.
TAKE A HIIIIIIIIIKE!
YOU GUYS SUCK!
GET OFF THE FUCKING STAGE!

AND YOU CAN HAVE YOUR GODDAMN AMP BACK WHEN YOU'VE PAID FOR THE DAMAGE!

CHRIST, SEWELL! A FUCKIN' GOTH CLUB! DO YOU NEED STRONGER MEDICATION?
WELL THE DAMNED WERE SORT OF GOTHIC PUNK. THERE IS AN OVERLAP.

THAT'S MY FUCKING AMP IN THERE, JOHN!
DON'T EVEN BOTHER CALLING ME UNTIL YOU'VE GOT IT BACK.
DON'T BE LIKE THAT, PUCE. PLEASE...

PUCE!
STAY HERE, MAN. YOU'VE DONE ENOUGH.
I'LL GO TO HER.

HI, MRS. SILVERMAN.

GEWALT IST MIR! ES HAT EIN *TEUFEL* IN ES.

LORDS AND LADIES OF THE REALM *INFERNAL*--

--MIGHTY *KINGS* OF THE DEMONIC DIASPORA--

THIS IS A SOLEMN OCCASION, CONFRERES. WHEN SOME OF US TOOK UP RESIDENCE IN LUCIFER'S HELL, AND OTHERS REFUSED TO FOLLOW, WE PARTED COMPANY.
LET ME REMIND YOU WHAT IT IS THAT HAS BROUGHT US TOGETHER AGAIN AT THIS TABLE.

GOD IS GONE FROM THIS COSMOS.
AND HE'S NOT COMING BACK.

YOU PRESUME TOO MUCH, DERUKIM! WHAT WE KNOW IS THAT THE SILVER CITY WAS ATTACKED.
--WHICH YAHWEH MAY HAVE ALLOWED FOR REASONS OF HIS OWN.

LUCIFER HAS LAID WASTE THE MANSIONS OF THE SILENCE. WOULD YAHWEH HAVE ALLOWED THAT?
PERHAPS LUCIFER IS AT LAST STRONGER THAN HIS FATHER.

AYE, YOU HELL-KIN WOULD LIKE TO BELIEVE THAT, SINCE YOU CHOSE TO SERVE HIM.
BUT WHERE IS LUCIFER? HE COULD SETTLE THIS IN A MOMENT.
LUCIFER WAS INVITED TO THIS GATHERING--AND HE MAY YET ATTEND.
IN THE MEANTIME, LET US REVIEW OUR OPTIONS.
AND YADA YADA YADA. SWEAR TO GOD--OR THE SPACE WHERE HE USED TO BE--
--IT'D MAKE YOU VOMIT YOUR OWN LUNGS UP TO HEAR THESE GUYS BANGING THEIR DRUMS.
THIS IS AN IMPRESSIVE VENUE, UNAGOR. YOU CHOSE WELL.
UH... THANKS--
ETHOR. OF THE LILIM, RIGHT?
WELL, A HUMAN SOUL IS A NICE, DISCREET LITTLE PLACE. BUT I'D BETTER GO GET A READING ON HIS VITAL SIGNS.
WOULDN'T WANT HIM TO CROAK WHILE WE'RE STILL IN HERE. CATCH YOU LATER.

HEY, JOHN! HOW'S IT *HANGING?*
SORRY ABOUT THE *INCONVENIENCE.* NORMAL SERVICE WILL BE RESUMED IN A WHILE.

TRUTH TO TELL, PAL, YOU GOT THE *BEST* OF IT. AT LEAST YOU'RE JUST BORED.
IF I HAVE TO LISTEN TO MUCH *MORE* OF THAT SHIT, I'M GONNA GO--

SON OF A BITCH.
I JUST HAD THE MOST *AMAZING* IDEA.

WE'RE GONNA HAVE US SOME *FUN,* JOHN.
DON'T WORRY. I'LL *DRIVE.*

WE WENT TO A COUPLE OF BARS, FIRST. THEN TO A CLUB, WHERE WE SET UP OPEN HOUSE WITH JOHN-BOY'S CREDIT CARD.
GOD FORBID WE SHOULD LOOK CHEAP.
OF COURSE, HUMAN FEMALES ARE ABOUT AS INTERESTING TO ME AS LINT.
BUT I WAS RIDING JOHN'S NERVOUS SYSTEM, SO WHAT HE FELT, I GOT TOO. LOTS OF LAUGHS.
UNTIL HE STARTED IN WITH THE WHINING.
WHY ARE YOU DOING THIS TO ME?
IN THE NAME OF GOD, WHAT HAVE I DONE? WHAT WAS MY SIN?
YOU MEAN BESIDES BEING A LAWYER? YOU WERE JUST NEUTRAL GROUND, JOHN.
HEY, WOULDN'T THOSE KEEP YOUR EARS WARM IN WINTER?
BUT HE JUST WOULDN'T GET INTO THE SPIRIT OF IT.
SO WE HIT THE ATM AND WENT OFF IN SEARCH OF PASTURES NEW.

WE FOUND A CARD GAME IN THE BACK OF A BROTHEL WHERE WE SCOOPED SEVEN HUNDRED BUCKS AND ABOUT A HALF DOZEN SOULS.
BEST GAME I'VE HAD IN A THOUSAND YEARS.

AND WHO'D'VE THOUGHT YOU COULD EVEN BUY A 1972 ELECTRA GLIDE IN SAN FRAN AT MIDNIGHT?
LET ALONE STEAL ONE?

THE HUMAN BODY'S AN AMAZING THING, JOHN.
OH CHRIST! OH CHRIST!
BUT IT JUST ROTS IF YOU DON'T USE IT, YOU HEAR WHAT I'M SAYING?

DO NOT MOVE! REPEAT, DO NOT MOVE! WE'RE COMING TO GET YOU!
FUCK, BRING THAT CHOPPER IN! HE'S LOSING HIS BALANCE!

SORRY, JOHN. I'VE GOT TO GO CHECK ON THE DELEGATES.

THEIR COMFORT IS MY REP. I KNOW YOU UNDERSTAND.

TO BE HONEST I NEEDN'T HAVE *WORRIED.* THEY'D ONLY JUST GOT UP TO INSULTING EACH OTHER'S MOTHERS.

WHICH WAS AGENDA ITEM *THREE.* TWO HUNDRED SEVENTY SIX TO GO.

HEY, CALL ME CYNICAL, BUT THIS IS JUST A *JOB* TO ME. I PROVIDE A SERVICE.

HEY.
AAAAAAA!
DON'T BURST AN ARTERY, JOHN. IT'S JUST ME.

YOU'RE NOT REAL! YOU'RE NOT REAL!
OH JESUS, I'M GOING CRAZY! I'VE GOT TO GET OUT OF HERE!

YOUR WISH IS MY COMMAND.
RATCH
CLICK
LET'S GO.

NO! JESUS, NO! DON'T DO THIS!
DON'T DO THIS TO ME AGAIN!
IT'S NOT TO YOU, JOHN. IT'S FOR YOU.

YOU'RE IN A JAIL CELL, ALL BY YOURSELF AND NOBODY HAS SEEN YOU LEAVE.
I'D CALL THAT THE PERFECT ALIBI, WOULDN'T YOU?

WHERE ARE WE GOING? WHERE ARE YOU TAKING ME?
TO WORK. HEY, JOHN, CHECK IT OUT.
THAT MAMA IS SO HOT FOR YOU SHE'S GONNA SKID OFF THE SEAT.

IT'S TOO EARLY. THERE WON'T EVEN BE ANYONE THERE.
THE DOORS WILL STILL BE LOCKED.
JOHN, YOU'RE NEVER GOING TO BECOME A PARTNER WITH THAT KIND OF ATTITUDE. GIVE ME SOME COMMITMENT.

MISTER FULBRIGHT.
SEWELL.
WHAT IN GOD'S NAME HAPPENED TO YOUR SUIT?

OH WELL, YOU KNOW HOW IT IS. YOU GET TANKED. YOU GET STONED.
YOU GO TO SLEEP IN YOUR OWN PISS.

I MEAN, WE'RE BOTH GUYS, RIGHT?
WE GO WITH OUR URGES.
WH-- WHAT? WHAT ARE YOU--?

AS KILLINGS GO, IT WAS VANILLA RATHER THAN SUPER FUDGE CHUNK.
THE ONLY BUZZ I GOT WAS FROM HAVING JOHN SCREAMING INSIDE HIS OWN HEAD THE WHOLE TIME. BEGGING ME TO STOP.

BUT I HAD TO SHUT HIM UP WHEN I GOT ON TO THE TECHNICAL STUFF.
SOME OF THE RECORDS I WAS MANIPULATING WERE THOUSANDS OF MILES AWAY. I NEEDED TO CONCENTRATE.

WHAT HAVE YOU DONE? OH GOD, WHAT HAVE YOU DONE?
I'VE MADE YOU RICH, YOU STRANGULATED LITTLE TURD.
WEREN'T YOU EVEN WATCHING?

ALL THAT MONEY FULBRIGHT WAS EMBEZZLING? WELL, IT'S ALL TUCKED UP NICELY IN YOUR BRAND-NEW OFFSHORE ACCOUNT.
HE TAKES THE RAP, YOU TAKE THE GRAVY TRAIN.

NOW--
--LET'S GO SORT OUT YOUR OTHER NEEDS.

THE DELEGATES HAD REACHED THE *BONDING* STAGE, WITH SURPRISINGLY FEW CASUALTIES.

THEY WERE TALKING ABOUT RUNNING THE *ANGELS* OUT OF HELL--ABOUT FUCKING *TIME*, IMO.

DID SHE GIVE YOU A KEY, BY ANY CHANCE?
NO!
WE DON'T-- WE DON'T HAVE THAT KIND OF A RELATIONSHIP YET.

OKAY. NO PROBLEM.
IT WOULD'VE SAVED SOME WEAR AND TEAR ON THE DOOR, IS ALL.

BEDROOM, BEDROOM, WHO'S GOT THE BEDROOM?
PUCE! PUCE, JUST RUN!
I CONTROL THE BODY, JOHN.THAT INCLUDES THE MOUTH.

OOH! BUT MAYBE I'LL LET YOU BORROW IT FOR A WHILE.
YOU'VE PROBABLY GOT SOME COMMENTS YOU'D LIKE TO MAKE AT THIS POINT.

P--PUCE! MARKY?
YOU DON'T OWN ME, JOHN. AND YOU'RE GOING TO PAY FOR THAT DOOR.
FUCK, MAN, I'M SORRY. THIS WASN'T--

TONGUE-TIED, JOHN-BOY? CAN'T SAY THE SAME FOR MARKY, CAN WE?
DON'T WORRY.
I'LL HANDLE THIS PART.
HEY, DON'T TOUCH MY AXE, MAN. THAT'S NOT COOL.
IT'S MY AREA OF EXPERTISE.
UKKKK!
YOU KNOW, THAT WAS PROBABLY THE BEST CHORD YOU EVER GOT OUT OF THAT FRIGGING THING.
YOU OUGHT TO BE THANKING ME.
THERE'S NOTHING SHARPER THAN INGRATITUDE, MARKY.
WELL, MAYBE BROKEN GLASS.

KRESCHHH!

SO. YOU'RE PRETTY **WET** ALREADY, I'M GUESSING.
NO SENSE LETTING MARKY'S SALIVA GO TO **WASTE.**
DON'T COME **NEAR** ME!

BUT JOHNNY LOVES YOU, PUCE. HE'S **ALWAYS** LOVED YOU.
HE'S PREPARED TO FORGIVE AND **FORGET.**

I **MEAN** IT, YOU FUCKER!
YOU--YOU TRY TO TOUCH ME AND I'M OUT OF THIS FUCKING **WINDOW!**

HMM. INTERESTING. I COULD PUT HER **TOGETHER** AGAIN, MORE OR LESS, BUT IT'D BE TOUGH TO GET THE **SOUL** BACK...
NO! DON'T **HURT** HER!

OKAY, JOHN, YOU'RE PISSING ME *OFF* NOW. I'M GOING TO JUMP OVER THERE AND FREEZE HER LIKE I DID YOU.
AND YOU'RE GOING TO DO YOUR *DUTY*. OR ELSE I'LL MANIFEST IN FLESH AND FUCK THE BITCH *MYSELF*.

OF COURSE, THIS WILL ALSO CHANGE THE VENUE FOR THE WHOLE *CONFERENCE*.
BUT WITH A BIT OF LUCK, NOBODY WILL *NOTICE*.
COMING THROUGH.
UHHH!

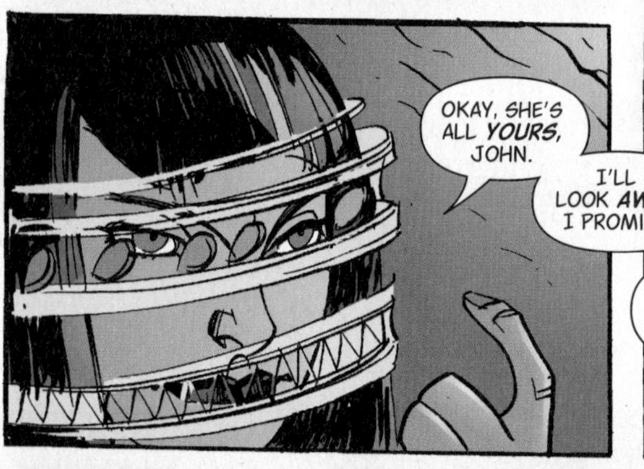
OKAY, SHE'S ALL *YOURS*, JOHN.
I'LL LOOK *AWAY*. I PROMISE.

OH JESUS, I'M *SORRY*, PUCE.
I REALLY AM.

BUT THERE'S NOTHING *LEFT* FOR ME.
NOT WITHOUT *YOU!*

GENTLEMEN.
I HATE TO INTERRUPT--
LUCIFER MORNINGSTAR! YOU ARE MOST WELCOME, LORD!
AND THE-- THE CHAIR BELONGS TO YOU, BEYOND DISPUTE.

THANKS, BUT I'M NOT STAYING. I JUST WANTED TO MAKE A POINT.
REALITY HANGS ON A KNIFE-EDGE, JUST AT THE MOMENT. AND IT IS IN MY INTEREST THAT REALITY ENDURES.

DOUBTLESS, YOU ONLY MEAN TO TAKE ADVANTAGE OF THE CURRENT DISORDER.
BUT IN THE PROCESS YOU DEEPEN IT INTO CHAOS. CHAOS, AS I SEE IT, IS THE TRUE ENEMY.

SO I'LL BE LOCKING THE DOORS BEHIND ME.

MY APOLOGIES TO...SOME OF YOU.

NINE POINT EIGHT METERS PER SECOND.
HOW RIDICULOUS IS THAT?
I MEAN, I COULD BE DOWN THERE SELLING SOUVENIR GLASS SHARDS BEFORE THESE TWO SACKS OF MEAT GET PAST THE MEZZANINE.
BUT I'VE BEEN FUCKING ENDPLAYED.
CAUGHT BETWEEN JOHN-BOY'S SCRUPLES AND LUCIFER'S LACK OF THEM LIKE--
--LIKE A BUG IN A FUCKING BIBLE.
THAT WAS A WEIRD LOOK HE HAD ON HIS FACE.
LIKE WE WERE JUST A DETAIL HE WAS CLEARING UP IN PASSING. LIKE SOMETHING BIG WAS ABOUT TO HIT.
SHAME TO MISS IT.
The End